Lessons from the Last Revolution …

Standin' in a Hard Rain,
The Making of a Revolutionary Life

Joel D. Eis © 2023

<u>By the Same Author:
Books about Theatre and Politics</u>

A Full Investigation of the Historic Performance of the First Play in English in the New World, Ye Bare and Ye Cubbe, 1665 (Lewiston: NY, Edwin Mellen Press, 2004)

The Function of the Ekkyklema in Greek Theatre, (Lewiston, NY: Edwin Mellen, 2014 Press) (Adele Mellen Award for academic contribution)

The First Play in English in America and its Contribution to the First Amendment, (Lewiston, NY: Edwin Mellen Press, 2021).

Activist theatre is a long-standing traditional American revolutionary weapon. The author in 2010 at the now-confirmed site of the performance of the first play in English in the New World, 1665. (Photo. Toni Labori-Eis)

Lessons from the Last Revolution ...

Standin' in a Hard Rain

The Making of a Revolutionary Life
Joel D. Eis © 2023

Published by
World BEYOND War
Charlottesville, Virginia

Standin' in a Hard Rain: The Making of a Revolutionary Life

© Copyright 2023 by Joel D. Eis. All rights reserved

    No part of this publication may be reproduced, stored in an information storage and retrieval system, or transmitted in any form by electronic or mechanical means without the prior written permission of the copyright holder. Reviewers may quote brief passages in a review.

    Every reasonable effort has been made to obtain permission for copyrighted material in this work and to ensure accuracy at the time of publication. All photos and other documents herein appear as public domain or with permissions from their legal owners. Captions denote permission by owner. Participants or witnesses who could be located have attested to all incidents in this document.

    Lyrics to Bob Dylan's, "Hard Rain's Gonna Fall" appear de facto-permission, Universal Music, Inc.

979-8-218-11060-4 ISBN paperback
978-1-0880-7558-6 ISBN e-book
LC# 2022917892

Book cover designed by David Mortonson

First Edition 1 2 3 4 5 6
Printed in the United States

Cover photo: Property of the Fresno Police Department, stolen from the evidence file at my trial, 1970. (Cover crowds*, Wm. Haigwood)

For David Harris,
Organizer of the Draft Resistance
during the Vietnam War,
who taught me where to plug in my Karma

CONTENTS

Foreword by David Swanson   i

Acknowledgments   iii

An Introduction that Fits the Mood   1

Introduction: The War at Home   3

Section I: Before I Knew What I Knew

Chapter 1: Jew Boy   11
Chapter 2: Bikinis and Molotov Cocktails,
    Fresno, California, 1960   18
Chapter 3: Becoming a Certified Regular Guy   22
Chapter 4: 1963—The Murder of Hope   25

Section II: There's Something Happenin' Here

Chapter 5: 1964—What I Did on My Summer Vacation   29
Chapter 6: A Southern Girl and the End of the Civil War   37

Section III: My Own Road

Chapter 7: Off to College, 1964   47
Chapter 8: Radical Politics Enters My Life   52
Chapter 9: 1965-1966—Coming Home, Frank Verges,
    and the Revlon Girl   55
Chapter 10: The Beginning of Bigger Things   61
Chapter 11: Love and Unsettling Revelations   68

Section IV: The Hard Rain Begins To Fall

Chapter 12: San Francisco and Big Trouble   99
Chapter 13: Radical Theatre and the Student Strike
    at San Francisco State   104

Chapter 14: Billy Clubs, Not Books — 111
Chapter 15: I Make a Circle — 123

Section V: *Que Viva La Huelga! Que Viva La Revolucion!*

Chapter 16: 1969—*El Teatro Campesino* — 133
Chapter 17: Breaking In — 141
Chapter 18: Back to School and Into the World — 145
Chapter 19: The Jew Boy *Con Los Chicanos* in France — 146
Chapter 20: Coming Home … Again — 154
Chapter 21: Parting More Sorrow than Sweet — 161

Section VI: Coloring in the Full Picture

Chapter 22: The Fresno Draft Resistance Movement — 189
Chapter 23: 1969—The Battle of People's Park, Berkeley, CA — 207
Chapter 24: Security Detail and the Brass Workers' Strike, 1969 — 211
Chapter 25: Not Sex—Sex and the Revolution — 215
Chapter 26: About Drugs and Revolution, for the Record — 220
Chapter 27: Some Other Encounters — 226
Chapter 28: More Front-Line Tales and "Your Friendly Movers" — 229
Chapter 29: 1969—Woodstock and the Politics of Love — 235
Chapter 30: Becoming the People We Were Warned Against — 237
Chapter 31: 1970—A Purge at the University,
    A Little Extra Attention — 245

Section VII: Breakdowns

Chapter 32: Caught in the Crossfire — 249
Chapter 33: 1970—Progressive Theatres Reflect the Times — 256
Chapter 34: Days Of Rage: The Cambodian Invasion and After — 261
Chapter 35: 1971—Going to Court, Fresno County Jail — 269

Section VIII: Times Changin'

Chapter 36: 1971—*Say 'Uncle' Sam!* and the Unraveling Times　307

Chapter 37: Smokin' with "A Few Good Men"　321
Chapter 38: Angela Davis and a Few Other Things　325
Chapter 39: David Harris, the Vets Against the War,
　　　　　　and "The Building"　330
Chapter 40: Riding Off Into the Sunset　333

Section IX: The Rustic Interlude and Beyond

Chapter 41: Political Theatre Where You Can　341
Chapter 42: Unexpected Challenges　352

Section X: You're Never Through When You Think You Are

Chapter 43: "Seize the Time"　361
Chapter 44: Ghetto Time and More Trouble　369
Chapter 45: Under My Own Stars: Some Late Revelations　380
Chapter 46: Off to Do My Thing, Somewhere　384
Chapter 47: Afterward and Now　393
Chapter 48: Back In the Saddle Again…　397

Coda: After a Hard Rain…　419

FOREWORD

By David Swanson
Executive Director, World BEYOND War
Charlottesville, Virginia

Standin' in a Hard Rain is a fascinating and entertaining account of one California Sixties activist's experience, overlapping with many others, some well known, some not. Joel Eis was active against war, racism, and unfair labor practices, among various interlocking causes taken up by a significant movement of dedicated young people pursuing a better culture as well as better systems of business and governance.

Eis took part in rallies, sit-ins, protests, strikes, counseling young men to resist the military draft, making speeches, and organizing events. But his particular focus was theatre. He wrote, directed, acted in, and produced plays for political theatre groups with a great deal of success.

The United States has inherited the victories of that generation's struggles. Today we eat healthier food without being told it's a hippie diet. We have expectations around consumer safety, environmental protection, and fair treatment of other people that are so ingrained that it's hard to recognize them as victories won by radical activists in the not too distant past. *Standin' in a Hard Rain* gives us an inside view of a movement that was exciting, sexy, and fulfilling, but also effective. This does not mean it was without severe hardships or missteps, or that its work is finished.

Eis had parents who both inspired his leftist politics and condemned them. He had an understanding of bigotry from experiencing anti-Semitism and perhaps also from experiencing homophobia directed toward him as a theatre person even though he was not gay.

Eis stayed out of the military as a Conscientious Objector and a known troublemaker who the military did not want. Yet he had nightmares about the death and suffering in Vietnam. The horror many miles away is always in the background as Eis recounts numerous creative and successful actions that slowly changed the world. Eis engaged in draft counseling to turn young men away from war and performances of antiwar plays to turn everyone else against it as well.

Back then, an ironic reminder of one's power as an activist was confirmed in the amount of government surveillance. Today, the U. S. government knows how to spy on you without telling you it is doing so. Back then, the taps on your phone could be recognized by the clicks, the cameras identified, the observers in meetings recognized. The low flight of a military helicopter taking photos over Eis's house (a true incident) was the level of subtlety involved. I can't help but think this harassment was not only aggravating but also a little bit encouraging.

When "the Sixties" ended sometime in the 1970s, many, including Eis, continued doing much of what they'd done before, but it was modified and no longer thought of as a movement. Aging Sixties activists continue to make up a good percentage of current peace activists, and many of them have never stopped being active. However, it's not full-time anymore, not full-person, not all-in existence in a counterculture.

If what's needed for a new upsurge in activism is for conditions in the world to worsen again, we must be well on our way. If what's needed are examples of how to win in the struggle, keep reading.

David Swanson is an author, activist, journalist, and radio host. He is executive director of **World Beyond War** and campaign coordinator for **Roots Action**. His books include *War is a Lie,* and he hosts *Talk Nation Radio.* David is also a **Nobel Peace Prize nominee**, and he was awarded the **2018 Peace Prize** by the **U. S. Peace Memorial Foundation.**

ACKNOWLEDGMENTS

This work is dedicated to my parents, who taught me always to finish my vegetables and to never cross a picket line; to James R. Bertholf (1933- 2006), who taught me always to seek a creative rendition in everything; to Roger Alvarado, David Harris, Luis, Lupe, Daniel Valdez, to Mark Loring and his bitter laughter, and to June Loring, who saved my life.

It is for the men and women who died in the jungle for the selfish, craven dreams of a few; for those who came home from the war, broken in body and soul; and for the people of Vietnam, upon whom we wreaked unspeakable havoc.

It is also dedicated to my sister Sandy, who endured more personal suffering during the Vietnam War than I can imagine, and who is always there for me. Many thanks to the best old man there is, Ian Swift, for his patient editing of this whole *megillah*. to Paul Dunham, Patrick Conroy, Don Teeter, John Walke, Ron Thiesen, Tom and Carol Valentine, and many others for correcting and approving the stories of our struggles together; special *abrassos* to my comrade Doug Rippey, Draft Resister, fellow organizer, and early member of *El Teatro* for advice and for fixing my *pinchi pocho* Spanish. To Bob Cooper for his patience advice and encouragement in the editing of this thing several times.

To Mike Rhodes of Fresno, California, who shared the contact info for the many old peace warriors who gave a nod to this document; to Bettina Aptheker, Free Speech Movement soldier, fierce defender of Angela Davis and the rights of all women, a thank you for important revisions and guidance at the last. Most of all, to my wife Toni, who demands that I tell the truth always, and who has heard each of these stories countless times.

"Don't start me talkin'. I'll tell you everything I know."
(Sonny Boy Williamson II, blues musician, 1955)

AN INTRODUCTION THAT FITS THE MOOD

Body of War

Joseph Zaccardi
(Published in *Vents* and *Cloud View Poets,* 2012)

I remember a flower floating on water.
What do I call it? White blossom swimming
in place? Brother holding brother?
To stanch bleeding apply gauze and pressure,
then bandage. I remember trawlers.
Lean brown men. Nets laid in the brine
like fine doilies. Where red tide meets blue,
sister caressing sister. If there's a wound
to the abdomen, inject morphine, tell them
it doesn't look bad, you've seen worse
and theirs looks good, pretty good.
I remember gathering this part to fit that part.
How can I tell you? That it didn't bother me?
There was no time to think? That it was just
a bad dream? Some nights I lie in bed trembling,
and if I try to speak, only consonant sounds
come out, words without vowels. Arm without
"a." Leg without "e." And head.
How do I say, "head?"

    Joseph Zaccardi joined the Navy and served as a corpsman on the USS Mars ASF1 in Yokosuka, Japan. He saw plenty of men leave for Vietnam and never return. He did not begin to write about it until 1970.
    He was the Marin County, California Poet Laureate from 2013 to 2015. Joe has been writing poetry for 55 years.

INTRODUCTION

> "Excuse me while I kiss the sky."
> *(Jimi Hendrix, 1967)*

> "In the war against meanness, selfishness, and cruelty, and its full manifestation in Fascism, joyfulness is a powerful weapon."
> *(Anonymous)*

THE WAR AT HOME

It was the summer of 1964 just after my high school graduation. As a graduation gift, I'd asked my parents for a roundtrip bus ticket across America. On my way east, I'd gone into the Memphis bus station washroom and came out to find history staring me in the face. A large crowd of Black and white students from all over America had convened in Memphis on their way into the Deep South to register Black people to vote. Outside the big windows of the bus station, a crowd of angry whites was gathering. Police and sheriffs were standing with them, clearly socializing with the good ol' boys. This was big trouble I hadn't planned on.

Something was happening to America right in front of me.

In that period loosely described as "the Sixties," roughly a million people, young and old, became passionately committed to profound aspects of revolutionary change. There wasn't any school to teach what was needed. It had to be learned on picket lines, at meetings, demonstrations, sit-ins, and rallies, and while running from the cops. This document is an up-close picture, without the soft lens and background music, of what it was like to navigate within those times.

The Movement was utterly opposed to Capitalism. What's wrong with Capitalism, you ask? To *capitalize* on a situation means to get more out of it than you put into it. Capitalism is therefore inherently a system of exploitation. It's based on *taking*, not *sharing*. In this system, a single individual, family, or nation acquires wealth out of balance with their neighbors by unfair exploitation, then holds onto it by force of arms and manipulation of the truth. It's basically criminal in intent and in practice. This is what's destroying America by send the young to war, pitting races against each other, and polluting for profit.

My generation found itself fighting a war at home. Revolution was—and is—our right. Did we advocate the overthrow of the Establishment? By "the Establishment" or "power-elite," we meant the entire matrix of both official and unofficial institutions with which unfair power is exercised, so the answer is "yes."

In this struggle, we were either part of the problem or part of the solution. We discovered—I discovered—that our role in history began with bearing witness. This was a very Jewish/Zen thing to do. But as the swelling tide of events rolled over us, this was not enough.

Voting, signing petitions, and marching with the crowd was not enough. Against a system of exploitation and violence, we armed ourselves with acts of kindness. This was inherently *revolutionary.* We found ourselves fighting a war at home. Something had to be done and we were the ones who had to do it. We figured out what that meant on the run. Every one of us involved in the Movement considered what we were doing to be a patriotic act. We became soldiers drafted into a struggle guided by the Golden Rule: "Treat others as you wish to be treated yourself."

Whether it was a blessing or a curse, I seemed to have been in the right place at the right time to grab the handles of history. I was followed. My phones were tapped. I was slammed up against police cars. Attempts were made by FBI plants to trick me into illegally advocating sedition. I was shot at. I got busted and went to jail.

Drugs, alcohol, or sexual distraction couldn't obscure what was happening around us. The Ruling Elite cleverly dressed up the Vietnam War in the slogans of our fathers to look like a noble enterprise and then sent us to die for their private profit. No amount of repeating these threadbare slogans could make it right.

Jailing those who could see it was wrong did not change its wrongness.

No one is a "born revolutionary," but I came pretty close to it. Leftist politics was a family tradition. My paternal grandmother was a suffragist early in the twentieth century. My paternal grandfather, a tiny Jewish tailor, was jailed for organizing for the Garment Workers' Union before the First World War. My own parents were staunch unionists. More than once, my mother walked us away from a picket line in front of a department store.

If every soldier and every peasant killed for our greed during the Vietnam War could rise from their graves, they'd tell you that history is personal. Our purpose was to end the crime that was that genocidal war. We were not traitors. We were patriots with a different vision. While we hated the war, we understood the soldiers' need to be part of something bigger than themselves. We felt this as well. The Capitalist Machine used the desire of young people to do something important and enlisted America's youth to fight and die for their personal profit. This was unconscionable beyond imagining. We were committed to bringing our soldiers—my own high school buddies—home even as they marched for empty slogans to their bloody end.

We were labeled as paranoid, hopped up on drugs, or were unwitting Communist dupes. (DOCUMENT #1: Anti-communist poster) However, the truth couldn't stay hidden for long. Somebody had to be part of the solution instead of being part of the problem. In doing so, we had to become the people our parents warned us against.

The "Generation Gap" was a fact of life. The first skirmishes in the struggle were fought around our own dinner tables. My father announced to me, "If you ever burn your draft card, you're no son of mine." The Movement was filled with young men who had experienced this shocking encounter. We could not live in homes where weekend Bible-carrying parents went out on Monday to make weapons, pollute the air, exploit minorities and women, then vote for the thieves and liars who sent us off to die to protect their right to keep doing it.

The FBI spent millions to spy on Americans involved in legitimate activities. It engaged in disinformation and disruption involving spies, lies, and outright murders. My generation was expected to embrace this system of repression and brutality as our birthright without asking questions.

It was the questions that got us into trouble…

Each of us took up the weapons at hand. I found my weapon for change in doing political theatre. Theatre moves people to think and feel at the same time. In political theatre, the last scene takes place in the street and in the hearts and lives of those who witness it.

How—*and why*—did a boy raised in a cozy home in American suburbia become a committed radical? What was the cost of such a life? What were the rewards? Finally, what was it like to return to a relatively "regular life" yet maintain an active exercise of my beliefs? I entered this struggle with everything I had.

As active revolutionaries, we lived by a basic principle: "Those who know don't tell. Those who tell don't know." This code of secrecy was necessary to protect our comrades. Even in this document, the names of many deeply involved people are altered. Nevertheless, I'm hereby ratting on all of us. I'm turning us all in. We are still engaged in a revolution to uproot our power-hungry, greedy society and plant something new in its place.

After the Vietnam War ended, times changed. Our tactics changed. We went underground. Driven by Kennedy's "Ask not what your country can do for you," we became teachers, went into medicine, the sciences, and nongovernmental aid agencies. We became writers, artists, musicians. We became parents of our own children. We considered this a continuation of the revolution, acting out our commitment to making a better world. There were battles won and battles lost, but we kept our soul. That is the greater victory. That is the lesson.

On my bookshelf is a lump of concrete the size of a canned ham. This ugly rock is a hefty chunk of the Berlin Wall, brought home from Germany by my good friend, Jim Brightwolf. It's solid proof of the power of the people who take up the hammer of truth against iron-booted repression anywhere. That's what "the Sixties" was all about.

The wheel has turned again. I wrote this book for you because in times of trouble, the voice of experience can matter a great deal, and most surely, we are headed for troubled times. This document is meant to be a guide through the dangerous territory you must cross.

Do not be afraid.

SECTION I

BEFORE I KNEW WHAT I KNEW

"Oh, where have you been, my blue-eyed son?
And where have you been, my darling young one?

I've stumbled on the side of twelve misty mountains
I've walked and I've crawled on six crooked highways
I've stepped in the middle of seven sad forests
I've been out in front of a dozen dead oceans
I've been ten thousand miles in the mouth of a graveyard

[Chorus]
And it's a hard, and it's a hard, it's a hard, it's a hard
It's a hard rain's a-going to fall"

"A Hard Rain's A-Gonna Fall"
(Verse 1, Bob Dylan, 1962)

CHAPTER 1: JEW BOY

I probably absorbed my politics *in utero*.

I must have been four or five years old. I remember walking towards the department store with my mother. There was a picket line in front of the store. Though it was cold and windy and the errand was important, she turned me around and said, "C'mon, Joely, we're not going in there."

"Why?"

"Those people aren't being treated fairly. We don't cross a picket line, *ever*."

My parents always stressed fairness and empathy for the other guy's situation. The most important teaching in all of the Jewish faith is, "Do unto others…" This means all week, not just on the Sabbath. For as long as I can remember, my father tied this sense of concern for others to his sense of himself. Dad was always quoting Polonius from Hamlet, "To thine own self be true, and thou canst be false to no man." They aren't the words exactly, but the sentiment is there.

My mother never quoted anybody. She was an original. As the daughter of an organizer for the Garment Workers Union before World War I, she grew up in a leftist household. As was usual for most women of her generation, she did her organizing around the dinner table while passing out seconds on mashed potatoes. Her final opinion came out while my father was eating, so he listened. This example stood me in good stead with women who spoke up some twenty years later. Timing is everything.

Tales of anti-Semitism in America were common in our home. My father once shared a story about his time in World War II when his fat Alabama commanding officer cornered him alone in his barracks and made a crack about him being "a kike." Dad—

who was all of five-foot-seven and one-hundred-and-forty pounds—reached up over his locker and took down his parade dress bayonet. He quickly unsheathed the blade and then slammed it, flat-sided, against the guy's gut, pushing him back against the lockers. He walked away leaving the weapon in the man's hands and a lesson in his bulging eyes. Great exit.

My parents got married in 1943 when Dad was on leave. (DOCUMENT #2: Parents' picture) My parents were staunch left-wing unionists. When they moved to Washington, D. C., in the McCarthy Era to open a family business with my Uncle Joe, they kept their leftist politics low-key but paid their workers fairly.

Dad was not always such a hero. On one occasion when I was six years old, he and I went to a park. I climbed up a steep wooded hill then started down. I tripped, fell, and rolled like a sack of rocks all the way to the bottom. For some reason, Dad was laughing when I tumbled to a painful stop at the bottom.

I was in real agony. I was expecting to be picked up in his arms. No such luck. He just stood there laughing. The absence of any comfort wounded me more deeply than the physical pain. From that moment on, respect for someone's feelings in their hour of need became my visceral understanding of justice. People in power have an opportunity and a responsibility to affect others' lives. It's what governments should do, always.

A New Game at School

One warm spring day in my third-grade year (1956), I came out on the playground and found myself the unexpected star of a new game.

The game was called "Jew Boy."

As I crossed the schoolyard, a line of children swooped down on me, chasing me, herding me into a closing circle. When they'd entirely encircled me, they picked a boy to egg me on to a fistfight. They pushed my friend and yelled at him until he hit me in the nose. The blood began to run. He had the confident look of victory on his face because he had their support. I looked at my "friends" surrounding me. There may have been other Jewish kids in that circle, but they didn't help me. I felt scared and cornered. I had no place to go and only myself to rely on. There was only one thing to do. I fought back.

We both ended up in the nurse's office. My parents came to the school the next day. I can only imagine my father in the principal's office, even without a bayonet in his hand. That game was never played on the playground again. My defending myself taught me not to waste time with anything less than a definitive response to oppression.

I was already feeling a sense of "otherness," of being on the outside looking in. I was getting the idea that my life was not going to be like the smiling, fair-haired kids in the milk posters on the school wall.[1] (DOCUMENT #3: Milk poster) I was becoming a recruit in a war I didn't even know needed to be fought.

Hot Coffee and Union Troubles

I was ten years old. It was a freezing-cold, stormy winter day in Rockville, Maryland, a suburb of Washington, D. C., where the snow can be like wet cement. While I suited up to go to school, an African American garbage man knocked on our back door and asked my mother for a glass of water. This was pretty brave. White people would throw away a glass after a Black person used it if they gave it to him at all. He could have lost his job. He must have known my folks were okay or he wouldn't have even dared. There were no Black people in our neighborhood, no Black children in any of my schools. I never saw any at the grocery store or the movies. This was Jim Crow America.

My mother asked him in, gave him the glass of water, and then poured him a cup of hot coffee. She passed him the cream, sugar, and a spoon, just as if he was one of our friends. After he left, I asked why she'd done that.

---

[1] These were posters of an idyllic world, usually warning us of the dangers of not drinking enough milk.

She said, "You give a person what they deserve whether they ask for it or not."

****

My dad and my Uncle Joe had a printing business in Washington, D. C. They often went in on Saturdays to finish work to be shipped out Monday morning. Sometimes I got to go along with the men and actually help. My job was to stand near the on/off button on the printing press and listen for the sound of a misfed sheet of paper. If a wrinkled or folded sheet got as far as the metal type, it would smash the lead-cast letters. Production would stop while the type was reset by hand, a job that could take hours. I had to be lightning-fast to trip the "off" button in less than an instant after the "whoosh" of the suction cups registered a missed feed. This was a big responsibility for a kid too short even to see inside the press.

A Black man named Willie worked in the shop. Willie broke up boxes, wrapped orders, loaded trucks, and cleaned up. Willie was learning to use the bindery equipment. Willie worked as hard as everyone did, and his contribution was important to running the shop. He earned a living wage like everybody else.

On one particular Saturday, my Uncle Joe was in his office. Through the delivery door came an "enforcer" from the Printers' union. I was having lunch right next to my Uncle Joe's cubicle. I heard the whole exchange.

Union Guy: I hear you got a nigger workin' here.

Uncle Joe: Yeah, so what?

Union Guy: We also hear you're payin' him the same as a white man. You can't pay a nigger the same as a white man.

Uncle Joe: You see that carton of milk there on my desk?

Union Guy: Yeah, I see it.

Uncle Joe: Until they sell that milk to Negroes for half price, Willie needs a full wage to feed his family.

Union Guy: If you pay that nigger the same as a white man then all the other shops will have to do the same.

Uncle Joe: You're breakin' my heart.

Union Guy: We can see to it that you don't get no government contracts. In this town, that's most of the printing work.

Uncle Joe: Get out of my shop before I take that two-by-four behind you to the side of your head.

I don't think Uncle Joe ever told Willie about that conversation.

****

Two years later, when I was twelve, I was at my friend Danny Welsh's house on a Saturday afternoon. His father, Charlie Welsh, was also a printer. He knew and respected my dad. Charlie had just read a story in the paper. He was really upset. He sat us down and read the story aloud. In a Southern city, the KKK had kidnapped a Black man who'd looked at a white woman for a few seconds too long. They took him out into the woods, castrated him, and then poured kerosene on the wound. The poor man was saved from bleeding to death, but the pain must have been horrible. I thought about Willie. This story still makes me angry.

From learning of these kinds of events, I knew what I was seeing when I saw images of police dogs, ax handles, and fire hoses used on innocent Black people. When I was a toddler, my mother had hired a Black woman named Josephine who came to take care of me when my mother went to work. I tried to wrap my head around how people could hurt Josephine or Willie, how there could actually be laws that made it okay to treat them as less than human.

Even before my teen years, I'd conjured up a connection between how my own people were treated in Germany and how Black people were treated in America. I didn't have a name for it, but I knew what it was. One side had guns and hate. The other had hope. I knew which side I was on.

My Hebrew School teacher at the time wore a black patch over one eye. He'd lost the other eye fighting for *the Haganah* (Jewish volunteer liberation army) in the War for Israeli Independence (1948). He told us a story about how they had one cannon for about five miles of front line. They moved the field piece all over the place so the British would think they had a lot of artillery. His stories taught me: (1) You have to be more clever than your enemy. (2) Determination is the most powerful weapon there is. I remember thinking, *If this skinny bookish guy in rimless glasses with a patch over one eye could be an independence fighter, then anybody can.*

I didn't know it then, but things were beginning to add up.

Jesus and I Go *Mano-a-Mano*

In 1958, I was in the seventh grade at Belt Junior High School in Silver Springs, Maryland, ten miles outside of Washington, D. C. It was required that the New Testament be read every day in homeroom. When your name was called, you had to go up and read from the New Testament. In that class of thirty students, there were at least sixteen Jewish kids—maybe twenty if you count the ones with blond hair who were trying to pass as gentiles.

In front of me sat Ruby Compton. Ruby was a thirteen-year-old blonde with a sensuous pout and early, noteworthy curves. Ruby looked how Marilyn Monroe must have looked at the same age. That morning, Ruby read some of the Bible (an incongruous image in itself). Then it was my turn.

Our teacher, Mr. Schussler, had been a Marine in the Korean War. He was the wrestling coach. He was over six feet tall and built like a weightlifter with a blond flattop haircut and hands like sledgehammers. He was a nice guy. With those hands, he could afford to be a nice guy. Mr. Schussler called my name and held out the Bible for me to read. I have no idea what possessed me. Perhaps I was channeling my television hero and moral compass at the time, Davy Crockett, who always said, "Be sure you're right. Then go ahead."

"No thanks," I said, "I'll pass."

I could feel the shocked, cold stares all around me.

Mr. Shussler's voice got deeper. He said, "It's *your* turn."

Again, I said, "No thanks, I'll pass." It wasn't my holy book.

Miraculously, at that moment, the bell rang. I was saved.

However, somebody must have called my house. When I got home, my mom asked me the whole story. The next day, my parents went with me to school. The office was crawling with more lawyers than ants on a chocolate cake.

At that age, I was mostly interested in getting a peek down Ruby Compton's blouse. I'd never heard about the "prayer in the schools controversy." I must have pushed a pretty hot button by opening my big mouth. This became the story of my life.

On the next Monday homeroom, instead of passing the Bible around, Mr. Schussler—staring daggers at me—said, "You don't have to read the Bible. It's *vol*untary." The last word sounded like a curse.

My innocent action had contributed to a shift in the entire school district, perhaps even beyond. A single small action by one person at the right moment can change things big-time. I'd become that one cannon on the five-mile front line of the First Amendment.

I'm pretty sure Ruby Compton didn't give a damn, but I had a hunch that my reputation as a troublemaker was going to follow me. I prayed to be airlifted out of there. My prayers were answered. That summer, we moved out to California.

CHAPTER 2: BIKINIS AND MOLOTOV COCKTAILS, FRESNO, CALIFORNIA, 1960

In 1959, during my seventh-grade year, my father had bought a printing business in Fresno, California, a region with a dry climate and crops of cotton, figs, grapes, olives, oranges, and melons growing even within the city limits. We'd moved to the Promised Land. I expected to see movie stars all over the place—maybe Marilyn Monroe, maybe Annette Funicello. I'd have settled for Sandra Dee.

It seemed like a big farm town with a far slower rhythm of life than the East Coast. When we arrived, it was midsummer in the desert climate of the San Joaquin Valley. The temperature reached eighty degrees about ten minutes after sunrise and skyrocketed to a hundred before noon. However, there was no humidity. We moved into a bunker-esque, cinder-block duplex apartment with a "swamp cooler" that drove air through straw pads that sucked up moisture from the bottom of the device, cooling the air and making it damp. However, as our valiant machine labored, the fan belt squeaked like a panicked little animal. We endured because it kept the place cool.

We lived in a neighborhood that was perhaps twenty years old or more; all around us were small, single-story apartment buildings and little stucco or clapboard houses. Most of the people were brown-skinned with black hair. They all spoke Spanish. The lawns were too small for recreation, so the families picnicked and played on the big lawns of the hospital in the center of the neighborhood. Because of the hospital and the neighborhood, the ambulance and cop car sirens wailed all night. We had moved in the Latino area but didn't know it.

I discovered that only a few blocks away was a community swimming pool. Though it was close to the Mexican enclave, the people at this swim park were all white. The girls at the swim park splashed and cavorted in the tiniest bikinis I'd ever seen. I thought I'd died and gone to heaven. There was one girl with short black hair and very brown skin, but she was not Latina. She was always in a small black bikini. She was my new Reason for Living. She wrestled with the boys and danced to the music coming over the loudspeaker. I had to go and sit down with my towel over my lap. At synagogue, I gave thanks for deliverance to the land of reckless girls in minimal swimwear.

I had completed my bar mitzvah training in Washington before we moved. In November, it was time for my rite of passage at Congregation Beth Jacob in Fresno. As I became a man in the rites of my tribe, I played to a good house. And there were girls. (DOCUMENT #4: My Bar Mitzvah picture)

At our congregation was a boy named David who was five years older than me. He had a number tattooed on his forearm. When he was an infant, David had been branded like an animal in a German concentration camp. David had the eyes of an old man.

In January, only a few weeks after my bar mitzvah, trouble found our congregation on the corner of Nowhere. One Saturday, everyone arrived at the synagogue to find police cars filling the parking lot. The rabbi and congregation leaders were all standing around in shock and fear. The women were all huddled in the car seats. Swastikas had been spray-painted on the doors, walls, and windows. Molotov cocktails had been thrown at the wooden doors of the sanctuary. They were all scarred and burned. (DOCUMENT #5: Swastikas on temple doors) That night, homes of some in the congregation were also targeted with vandalism and hate phone calls. It was our own little *Kristallnacht* right there in Paradise. The community—some of them German concentration camp survivors—was scared shitless. Until then, I only saw this kind of thing in history books or newspaper stories about the Deep South.

Now here it was in my beardless face. The men divided their nights standing guard at the synagogue for weeks thereafter. Just having become a man, I wanted to go with my dad, but he said "no."

History had become personal.

Two big, blond, blue-eyed football stars, the valedictorian and salutatorian of the richest high school in town, bragged about it in the locker room. The cops came calling. The boys lost their spots at the top of the class. They were denied Harvard. Did this put a fire under my feelings of dissociation from America's mainstream? You bet your bagel knife it did.

Even in laid-back California, I learned that I was carrying my future politics on my face. I was getting the idea that manhood was going to include a hell of a lot more than shaving, driving a car, and getting laid.

There is a happy end to this tale. I discovered that Adrian, the Princess of Blackstone Swim Park, was a Sephardic Jew, thus the dark skin and hair. We dated and stayed friends for years.

High School Debate Team

In 1961, I entered C. L. McLane High School. I exercised my growing interest in politics. I joined the debate team. We had to read widely on a subject for our debate cases. Carrying briefcases and file boxes full of quote cards and case outlines, we all looked like lawyers with pimples. Debate competition taught me to have my facts right and not to be fooled by twisted rhetoric. I soon discovered that the "evidence" put out by government spokespeople was often bullshit.

In class one day, our coach, James C. O'Bannon, gave us an example. "The State Department reported that the U. S. was involved in an international automobile competition. Of all the nations in the contest, the United States came in second."

"What's wrong with that, 'Mr. O'?"

"There were only two countries involved. The USA came in second and therefore actually lost the competition. You have to question the facts behind the statements you read."

"Jeez..."

"Don't say 'jeez.' It makes you sound like a cartoon."

Jim O'Bannon taught me to smell a lie a thousand words away and sharpened my Government Suspicion muscle. My vague political interest was taking a confident shape.

High school debate was where I met and befriended David Harris from Fresno High. We went up against each other in many tournaments. David was later to become the organizer and spokesperson for the National Draft Resistance. David was a great speaker with a way of trusting his audience (the judge) to come to the correct conclusion. Faith and respect for the inherent wisdom of his audience was a hallmark of his style. I learned a lot from him at the time. I was destined to learn a lot more.

CHAPTER 3: BECOMING A CERTIFIED REGULAR GUY

I was bookish (I'd joined the debate team), I was Jewish (Jews don't fight), I was in the school play (probably a sissy), and not exceptionally athletic. It didn't matter that I dated girls; I was queer-baited from the moment I got off the school bus. I resolved to become a "Regular Guy."

This obsession became even more intense after I met David Kohlman. Dave was one of those rare, blond-haired, blue-eyed, Sandy Koufax-type Jewish boys. David actually played varsity football. I thought, *I might become a Regular Guy and still actually stay Jewish.* What a concept.

Dave had been "outed" as a Jew by the racist football coach. David related his story. "I was supposed to be a starting varsity quarterback. Coach thought 'Kohlman' was a good German name![2] Coach saw my Star of David necklace in the locker room. When I came back from the High Holy Days, my number was benched. Coach called anybody else to take the field but me.

"My folks told the principal they'd call the newspapers and the lawyers, so the principal okayed a transfer to another school, but I wanted the bastard to pay."

Dave got a big smile on his face. "I heard the coach braggin' about movin' into a new house. I called a nursery and had a half-ton of fresh, ripe steer manure dumped in the driveway. The bill was delivered to his address."

---

[2] I heard this coach (at my own school) call the Black neighborhood "nigger heaven" and use the phrase "Jew him down" more than once.

When all you're trying to do at age sixteen is keep the zits off your nose and be cool, this kind of racist stuff feels like a half-ton of shit delivered into your ordinary life.

David Kohlman's thousand-pound prank taught me that theatricality in your politics raises it to another level.

Becoming a Regular Guy

This Regular Guy thing was going to take some doing.

I was a Jewish kid in a town that was seventy-percent Oklahoma Dust Bowl refugees, twenty-five percent Mexican, and about five percent Black and "other." We Jews were "other," like Samoans. Being on the debate team and in the school plays gave me status with the eggheads, the beatniks, and gay kids. I would never have a chance to date a cheerleader or even a song girl.[3]

I devised a plan. I tried out for the "red trunks" P. E. class, filled with all the school's athletes. You could paint a house with the testosterone in the weight room after these guys hit the showers. I busted my butt and scored exactly two points over the required three hundred points on the tests. I was in.

I was soon doing the same lifts as guys who were thirty pounds heavier. I could do fifty Marine pushups, a hundred sit-ups, and ran a half-mile in a respectable time. My neck looked like a walrus. The Regular Guys stopped towel-swatting me in the shower room.

My gym class took to the playing fields at the same time as the cheerleaders and song girls, mostly certified blondes. Aside from one Armenian girl, not a nose job in the bunch. They eyeballed us guys in red trunks as if we were lunch. I met and started dating Janis McFee, a perfect, button-nosed, freckle-cheeked, blue-eyed song girl right off a milk poster. The absolute coolest guy in school decided we were friends. A few times, we even double-dated in his car. Real America and the likes of Janis McFee were within my grasp.

---

[3] Cheerleaders for the junior varsity teams.

I felt so cool that I ran for Class President and won. (DOCUMENT #6: The Regular Guy, high school senior picture) I was learning that if I dropped my self-conscious paranoia and didn't buy into racially stereotyped behavior, I could get along with pretty much anybody. This saved my life at least once.

CHAPTER 4: 1963—THE MURDER OF HOPE

While I was flexing my pecs in front of the bathroom mirror and learning how to drive, the connection between unjust racial practices and excessive accumulation of wealth was becoming clearer. The Black ghettos were ablaze with pent-up rage, and the war in Asia was creeping toward the newspaper front page. Soon these wouldn't be drowned out by sit-com laugh tracks. My generation was headed for a political tsunami.

Jewish progressives like my parents were accused of being communist sympathizers for their stance on labor and minorities.[4] I remember watching Dr. King's speech on TV. My cousin Laura, who lived near Washington, D. C., had gone to the March on Washington. She sent me an SNCC (Student Nonviolent Coordinating Committee) button that I wore at school. There was a personal message in Kennedy's challenge, "Ask not what your country can do for you. Ask what you can do for your country."

Something was going to happen.

The fall of 1963 was my senior year. I was finally growing hair on my face. My voice had finished cracking. I discovered Beat literature. Ginsberg's *Howl* and Ferlinghetti's *I am Waiting* spoke to me. The war in Vietnam had not yet hooked our full attention, but it began to grab more headlines. The news spoke of our "victories" there, but the number of protests was also growing. Then, in June 1963, the Buddhist monk Thich Quảng Đức doused himself with gasoline and set himself ablaze on a street in Saigon

---

[4] I never figured out how the Jews could be blamed as evil capitalists who owned every exploitive business interest *and* were the spearheads of the conspiracy to undermine Capitalism. Neat trick.

to protest the corrupt government in Vietnam. After that, damned little was funny anymore.

It was Thanksgiving week of 1963. Everybody was thinking about football and the four-day weekend. I was in Mr. Mario Chavez's third-period English class when the school intercom crackled with the surreal announcement. The President of Our Hopes had been gunned down in Dallas. You cannot imagine what this felt like. We felt JFK was one of us. Kennedy had put the future back in our lives with a belief that we could do anything.

When Mr. Chavez put grades in the book, he would smile wryly and quote the *Rubáiyát* of Omar Khayyam: "The moving finger writes, and having writ, moves on. All your piety nor wit shall draw back half a line, nor all thy tears wash out a word of it." How true this was on that day. Mister "C" left the news on in his classroom. At first, everybody just sat listening, too shocked to move. Mister "C" went out in the hallway and stood facing the wall. He was weeping.

Classes stopped. The bells stopped. Everything just stopped.

Somehow, I got home. The bomb bay doors of fate had been opened under us, and we'd been booted over the edge into the open sky of history. We were in freefall without a parachute. When Kennedy's blood ran in the street, hope poured out of our hearts. It was clear our generation was now on our own. What we'd have to do for our country was not going to be easy.

It felt like "Jew Boy" to me. However, we had more going for us than we ever imagined.

SECTION II

THERE'S SOMETHING HAPPENIN' HERE

"Oh, what did you see, my blue-eyed son?
And what did you see, my darling young one?

I saw a newborn baby with wild wolves all around it
I saw a highway of diamonds with nobody on it
I saw a black branch with blood that kept dripping

[Chorus]
And it's a hard, it's a hard, it's a hard, and it's a hard
It's a hard rain's a-going to fall"

"A Hard Rain's A-Gonna Fall"
*(*Verse 2, Bob Dylan, 1962)

CHAPTER 5: 1964—WHAT I DID ON MY SUMMER VACATION

I met Robert Keith "Bob-B" Hobbs in my varsity athlete's gym class He was a football player and a rock 'n' roll drummer with a prankster's sense of humor. We became a recognized duo at school, more like Laurel and Hardy than Batman and Robin.

We planned to spend the spring break of 1964 (our senior year) at Avila Beach, a small beach town near San Luis Obispo. During spring vacation, Avila Beach crawled with girls from nearby schools. The motels were cheap. You could always find a "local" who'd buy you a six-pack if you paid for beer for him. There were surf parties everywhere. This was where it was at.

Bob-B had a white 1956 Ford Victoria with a red leather interior. It was a real party wagon. Somehow, despite Bob's good looks, his certified cool car, my buff bod (thank you, red-trunks class!), and my gift as Master of the Smooth Pickup Line, we didn't score with any babes—not even the drunk ones.

By Friday night at the end of the week, we were low on cash and getting tired of lumpy motel beds. We scored two six-packs of beer. We took our beer, snacks, and sleeping bags and ducked under the bridge at the north end of the beach. A bright moon was out. The sea was calm. It was a beautiful night. Bob and I got good and plastered then crawled into our sleeping bags under the bridge. We soon passed out.

I awoke just after dawn. The entire expanse of beach—a football field's distance down to the normal shore break—was wet within mere inches of our sleeping bags. It was strewn with all manner of flotsam. This was very odd.

Bob was still passed out. I got into my pants and headed for the bait shop, the only store open at that hour. I bought a coffee and a Hostess Cherry Fruit Pie. In the rusted metal rack in front of the shack was an *L. A. Times* with a headline in three-inch letters:

KILLER QUAKE HITS ALASKA, TIDAL WAVES SLAM WEST COAST BEACHES

I almost dropped my cherry pie. Bob and I had been blissfully passed out mere inches away from the worst tsunami to hit California in decades. *Christ on a crutch! My ticket could have been punched before I'd even got laid!* With the half-finished pie and the Dixie cup in hand, I decided all I had time for was pursuing what was most important.

The tide of History was soon to catch our dreams.

****

I had been deeply affected by John Howard Griffin's book, *Black Like Me*, in which the writer tinted his skin to look African American and traveled throughout the South and then traveled the same route again as a white man. He painfully recorded their bias to two skins on the same man. This book, along with Steinbeck's *Travels With Charley,* about the author's sobering discoveries about American life, started an itch to see for myself.

I also read books on Zen Buddhism. I dug the principles of Karma Yoga. Doing good in the world as a simple but profound spiritual practice resonated in me like a plucked guitar string. It was the Golden Rule and the cornerstone of socialism. From this moment of *Sartori,* I became a "Zen Marxist." Practicing Zen's precept of right living seemed like a dare. Nothing gets a teenager's attention better than a dare.

When I was a child, my dad had always sung and played the guitar to me. One of our favorite songs was *The Bear Went Over the Mountain*. I surprised my parents with a request for a roundtrip bus ticket to New York as a graduation present,. When they questioned the reason, I retorted, "If you have to ask why I want to make the trip, you wouldn't understand." I didn't believe there was nothing but the other side of the mountain. A little Zen goes a long way.

Eventually, they ran out of reasons to turn me down. I could stay with relatives near Washington, D. C., and in New York. I even arranged a job at my uncle's garment warehouse in New York City. (God forbid I should look like a freeloader...) They went for it because it was cheaper than buying me a car.

The cool thing about a prepaid bus ticket is that you can get off and then get back on a later bus to continue. I pored over the map. I would head south to the Grand Canyon, then to Dallas, and up into Tennessee and Virginia. The summer swelter and humidity would be bad enough without going through Alabama and Mississippi. I didn't cotton to the social climate down there either. With my California accent and my Jewish face, trouble I didn't need could find me.

Two weeks after graduation from C. L. McLane High School, class of '64, I stepped into the Greyhound bus in downtown Fresno. The first stop was the vast, unbelievably beautiful and dangerous Grand Canyon. My mouth stayed agape for two days. It was like another planet. I don't know where that bear in the song had been looking, but there was a hell of a lot more out there than just the other side of the mountain.

The next stop was Gallup, New Mexico. The streets of Gallup seemed to be made of dust and poverty. The earth and the people were the same color. Native American men wore heavy boots. The women wore sandals. The men all wore sweat-banded, weather-beaten Stetsons. They all seemed to be looking down. Traffic moved slowly as if trying not to disturb the dust. I bought a small silver ring with a square turquoise stone from a Zuni jeweler on the street. I returned to the bus station as a refuge from the heat and the grit. I cherished that ring until the band wore through.

The bus pulled in to Abilene, Texas, at four in the afternoon. Weary of schlepping my big suitcase, I bought a small overnight bag. I hastily packed it with clothing to get to family friends in Richmond, Virginia. I checked my big bag through and found a cheap, clean motel for a night's rest. After stepping out of the shower, I discovered I'd packed all my underwear in the other bag. At that moment, my Fruit of the Looms were rolling toward Richmond, Virginia.

I faced the possibility of a fate even worse than a Jewish mother's greatest fear. I could be in an accident *without any underwear at all*. I'm sure that this is mentioned as a sin in the Old Testament. As the sun set in the West, I found a "five-and-dime" and bought a package of underwear. I think the sales girl knew my predicament as I stood at her register. Nevertheless, I'd averted the first crisis of my solo mission.

After a night's sleep, I headed for parts East with *my* parts protected. I was off to where John F. Kennedy had been shot.

Dallas in the Heat: Welcome to America

A Texan in his cowboy hat feels as if he's wrapped in the flag. His Stetson is like the skullcap for Orthodox Jews in Israel. There were cowboy hats of every size and color, but very few were beat up and dust-encrusted like those in Gallup. I arrived on a sweltering muggy day. I stowed my bag in a bus station locker, sucked down an iced tea, and hopped on a city bus to the crossroads where JFK had been gunned down.

It was just six months after Kennedy's murder. The stain of his killing was still etched on everyone's faces. People on the city bus knew when we were approaching the spot where Kennedy was killed. This corner was the monument to a burned-out hole in History. As the bus approached, the locals set their expressions to deal with the anguish. When the bus stopped, the driver looked away. As I stepped off the bus, all the feelings of that terrible day washed over me like a tidal wave. Those stepping off the bus tried not to see the question, *"Now what?"* in everyone's eyes. We all looked off into the shimmering air and an uncertain future that seemed more treacherous than the Grand Canyon.

If there ever was a location that had a feeling of negative spiritual energy, it was the area between where Lee Harvey

Oswald laid in waiting and where the president's motorcade had passed under his sights. My generation's dreams and hopes had been burned away by his bullets in the air around me *right there*.

I was not ready for this. I couldn't breathe.

I got on the next city bus back to the Greyhound station, grabbed my bag, and got on the next bus out of there. I would now have to ride through the gauntlet of the Deep South and let it ride through me. Not long before this day, the FBI had found the bodies of the three Freedom Riders who'd been murdered in Mississippi. The whole world was watching. I had bought a ticket on the highway of history. As I left Dallas, I already felt as if I were carrying something far heavier than my luggage.

A Breakfast Served with Billy Clubs

I tried to sleep on the bus as it rolled and rumbled through the sweltering Southern night. The air conditioning couldn't keep up. The night was anything but quiet. The roar of the katydids off into the deep woods was deafening.

At midnight—probably as we passed into Arkansas—the new civil rights law signed by Lyndon Johnson went into effect. Jim Crow and "separate but equal" were dead. Bitter anger washed over the white South while a mix of quiet "hallelujahs" and fear energized the Black population. The world of Southern white people had shifted under their feet. Southern whites didn't seem to know their place in a world unless they had somebody else *to feel better than*. Every discussion about their problems invariably ended with, "At least I ain't no nigger."

The whites knew what they'd done. They knew why being Black was such a hardship. They rightly feared retribution when the Black population began to vote—and run for office. When Black people went to register, white authorities invented impossible tests only for Blacks. If a Black person parked in front of the registrar's office, the car was ticketed or towed.

Everyday life for Black people in the South was negotiated in a state of siege. If a Black man walked down the street, a group of white boys would stand in his way just enough that an accidental body touch—real or imagined—turned into a fight for which the Black man was arrested. Young Black couples were ruthlessly intimidated. The boy might be held down to watch helplessly while his girl was insulted, ogled, fondled, or even raped. If the law even showed up, the victims were charged with causing the disturbance. If they won their case in court, their houses were torched.

  I stepped off the bus bleary-eyed and body-stiff in the Memphis Greyhound station at five a.m. I ambled into the bus station washroom—labeled "WHITES ONLY"—to wash my face and wake up. The sign was shocking. A crowd of young white and Black people filled the bus station. I could tell from their accents that they were from the East, West, and North coming to register Blacks to vote.

  Both joy and fear hung in the air thicker than smoke. The civil rights law had gone into effect the night before, yet there was the sobering news of the discovery of the bodies of their companions from the previous summer. Here was the tidal wave of History flooding over my freshly washed face.

  Outside the bus station, there was a different sort of gathering. Filling the sidewalk was a seething mass of angry Southern "Crackers." Clearly, they didn't know what to do with the history in *their* faces. Cops by the busload were arriving.

  I walked up to a tall, smiling black man, probably in his early thirties, wearing almost-new overalls and a clean white shirt. Robert (Bob) Moses, organizer of the Freedom Riders, (DOCUMENT #7: Bob Moses, leader of the Freedom Riders) shook my hand then asked me to join them into Alabama and Mississippi. The news about three murdered Freedom Riders from the previous summer was not encouraging. I was underage, I already had plans for my summer, and I didn't have enough clean underwear. I demurred. Robert sighed and said, "Well then, we're all goin' to sit down to breakfast *together*. Why don't you join us?"

  I did.

This was the first time that whites and Blacks sat down and ate together at this lunch counter, sharing the sugar and cream for their coffee, passing the syrup and butter for their grits and biscuits. The white wait staff was not shy about how they felt about this little revolution. My eggs came out of the kitchen raw. The bacon was burned. The biscuits were cold, and the grits were lumpy. They poured hot coffee out of the cups as much as in them.

The white crowd was gathering behind us. They started to shout things. I looked Jewish, I talked like a Yankee, and I sounded *educated*. To the white crowd behind us, that was three-out-of-three. I was sure that if I opened my mouth, I'd never make it to the Mason-Dixon line alive.

The cops pushed in between us and the crowd. I thought, *Oh good, the police are here. Now we're safe.* How wrong I was. As the cops paced behind us, they swung their billy clubs. All of us at the counter ducked our heads close to our plates. Anyone who lifted his head was clubbed, dragged off, beaten, and jailed.

The group's organizers could see a bloodbath brewing. They struck a deal with the cops. If we all left at once, *Jewish lawyers* from New York wouldn't descend on the town. There would be less paperwork. Cops hate paperwork. There were rumors that Federal Marshals were coming. The cops agreed. I threw two dollars on the lunch counter and went to find my bus to Nashville.

My bus would leave in an hour, but waiting alone with the white crowd still angrily milling around didn't sound like a good idea, so I opted to swelter outside by the buses.

I prayed for the Freedom Riders, fighting for ordinary things I took for granted. *I can vote for my candidate of choice or walk with my best girl on a summer evening without fearing for my life. What a different America it is for Black people.*

Finally, the driver opened the door to the bus and started the air conditioning for early passengers. As I sat in the muggy bus, it sank in that my generation was going to pay a heavy price for remaking the world. The headlines were getting closer to my own life. I had the feeling that I was going to be in one of them someday. My mother was not going to like this news.

    I was seeing what was on the other side of the mountain.

CHAPTER 6: A SOUTHERN GIRL AND THE END OF THE CIVIL WAR

The trouble had passed. I found a window seat in the middle of the bus and began to read. Passengers began to file in. I looked up to see a pretty blonde girl and a middle-aged woman working their way down the aisle. The older woman took the aisle seat across from me, pointed to the seat next to me, and told the girl, "Sit there, honey. He looks normal enough."

I went back to my book.

Five-foot-two, with blue eyes and very blonde, this "Gidget" oozed into the seat and gave me a smile that could stop a truck. In an accent like melted butter, she said, "I hope y'all don't tawk much. I'm fixin' t' git some rayast."

I said something non-threatening and went back to my book. Despite her admonition, she started to chat. Her name was Liz Whalen, from Red Bay, Alabama. The older woman was her aunt. They were headed someplace north. "Not *too fah* north," she assured me, as if they might catch something terminal. Casually, I mentioned that I was going to college in California. She was a high school junior who had just been made cheerleader. I was not surprised.

We chatted through the afternoon and into the evening. When it got dark, the aunt fell dead asleep. Liz and I had become downright chummy, talking with our heads close together. She claimed that she wanted to nap for a while. A few minutes into her nap, she dropped her hand on my thigh as if she didn't realize she was doing it. Yeah, right. And Jefferson Davis was a rabbi. You can bet your corn fritter I wasn't sleeping with her hand where it was.

When the bus pulled into a small town for a rest stop, the aunt and most of the other people left the bus for a breather. Liz looked up, saw we were alone, and began to make out with me. When the bus got back on the road, there commenced some serious hand wandering under various garments. Someplace deep in the South, the Cheerleader made me very happy.

History found me again in the morning. We got to the Nashville Greyhound station early. Mercifully, there was no political gathering, and the air conditioning was working. Liz was as prim and daisy-cute as she could be.

Then a quiet revolution took place in front of us. A few minutes later, an old Black man in overalls appeared out of a back room carrying a small stepladder. He headed toward the bathrooms and water fountains across the lobby. He was armed with a big screwdriver in the back pocket of his overalls.

The order that the white supervisor had to give that janitor must have gone something like, "Ah, boy (the man was pushing sixty), check on the paper towels in them bathrooms, and...ah...take down all them 'COLORED' and 'WHITES ONLY' signs." The white station manager must have felt he was spitting a mouthful of red-hot nails.

The old man ambled across the forty yards of checkered tile floor toward the other side of the waiting area. Under his arm were two rolls of brown paper towels. Everybody in the waiting area knew where he was headed and what he was about to do. Nobody gave a damn about the paper towels. He went into each of the bathrooms and changed out the paper towel cores. He then came out and slowly placed the stepladder in front of each bathroom door. He carefully removed the "WHITES ONLY" and "COLORED" signs. He stuck them in the rear pocket of his overalls. He then liberated the water fountains.

Finally, the old man deliberately went back into the former "WHITES ONLY" bathroom. He was in there quite a while. I'm sure he took a piss in that urinal that had been denied his people since before his father was born. He came out and walked slowly back to the "EMPLOYEES ONLY" area. He was sweating as if he'd just lifted something that had lain across his shoulders all his life, but his head was held higher than when he'd crossed the lobby going the other way. There was almost a smile on his face.

The Black folks in the room tried to act as if nothing was going on, but the eye contact around the room was conspicuous. In street parlance, they were all "playin' dead." The Southern whites were ablaze with anger. I looked over at Liz Whalen. Her perfect, creamy, freckled face was twisted into the most hateful expression I have ever seen on a sober, sane woman. I'd seen this blazing mask of rage in newspaper pictures. I never thought I'd see it next to me on the face of a cheerleader-to-be. I said, "How can such a pretty face make such a hateful look?"

Never losing the expression, she said in a tone unbelievably harder than her years, "You just never mind. We'll see about all this."

Before all of this happened, we'd exchanged addresses. When her bus was called, Liz and her aunt said their goodbyes and walked away. Back in California at the end of the summer, I received a chatty schoolgirl letter from her as if nothing had happened. I brought myself to write her one letter in reply. I did not know how to reach into her and extract the curse of mindless hatred she had learned in her short lifetime.

Washington, D. C., and Old Friends

The unsettling experiences of Dallas, Memphis, and Nashville had left me in a state of shock. All of my worst expectations about the South were confirmed. I rode straight through the rest of Dixie to Richmond, Virginia. I was to spend part of a week in Richmond with a Jewish childhood friend and her crew. I joined them in their blissful, ordinary "regular-ness." We cruised around listening to Little Richard, Chuck Berry, Gladys Knight, and The Supremes, along with the Stones and the Beatles. After the events of the days before, this was a blessed respite.

From here, I would head north. I got back on the Greyhound bus and crossed over the lazy Potomac River into

Washington, D. C. I thought that all the racial troubles were behind me.

Back in 1959, I'd left Rockville, Maryland, a suburb of Washington, D. C., at the tender age of thirteen. In Rockville, I was to spend a week with the Wallachs, our former neighbors and family friends. The Wallachs' daughter Ellen and I had been childhood pals. I had always felt a brotherly affection for her. Now sixteen with dark hair, deep-brown (almost black) eyes, and pale skin, she had grown to be quite pretty. Ellen was a delicate, prim, dignified girl with a kind of Chekhovian reserve. She was the kind of girl my mother prayed for. Ellen didn't put out signals anything like Liz Whalen's. I have to admit that I am drawn to the rebellious type.

While at Ellen's, I hooked up with a former friend, Danny Wells. When we were both young boys, we explored the woods near our homes, went sledding in winter, and played sports. Just before I had left at age thirteen, Danny was beginning to turn arrogant and surly. Now, at seventeen, I didn't know what to expect.

Danny showed up in a four-door, bright orange cruising wagon with wire wheels, leather seats, and a rumbling V-8 engine. The car rocked on its tires just sitting still. It was up in an "Okie rake," as we called it in California, with the front of the car jacked up and the rear end lowered. The car looked like it was about to be airborne.

I got in. Danny introduced the other two guys. Danny started right in on me. "Hey, you like this rake? All you guys out there rake your cars nose down. Looks pussy to us."

"I drive my dad's car."

He chuckled and sneered at his friends.

"It's a new Pontiac V8, three-hundred-twenty horsepower, big stereo, air conditioning." This shut him up for about thirty seconds. The other guys looked nervous.

Danny was tapping the steering wheel. He turned on the radio to an R and B station. "Hey, you-all out in California loooove nigger music. You like nigger music?"

The other guys were snickering. I was shocked. It had been Danny's father who'd brought the horror of racism to our attention when we were no more than twelve. I'd never heard the term "nigger music" even once in California. Now I knew who I was with.

I played dead. "What do you mean?"
"You know, *nigger* music."
"Like Chuck Berry, Little Richard?"
"Yeah, like that."
"Sure. Surf music too."

I realized in a flash that I had misjudged Rhonda and her friends back in Richmond. They'd actually embraced Black music. This was a profound indicator that I had not understood.

Now I was back to Danny and the Regular Guys.
"Ever been surfing?"
"Yeah, I have." This was true.
"You ever score yet?"
"Sure," I said. Though I hadn't actually "done it," technically I had had sex. Several girls and I had our hands in each other's pants to the logical conclusion. For high school boys, that might not be a touchdown, but it counted as a field goal. He was such a jerk, I doubted he'd scored with a girl at all.

Now I went after him. "I've dated some cheerleaders, even a girl who was runner-up in the Miss Teen America contest." (This was the truth.) "Girls like that."

"Ever see any movie stars out there?"
The other guys could see that Danny was reaching.
"Naw. Just regular folks."

We cruised around, then he took me back to Ellen's. I thought, *If these are who I hang out with to be a "Regular Guy," it's not worth it.*

Two Dozen Japanese Tourists

I went to downtown Washington to do some sightseeing. A group of about two dozen Japanese businessmen was gathered in front of the Capitol. We don't think much about Japanese tourists all over America now, but 1964 was only nineteen years after the end of the World War. The anger over Pearl Harbor and the war was still simmering. It took some guts for them to show up in America at all.

They each wanted a group photo. Back in those days, if you wanted snapshots, you bought a Kodak Instamatic camera and then turned the whole camera in to a camera shop or processing booth nearby. You picked up your pictures a few hours later, or they were mailed to you. One of the men came over to me and bowed. He spoke no English. I spoke no Japanese. He pointed to the waiting group and to his camera. I took the picture for him. Then another man asked me, then another, then another… Twenty-seven pictures meant a snapshot on each of twenty-seven cameras.

Finally, I mimed for each of them to line up their cameras on the ground in front of me. I began to shoot the same group over and over. I began clowning with the cameras. Soon, instead of somber, austere poses, the men began to clown for the cameras too. Imagine serious, austere Japanese businessmen making faces in public! We were drawing a pretty good crowd. We were all laughing so hard, they could hardly pose for the pictures. I walked away from the group thinking, *Jesus Christ, twenty years ago, these guys—or their fathers—were shooting at my dad and his buddies. How utterly stupid and useless are wars!*

My next stop was New York City.

New York City, Unexpected

In New York City, I stayed with my Uncle Ben, my mother's older brother. Before the Great Depression, Benny started working as a stock boy in New York's Garment District. Just before World War II, he opened a small shop making nurses' uniforms. Then came the war. Uniforms of all types were needed by the thousands. By the mid-1950s, Ben was a millionaire.

While under Uncle Ben's roof in New York, I worked part-time in his warehouse. The job was eight-to-five in a hot, humid, dusty, poorly lit, upper-floor warehouse with no air conditioning. We uncrated mountains of toxic, newly-dyed pants. When we opened the crates, the chemicals in the dye made my eyes water. It was hard work. The handling of armloads of cotton pants made my hands raw. I was aware that for me, this was just a summer thing. For the other guys, this was their life.

On my days off, I visited museums, the Statue of Liberty, and the Empire State Building. I went to the Third Ear Comedy Club in Greenwich Village, where I saw Mike Nichols and Elaine May. There were real Beatniks. People of every color hung out in the clubs and cafes of the Village.

I thought I'd take a little trip up to Harlem, maybe go to some jazz clubs. These were the dog days of a very hot summer. It was "the Killing Season." I got off the subway at 125th Street and walked up the station steps into a ghetto under siege. In contrast to the nonviolent civil rights events in the South, the Northern cities were erupting in insurrections against crushing slum conditions and police brutality. After a hundred years, they were done with low wages, bad schools, and slum housing. They were finished with long jail sentences for petty crimes or being shot by cops in the street for nothing at all. Malcolm X and Stokely Carmichael were fueling the rage.

There were two cops or National Guardsmen on every corner—eight to an intersection—carrying machine guns. Truckloads of soldiers were parked mid-block on every block. This was the quelling of an insurrection. Harlem looked like the set for a war movie in Eastern Europe. This wasn't a movie, and it wasn't another country.

In the South, truckloads of angry white men would carry shotguns through the ghettos, taunting women and families just for fun. In the North, the white men were in uniform. In the South, the demonstrators were practicing nonviolence. In Harlem, the Blacks were throwing rocks and Molotov cocktails at the cop cars and shooting back from empty tenements.

I walked a few blocks, went into a corner store for a Coke then headed back to my uncle's place before the sun went down.

That night on television, I saw gunfire and burning stores on the same street corners I'd walked that very afternoon. I thought, *This is Baldwin's 'The Fire Next Time.' The people in the South aren't going to stay nonviolent for long.* I didn't tell Uncle Ben where I'd been that day.

That night, there were also reports about both growing hostilities in Vietnam and antiwar demonstrations. The same soldiers shooting Black people in Harlem were called out against antiwar demonstrators. America was at war with itself, and it was all on TV.

There had been unspeakable surprises on the journey. There was a hell of a lot happening on the other side of the mountain. Sure as hell, it was clear that History was coming over the ridge. I was badly shaken. On my return to California, I stayed on the bus and ate in or near the terminals. There wasn't a Regular Guy bone left in my body.

In a few weeks, I would be at San Jose State College, four hours north of Fresno and an hour from San Francisco and Berkeley. I was looking forward to college life. What could happen at a school rated by *Playboy* magazine as the number-two party school in America?

SECTION III

MY OWN ROAD

"Oh, what did you see, my blue-eyed son?
And what did you see, my darling young one?

I saw a room full of men with their hammers a-bleeding
I saw a white ladder all covered with water
I saw ten thousand talkers whose tongues were all broken
I saw guns and sharp swords in the hands of young children

[Chorus]
And it's a hard, it's a hard, it's a hard, and it's a hard
It's a hard rain's a-going to fall"

"A Hard Rain's A-Gonna Fall"
(Verse 2, Bob Dylan, 1962)

CHAPTER 7: OFF TO COLLEGE, 1964

I entered my freshman year at San Jose State College in September of 1964. I lived in an off-campus boardinghouse with thirteen other freshman jocks, surfers, slackers, and "eggheads" (nerds). There were probably one or two closeted gay guys in the house, but I wasn't paying attention.

I Compete for the Olympics, Meet a Future Hero

In my first days at San Jose State, I suited up for a P.E. class in track and field. The instructor showed up with his clipboard, silver whistle, and stopwatch. We formed heats of four boys each to test in the hundred-yard dash. On the starting line next to me was a tall African American kid. We crouched in the blocks. The starting whistle screeched. The Black kid shot ahead of me as if I wasn't even moving. After he cleared the finish line, the coach looked at his stopwatch in disbelief. "See the track coach right way!" he said. The kid was already known to the track coach. My time was slightly less awesome. I transferred to a gymnastics class where I could get some skills.

The Black kid was Tommie Smith. He won gold in the 1968 Olympics in Mexico City. He and John Carlos gave the Black Power salute on the podium, exploding the Black Power Movement into America's living rooms. I taught him everything he knew…

Registered

Just after I arrived in San Jose, I got my notice to register for the draft. I turned eighteen in early October of 1964. There was no explanation of my options. I received no counseling. I just went into the linoleum/neon office, checked the boxes, and turned the forms back in. I had no idea what I had done. It didn't seem real. It didn't fit in anyplace. I guess I felt like a man.

College life in 1964 was dominated by a frantic, post-adolescent, pre-political precociousness. On some level, we knew what was about to hit the fan but acted like we couldn't feel the wind. We manifested denial through sports, sexuality, fashion, and pre-political pranksterism before draft card burnings, drugs, campus protests, and girls burning bras. If you've ever seen the John Belushi film, *Animal House*, you get the picture.

One of my boardinghouse roommates was a guy from Los Angeles named Bryce Barrett. We nicknamed him "Pig-Pen" after the *Peanuts* cartoon character who couldn't keep himself clean to save his life. Bryce kept his laundry in a suitcase under his bed for weeks until he made a trip home. Every time he opened his Samsonite vault to toss something in, you could smell his gag bag all over the house. I'll get back to Bryce.

****

I had declared my major as Philosophy/Psychology along with perhaps four other people. However, I'd been bitten by the theatre bug back at McLane High. I'd even written and performed skits for the pep rallies. I found myself trying out for the university plays even before I'd gathered my own first load of laundry.[5]

The first production was Aristophanes' *Lysistrata*, an ancient Greek comedy about women who refuse to have sex with their men until a peace treaty is signed. Essentially, it's about

---

[5] As I look back on it now, these were like little agitprop skits, my first dramatic writing.

women who say "yes" to men who say "no" to war. Written in the fifth century BC, it still plays like gangbusters.

Lysistrata was my introduction to political theatre. Though box office was not the main consideration, the rising antiwar sentiment made this a business-savvy choice. I auditioned and landed the pivotal role of spear-carrier-on-the-left, the beginning of a meteoric rise in a theatrical career. (DOCUMENT #8: *Lysistrata*, San Jose State College, 1964) Hanging out in the Green Room (actors' lounge), a guy named Eddie Green told me, "What you see on stage is a lot of fear. The critics call it 'talent'."

I began to think about my interests in both theatre and politics. As more stories about the war in Southeast Asia showed up on the news, it dawned on me that registering for the draft without talking to someone was a colossal mistake.

I Meet the Drama Department Bad Boys

There was a small gang of "bad boys" in the SJS graduate program: Eddie Emanuel, whom I met working on *Lysistrata,* a big blond Viking named Jim Bertholf, and a short, cigar-smoking Mexican-American fireplug named Luis Valdez.

Eddie was big on Yiddish theatre. He turned me on to the Yiddish identity theatre from the 1920s and 1930s. Eddie was very encouraging of my acting and talked me into trying out for shows, a great confidence-builder at the time.[6]

Jim Bertholf was six-foot-six, part Norwegian and part Mandan Indian. He had striking high cheekbones, luminous corn-silk-blond hair, and blue eyes. Jim was an avowed leftist and apparent pacifist. We hit it off. He talked about political playwrights such as Bertolt Brecht, the Labor Theatre, the Federal Theatre Project during the Great Depression, and the McCarthy-era Hollywood blacklist. My parents had spoken about these topics as

---

[6] Eddie became the Chair of the Drama Department when I began to pursue my MA at Fresno State. He was a great supporter then as well. He was replaced in the rotating chair post by a guy who was my nemesis.

well.[7] Talking with Jim was like the best parts of being with my father.

Luis directed his own script, *The Shrunken Head of Pancho Villa*, for his master's thesis. *Shrunken Head* is a wildly farcical, deadly serious play drawn from the Mexican-American experience. It portrays the Chicanos' ethnic pride and the struggle to define their identity in the face of poverty and racism.

I was probably one of very few of the suburbanites in the audience members who'd seen firsthand the conditions that his play was about. The summer before my senior year, I'd gotten a job with a crop-dusting company out on the huge factory-like fruit and vegetable ranches west of Fresno.[8] Riding to and from the fields, we passed small armies of Mexicans stooped in the blinding sun moving through the crop rows that disappeared into the distance of the shimmering heat. I did not know how recently those fields had been sprayed with the poison in our planes.

The men and women were paid by the box, not by the hour. They moved like frenzied automatons, filling crates with melons, grapes, or bags of cotton. There were usually children following them or playing by the fields. Grim-looking white men in khaki uniforms and dark glasses, sometimes wearing side arms, watched the workers. A farmworker's life is not depicted on the milk posters at school.

Shrunken Head was saturated with the kind of identity politics I had grown up with in a post-Depression Jewish home. There was a nation of oppressed people around me who ate

---

[7] My parents had friends, such as the writer Artie Manoff, who were blacklisted. Manoff couldn't get work under his own name. He earned a poverty existence by fixing up others' scripts that became major motion pictures. Woody Allen did a film about him called *The Front*. It was years before I made the connection between such friends and my parents' politics

[8] A flagger stands at the end of the crop rows to be dusted and waves a flag (or a flashlight if we began before sunrise) so the low-flying plane won't over- or under-spray the field. He then quickly walks several paces to be clear of the plane's wings. I got the job because the flagger before me had miscounted his steps and was decapitated by the low-flying plane. I didn't tell my parents this detail of the job.

tortillas instead of matzo. I immediately identified with the struggle of being "other" just for being who you are. I watched a late rehearsal of *Shrunken Head* but missed the show itself, performed over Christmas break. Luis was to become an important playwright and director.

These three men—Luis Valdez, Eddie Emanuel, and Jim Bertholf, encountered during a rich political/theatrical season—would each return to my life again as important friends and mentors.

Meanwhile, concern over increasing troop call-ups began to eclipse discussions of sports, unfair professors, and dating. By Christmas of 1964, this fear became a billboard inside our heads. For some of us, History began arriving in the mail: "Greetings from the Commander in Chief. You are hereby ordered to report…"

CHAPTER 8: RADICAL POLITICS ENTERS MY LIFE

Soon after I arrived, I attended several antiwar rallies on the San Jose campus. The Free Speech Movement at Berkeley—an hour north of San Jose—was galvanizing the simmering student unrest all over America, especially in California. I went up to Berkeley as soon as I could get a free day. I listened to speeches in Sproul Plaza, absorbing the growing militancy in the student population. They were all *me*. I may have been on the campus at U. C. Berkeley on the day of the big confrontation. I remember that there was a crowd that looked like over a thousand and a lot of angry cops approaching in waves. I thought to step away.

Here's what Bill Haigwood, a witness to the events of that day, has shared with me:
"The cops approached Jack Weinberg at the CORE (Congress of Racial Equality) table and arrested him for soliciting funds. Jack went limp as they held him. The cops had stupidly driven their car onto Sproul Plaza. As they put Jack in the squad car, someone shouted, 'Surround the car!' Eventually, a crowd of more than two thousand formed. More police were called. Jack spent thirty-two hours in the police car while it was surrounded."

Mario climbed on the car roof and was handed a microphone. This was what he said.

"We're a bunch of raw materials that don't mean to be made into any product! ... We're human beings! ... There's a time when the operation of the machine becomes so odious—makes you so sick at heart—that you can't take part. ... You've got to put your bodies upon the gears and upon the wheels, and you've got to make it stop. And you've got to indicate to the people who run it, to the people who own it, that unless you're free, the machine will be prevented from working at all."[9] Mario had crystallized exactly what our generation was feeling.

One sunny Friday afternoon, I went to see an outdoor performance by the San Francisco Mime Troupe at San Jose State. I sat with Jim Bertholf and Luis Valdez. The Mime Troupe was doing a *commedia* version of Moliere's *Tartuffe* about being hoodwinked by unscrupulous con men. (DOCUMENT #9: San Francisco Mime Troupe, 1964) This kind of in-your-face, entertaining yet ideologically pointed theatre was exactly what I had been trying to imagine. I understood that my theatre skills could be a weapon. Meanwhile, my student deferment would keep me out of the draft… I hoped.

News of increasing troop call-ups made the headlines frightening and personal. The body counts and the call-up numbers raced each other higher and higher. Stories about demonstrations and arrests were increasing like a rising wave. The civil rights demonstrations triggered more and more violent government repression. I began to grasp just how serious (and dangerous) the world was becoming for my generation. Most of the guys in the boardinghouse were outwardly ambivalent about the war. However, every bone in my body knew the war in Vietnam was wrong. I expressed my opinion. This triggered pranks perpetrated by Bryce Barrett with encouragement from others in the house.

At the end of the term, I discovered that my year away had been a financial strain for the family. With sighs and sidelong glances, my mother made it clear that it wouldn't be a bad idea if I came home. Never ignore a sigh from a Jewish mother followed by a sidelong glance. As I packed up to return home, I discovered that Bryce "Pig-Pen" Barrett had pulled one last prank. He'd pissed into my cologne bottle—a product the same color as urine—

---

[9] From the text of Mario Savio's speech on the steps of Sproul Hall, University of California, 1964.

thinking I'd splash it on before I went on a date. However, as soon as I opened the bottle, I smelled what he'd done.

I went to him before I left for home. "Hey Bryce, I know how much you like my cologne, so I gave you the bottle. I put it in your suitcase. But I'm not sure the lid was closed all the way..."

This would not be the last time I connected with Bryce.

CHAPTER 9: 1965-1966—COMING HOME, FRANK VERGES, AND THE REVLON GIRL

I transferred down to Fresno State and cleaned up my old room. My dad matched funds with me, and I bought a white 1960 Dodge Dart with a red interior. The license plate was "EIS 476," my last name and my lucky numbers. It was my Car of Fate.

At the beginning of my sophomore year, things in my life seemed to fall into place. I scored an afternoon dishwasher's job at a nearby coffee shop (endless free burgers and shakes) and acquired a certified-blonde girlfriend with a natural small nose.[10]

I got into a play at the community theatre, *Life with Father*, working with my friend Mark Loring and his mother, June—my second mom. (DOCUMENT #10: June Loring and I, 1965) My part in *Life with Father* required that I have carrot-red hair. Because of my job schedule, the only P.E. class I could take was a morning weight-training class. As soon as I showed up with the professional carrot-top dye job, the queer baiting began. The very blonde girlfriend didn't seem to stop them.

My companion in the kitchen at the coffee shop was a middle-aged fry cook named Homer, a Cherokee from Oklahoma. On his most loquacious days, Homer never said a word. The only

---

[10] Every time I dated a Jewish girl, my mother started making up the wedding guest list. Jewish girls began to size you up for her mother's checklist even before my mother began the wedding invitation list. I couldn't stand the pressure, and besides, *shiksas* were different and usually wilder than proper Jewish girls. If something is working, don't fix it.

time anything coming out of Homer, it turned out to be one of the most important things that anybody ever said to me in my entire life. One afternoon, between flipping burgers onto plates set out with lettuce and buns, Homer turned to me and said, "Boy… Whatever ya do in life… Hurry!"

A Cherokee Fry Cook Guru. Who knew?

The fact that the Vietnamese were fighting just to keep their own country didn't seem to dawn on anyone. Then, on the first week of November 1965, Norman Morrison, a thirty-one-year-old American Quaker, set himself on fire outside Defense Secretary McNamara's Pentagon office, demonstrating a supreme self-sacrifice to end the war. Mr. Morrison was not a member of some obscure religious cult. He was not a fuzzyheaded rebellious adolescent. He was a mature suit-and-tie guy who was deeply affected by what his country was doing in his name. This was an act of bearing witness beyond anything I could imagine.

Most assuredly, the war was coming home.

Mr. Morrison's sacrifice brought out the deep wrongness of this war in a sense beyond words. What disturbed me deeply was that Americans weren't moved by the horror that we were torching whole villages with napalm that were full of women and kids, who most assuredly hadn't volunteered for excruciating immolation.

What is napalm? Napalm is a jelly that sticks to whatever it touches—such as the body of a child—until it burns away. It's impossible to extinguish. It rolls along the ground and finds you like the devil himself. Hitler would have loved the stuff. With this hellish concoction, delivered by air to unsuspecting villages, we racked up a score of a hundred little Dachaus every day. "Better things for better living…through chemistry," brought to us by Dow Chemical. Dow Chemical also owned Wonder Bread Bakeries. The war profiteers who made this evil stuff also made Hostess Cupcakes for kids' lunchboxes.[11]

---

[11] Eventually, the Movement began a boycott of these more accessible products, and the broad support of this effort stopped the production of napalm. Never say, "We can't do anything about what's going on."

In July 1965, Bob Dylan plugged in his guitar at Newport and electrified the protest song genre. It was now rock 'n' roll against the forces of evil, and we couldn't afford to fail.

****

To be not only nonviolent but *anti*-violent in a society that solves its problems with violence was to be against that system at its core. I understood that Capitalism inherently does violence to human relations. I hadn't considered an application for Conscientious Objector status, but I knew where I stood on what this country was doing. I didn't realize it, but I was slowly defining myself as a confirmed revolutionary. When Dad quoted Polonius in Hamlet, he was on the money. I found myself dedicated to a revision of this culture at its very roots. If I was true to myself, this was going to bring on a sea of troubles.

My father had gone to war against the Nazis partly because of what they'd done to our people. It was difficult for him to see that for the Black people in America and the Vietnamese, we were the Nazis. My father said, "If you were called, I'd go in your place."

I reposted, "That's not the point. The point is to end the war so that no one has to go at all." I had drawn my own line in the sand.

About this time, my mother saw an article in the paper about Cesar Chavez and the farmworkers strike based in the farm town of Delano, a hundred miles south of Fresno. It mentioned *El Teatro Campesino*, a theatre of farmworkers using guerrilla theatre in the fields to support the Grape Workers Strike. The director was Luis Valdez! *Maybe I can connect with him,* I thought.

Every time I heard President Johnson, Robert McNamara, or arrogant pundits talking about the nobility and necessity of the war, my reaction was visceral. Inexplicably, I also began to experience a kind of hellish waking dream. When I closed my eyes, I could hear and see screaming children and soldiers inside my head. I couldn't turn it off.[12]

Antiwar and civil rights groups were holding "teach-ins" on college campuses around the country. The purpose of these events was to cut through the shallow sound-bite lies spewed from Washington and share the truth. In this era of lingering McCarthy-style "Red baiting," this took great courage. Many professors around the country lost their jobs as a result of speaking out at these events.

During the spring of 1966, a teach-in was planned at Fresno State, organized by my Introduction to Philosophy professor, Frank Verges. Like Socrates, Verges was a gifted teacher who could connect ideas to experience. Also like Socrates, this kind of teacher draws attention from reactionary forces. Interest in the teach-in was high. Even the pro-war faction was to have a chance to speak. Then unexpectedly, the greatly anticipated event was canceled. The administration had threatened Frank's job if he went through with it.

This felt like "Jew Boy" to me.

After this shameful debacle, Frank's entire demeanor changed. There were no more jokes in class, no more spirited discussions sitting on the floor in the hall outside his office. He was thoroughly gutted. He completed the semester in lackluster fashion and left Fresno State soon thereafter. But I would cross paths with Frank Verges again.

What I Learned From the Revlon Girl

Though I didn't audition for shows at Fresno State, I hung out in the Drama Department Green Room. In mid-spring 1966, a gorgeous redhead started to hang out in this actor's lounge. She kept to herself, usually reading. She was serious as well as mysterious. After three or four chance run-ins, we began to chat.

---

[12] In his book *Our War*, David Harris confessed to experiencing the same phenomenon.

Carrie was actually in her mid-twenties but still an undergrad. Somehow, she looked familiar. I said to her, "Listen, I know this sounds like a line, but I feel like I've seen you someplace before."

With a sly grin, she said, "You probably have."

She reached into her bag and pulled out a women's glamour magazine. On the back cover was a picture of her in deep-red Revlon nail polish and lipstick.

"Holy shit! You're the..."

"...Revlon girl."

In the 1960s, there was only the *Cosmopolitan* cover girl, the *Esquire* cover girl, the *Playboy* centerfold, and the Revlon girl. Except for movie stars, that was it.

"What are you doing at Fresno State?"

"Trying to get some privacy while I get a degree. I was at UCLA, but talent scouts and movie agents wouldn't leave me alone. I gotta tell you, this face can be a real hassle when you just want to go out for a beer. Everything in pants tries to score on me."

"What's your major?"

"Pre-law."

I imagined her in front of a jury. *How could the other lawyer hope to get any attention with her in the courtroom?*

"I'm banking every dime I can with this modeling thing."

"I'd never have pegged you for law."

"You and everybody else. I'm thinking Columbia or USC. Probably USC so I can still make some bread[13] as a model."

One day, Carrie left to go on a Revlon PR tour. It would be a lot of money.

Carrie made me rethink my ideas about women. Why was the idea that she would study law so unexpected? Women were beginning to demand to be treated as more than decorative objects. Even the Revlon Girl was part of the revolution right under my nose.

---

[13] The hip term at the time for money.

As Mario Savio had said, "We need to liberate ourselves from what The System expects us to be." That was the last I saw of her. I hope she achieved her dream.

****

The cancellation of the teach-in along with my hankering to start a real theatre career made me look beyond Fresno State. I decided to pursue a degree in theatre at the University of California, Santa Barbara. UCSB was a serious theatre school. Shows at U. C. Santa Barbara were reviewed in the L. A. papers. This looked like a good move.

The conservative faction at Fresno State was emboldened by the suppression of the teach-in. However, Fresno was the location of one of only three U. S. Army Induction Centers in California. As the war in Vietnam escalated, it was inevitable that Fresno would become a hotbed for antiwar activism. The Grape Workers Strike and the Chicano Power Movement were energizing the political landscape in the Central Valley as well. Fresno was destined to catch radical fire with the inevitability of a Greek tragedy. But I'm getting ahead of my story.

CHAPTER 10: THE BEGINNING OF BIGGER THINGS

At the University of California, Santa Barbara, I expected to learn what I needed for a life in the theatre. I loved acting, yet I was equally attracted to the technical side. My dad had shown me how to use tools. The directing bug had bitten me back in high school as well. I'd written and directed many successful small skits for pep rallies. An undergrad theatre degree at UCSB would allow me to explore all of these options before choosing my path. This was a good thing because I wasn't ready to make up my mind about a direction in the theatre.

Soon after I arrived at this university-on-the-beach in the fall of 1966, I was cast in the character role of the itinerant peddler in Lynn Riggs's *Green Grow the Lilacs. Lilacs* became the musical, *Oklahoma.* My character was a traveling salesman, a Middle Eastern immigrant who was an outsider in the American frontier. (DOCUMENT #11: *Green Grow the Lilacs*, UCSB) The peddler wanted to belong, to fit in, but he didn't know how. I was playing myself.

A Los Angeles reviewer said I was "adequate in the role of the peddler." The reason I was merely adequate was that I hadn't yet discovered that the commitment to acting a part was the same as committing oneself to an action in real life.

One evening, on a break from rehearsal for *Green Grow the Lilacs*, an older actor and I were walking back to the theatre from the Student Union. Gordon bent over to tie his shoe, and a lumpy, hand-rolled cigarette fell out of his shirt pocket. He said, "Well, since it's out, we might as well smoke it." This was the first time I "turned on." I didn't become addicted. I didn't become a trembling, wide-eyed lunatic. I didn't stand on corners begging strangers for heavier stuff.

The media's penchant for disseminating misinformation and disinformation about our lifestyle was rampant. The same news agencies that lapped up hippie hoax stories about smoking banana peels and psychedelic smoothies with morning glory seeds[14] also slavishly reported "official body counts" of the thousands of Viet Cong killed in Vietnam. These turned out to be the bodies of women, children, and old men left in the torched and razed remains of their own villages. The mass-market weekly news magazines of the day, *Time, Newsweek, Life,* and *Look*, were all filled with these images. The news reported "decisive victories" of territory captured several times over. Meanwhile, the truth about the war was buried along with my high school buddies coming home in body bags.

****

In my classes, I learned about good, relevant, progressive plays in the traditional repertoire. I learned about the Theatre Guild and the WPA Federal Theatre, all-important developers of politically engaged theatre in the 1930s. These lectures resonated with my conversations with Jim Bertholf at San Jose State. It also rang some bells in a discussion with my dad who offhandedly remarked that he had been part of one of those left-wing theatre groups back in the 1930s.

I discovered Mordecai Gorelik's book, *New Theatres for Old,* on progressive theatre and community. Gorelik wrote, "To the degree that art is moving, it is propaganda. To the degree that

---

[14] It so happens that one of the guys who perpetrated the "Great Banana Peel Hoax *and* the Morning Glory Seed Hoax was a friend of mine from the scene shop at UCSB. He and his pals did it with a great piece of theatre, a hokey news conference in the Haight-Ashbury in San Francisco, complete with Indian print tapestry, peacock feathers in vases, and incense burning on the table. This ended up in Donovan's "Mellow Yellow" song thereafter. (Far out.)

propaganda is well done, it is art." Gorelik and others made the case that progressive material was commercially viable if done well. This was music to my ears.

The mood in the country was becoming more militant as the lies coming out of Washington became more desperate. With the immediacy of the Civil Rights Movement and the developing Vietnam War, more pointed political plays were regaining interest. Articles in such journals as the *Tulane Drama Review* kept mentioning the San Francisco Mime Troupe, the Bread and Puppet Theatre, and *El Teatro Campesino,* along with consistent references to Bertolt Brecht. I felt that somehow I was in the right place at the right time.

Joan Baez and Ira Sandperl

U. C. Santa Barbara hosted a lecture series featuring such thinkers as Buckminster Fuller, John Cage, and Joan Baez. I went to hear all of them. Joan came with an eloquent peace activist, Ira Sandperl. Their philosophy of nonviolence was sweeping the world. Its effectiveness as a religiously-based principle was eroding opposition to the Civil Rights Movement even within the segregationist community.

Two thousand people filled all the seats in the hall, sat in the aisles, and stood around the walls. Thunderous applause erupted as Joan came out on stage. She began, "I'm not here today as an entertainer. I'm here as a citizen of the world, just like you. All of us must live with what we do in the world every day. We have to decide if we are going to make it a safer place in the face of nuclear war or let all hell break loose because we did nothing." She was speaking to each one of us deciding what we were going to do with our lives at that very moment.

Mr. Sandperl then told a story from his own experience. Alone late at night at a train station in New York City, he was accosted by a man who demanded money. Ira said, "Listen, I really need to get home tonight. Why don't I give you half?"

The hapless thief was disarmed by this offer and told Ira his tale of woe. Ira gave him half of his money. They shook hands and parted friends. This story was beautiful in its almost biblical simplicity. Seeing the situation from the other guy's point of view became my dharma. When I walked out of that auditorium into the Southern California sunset, my feet were on a different path.

Picking up Some Chops

Completing a degree in theatre required lab hours spent in the production shops. I loved working in the scene shop. My father had taught me how to use tools and build things. I'd also taken classes in mechanical drawing in high school. After about two weeks, the university's tech director figured out that I could safely use pretty much every tool in the shop and could read the construction drawings. I soon became the unofficial Shop Foreman.

I moved on to the lighting lab. Because of my rock climbing hobby, I had no fear of walking the square steel grid over the room to hang or focus lights. I paid attention to which lights were used to create which effects and which colors worked for different moods on different actors' faces and costumes.

Near the end of my junior year at UCSB, I was cast in a one-act play, *The Bespoke Overcoat* by Wolf Mankowitz, a play about an old Jewish tailor who dies of pneumonia. His ghost returns to enlist his best friend to help him steal the promised (bespoke) overcoat, the lack of which was the reason for his death. It's a play about acting out justice.

My own grandfather had been a tailor who worked on overcoats exactly like the character in the play. When my parents came to see me in the play, my mother was unexpectedly shaken by my portrayal. The makeup was so good that I appeared to her the very ghost of my grandfather. But it wasn't just the grease paint, the hair dye, and the costume. In feeling the injustice in the character's life, I was expressing my own sense of injustice. I was truly transported in the role, and it came across to the audience. I was playing myself in the moment. I was *acting*. It made the ideas come alive.

After the production, my father said nothing about my performance. Instead, he expressed his fears and concerns about my choice of career. My father had never complimented me on any of my roles. It would be many years before I found out the root of his problem.

While all of my classmates in theatre were grooming themselves for commercial careers, I was pulled toward political theatre. With the growing antiwar consciousness and the Civil Rights Movement, the audience for progressive art was larger than it had been since the Great Depression. In show business, timing is everything.

****

Toward the end of my junior year, Ronald Reagan (or as we called him, "Ray-gun"), the B-grade film actor-turned-Governor of California, was pushing a huge tuition increase for public university students. This was a meat-and-potatoes issue that struck at the heart of the American dream for many families, including mine. This tuition hike would weed out working-class families from access to higher education, especially Blacks and Latinx families. It would force many current students to leave school. Many of us, including me, could be drafted. Reagan was well aware of this endgame.

The reaction to the tuition hike proposal was swift and strong. Busloads of students and professors from all over California planned to converge on Sacramento. I found a gap in my schedule and got on a bus. As our bus lumbered all night to make it to the rally the next morning, we talked about this situation. Something about what I said and how I said it made an impression on the leadership on the bus. Out of nowhere, they asked me to make some remarks from the stage when we got to Sacramento. It just seemed to happen, like the Bible-in-class incident back in the seventh grade.

When we got to the State Capitol, I was escorted to the speakers' platform in front of a crowd of thousands from all over the state. Years of oratory practice in high school and college theatre improv class kicked in. Both Ronnie Reagan and I will tell you never to underestimate the value of a good improv coach. What I said was well received.

There comes a moment when bearing witness is not enough. This was that moment for me. It can happen to anyone at any time. Something touches pushes you out of the anonymous crowd and into the tide of events. You step forward and *become History*. That is what happened to me, to us.

The overwhelming statewide response scuttled the proposed tuition increase. In this battle, I learned an important lesson about political organizing: If you don't share a real connection with the struggle, your words and actions are false. On the bus home, I tried to figure out what quality in me was perceived as leadership, what to do with it, and how "to thine own self be true."

Summertime Down by the Beach gets Heavy

I elected to stay at UCSB during the summer of 1967 to get some of the required tech lab hours done and thereby leave more time in the regular school year for acting in shows. During that summer session, UCSB hosted a special planning institute for African American theatre. During this "think tank" event, I took my breaks and my lunches sitting with the Black actors and directors gathered for breaks and lunches. Usually invisible to actors because I was a techie, and even more so to this gathering because I was white, I was privy to discussions rarely gleaned by people like me.

This was a rare window into understanding how racism affected their lives. Though they were at the top of their profession, they were never cast in classical roles or even the better roles in the professional repertoire. Up until only a few years before, in many parts of the country, they couldn't stay in the same hotels as the rest of their company. They and their whole community were barred from sitting in the front-row seats of the very theatres in which they acted. With artists like Ossie Davis and Ruby Dee roaming the halls talking about civil rights, even under the summer palm trees, the riots and demonstrations seemed near.

There were other unexpected lessons during this summer. UCSB had hired a hotshot New York designer for that summer's session shows. He'd conjured up *Camino Real* in a dreamlike New Orleans French Quarter. The set had to load in for a quick turnaround, so it was built on a monstrous single wagon. On load-in day, all hands available—even the secretaries from the office—came down to push the big wagon out of the shop and across the outdoor concrete breezeway toward the backstage load-in door thirty yards away.

As soon as the unit began lumbering toward the theatre, we discovered that the backstage load-in door was narrower than the shop load-out door. The moving unit, gathering speed, was not going to make it through the opening. The designer grabbed a power saw, attached it to a hundred-foot cord, then tossed it at me and yelled, "Cut it down!"

I jumped on the rolling Juggernaut and began cutting sections away, kicking them clear. It made it into the theatre with only inches to spare.

Sometimes you discover what you need to do on the fly.

Twenty years later, when I worked with African American theatre companies in the San Francisco Bay Area, I still heard references to this pivotal event. Most assuredly, I was also one of the inheritors of its legacy.

CHAPTER 11: LOVE AND OTHER UNSETTLING REVELATIONS

Everything my generation thought, felt, and believed was under fire. Every young man I knew in college was dealing with fear of the draft. As I entered my last year of undergraduate school, I was not only dealing with the mounting pressure of becoming possible draft bait. I was finding myself as an artist in the theatre.

In the midst of this turmoil, things in my life were about to take a different turn. In the very first week of my senior year, October 3 was my twenty-first birthday. I was in a study lounge in the Student Union. Into the room came Sharon. Sharon was a newly arrived freshman. She was tall with a glorious mane of (real) blonde hair, sparkling green eyes, and a Barbie doll figure. Though I have to admit a weakness for brunettes, I was lost. That evening, we went out for pizza. UCSB was crawling with pretty girls, but there was something in Sharon's spirit beneath the head-turning good looks. She was so magical that I forgot that this was the first day I could legally order beer.

It wasn't long before she was pretty much living at my apartment. She was unique among my partners, who were mostly dark-haired women. Outwardly, we were very different. She was very Peter Max/Bullock's/Macy's/Magazine Cover; I was *Village Voice/Berkeley Barb*/thrift store/coffeehouse. Sharon caused traffic accidents when she crossed the street. I was a scruffy, bearded, paisley actor. Yet somehow, inwardly we were very connected. She was to be the source of more than one unexpected epiphany that affected my values and my actions.

An Ordinary Friday Night Miracle, My Higher Calling

After we had been together for several months, Sharon asked to attend a Jewish Sabbath service. One Friday night, we went to a temple in Santa Barbara. At this service, a miraculous biblical legend was reenacted.

As the service began, a mentally retarded and physically handicapped adolescent walked to the bimah with his father. The shy boy held a clarinet. He lifted it to his lips and haltingly played a Jewish melody. This was his gift, the voice of his soul. Everyone in the place had tears in their eyes. On the way home, I explained the biblical connection of the story of Rabbi Hillel and the mute boy who played music as his offering to God at the old temple in Jerusalem. Sharon was quite moved.

I believe in the uplifting miracle of the spirit through artistic expression. This event confirmed my quest for something deeper than a scrapbook full of reviews and show programs. There *was* something more. I would find it.

A Little War Talk, An Unexpected Change of Heart

Sharon took me to meet her extremely wealthy family. Her father was the president and CEO of his second major national corporation. He prided himself on being a "thinking Republican." I was a skinny, Jewish, suburban kid, an aspiring actor, and obviously a left-winger with a beard. It would be safe to say I probably wasn't his ideal match for his daughter.

Paul was supportive of the Vietnam War for all the expected, bumper-sticker reasons. He and I had an after-dinner talk about the war over Scotch older than I was. He repeated all the cereal-box political slogans such as "saving the free world from Communism." So much for thinking Republicans.

After a second refill of twenty-five-year-old spirits, I said something like, "If we'd supported their struggle for self-government—like our own revolution—instead of roasting their women and children in front of their own farmhouses, we'd have a solid ally instead of an enemy, not to mention access to the natural resources."

Something in this grounded, meat-and-potatoes argument stopped him in his seventy-proof tracks. He said, "I'm having dinner with Nelson Rockefeller in New York next week. I'm going to share that line of reasoning with him."

Two months later, Nelson Rockefeller publicly reversed his position on the Vietnam War and began to talk about withdrawal. Though I have no proof of a connection between my conversation with Paul and his lunch with Nelson Rockefeller, the timing seemed auspicious. Never miss the chance to share your point of view. You have no idea where your ideas will go.

The Most Important Unexplained Event in My Entire Life

Close to the end of my senior year, Sharon was part of the most bizarre, unforgettable moment of my entire life. Had Sharon not been there, it wouldn't have happened. It remains unexplained to this day. Sharon wanted very much to get me something special for graduation. One afternoon, we were alone in my second-floor studio apartment. Sharon had her arms around my neck, and I had my hands on her hips. She pleaded, "What do you *really want* for your graduation?"

I closed my eyes and somehow cleared my mind of every other thought. I was about to say something when a deep voice *came from behind me*. It answered her question. It said, "Myself." This was what I was thinking. "Totally surprised" doesn't begin to cover both of our reactions.

When I opened my eyes, *Sharon was looking into the vacant space beyond me from where this voice had seemed to come.* It seems that both of us heard something in the room. That would be the only reason why Sharon would be looking over my shoulder. There was no one else in the room. The next-door apartment was vacant at the time. Wide-eyed, we ran out and didn't return for several hours.

It is entirely possible that the magic I felt in her when I first saw her was manifested in our combined conjuration of this experience. I will never know. Neither of us was a stoner or stoned at the time. I am not a crystal gazer or a spiritualist. I haven't a clue about what happened, but in that sober, focused moment, something did.

This unexplained event reflected my father's advice in an eerie, confirming way. It focused me as I had never been focused before, pulling together everything in my hopes, dreams, and experience.

Years later, I recognized that this disembodied voice was my own.

Those Best-Laid Plans...

Soon after arriving in Santa Barbara, I'd signed up as extra help with the local stagehands' and electricians' unions. I was soon called to work load-ins for large, professional road shows in the downtown theatres. I learned how to plan a load-in and load-out, hang, rig, and strike a big show, and how to pack a truck for a road show. At UCSB, I supervised aspects of construction in the shop. I learned to weld and to repair lighting equipment. I also directed several projects. By the time I graduated with a bachelor's degree (after studying at three different schools), I'd acted in, built, painted, lit, crewed, or directed nearly thirty shows.

I knew something about my style and an idea of what I might do with my training. I wanted to direct. However, my grade-point was not exceptional. Graduate school, therefore, was not a "given." I could still find myself in Vietnam dodging machine-gun fire in an outfit of stunning camo-green.

The political situation was turning critical. The Chicano Movement and Black Power struggles had turned militant. Both Robert Kennedy and Dr. King had just been assassinated. The combat in the cities were making the Harlem riot I'd seen look like a picnic. Hope itself seemed gutted and derailed. Then, at my graduation, a powerful voice came from on high. The commencement speaker up on the stage was Supreme Court Chief Justice Earl Warren. He spoke of our duty to make our own future. He said, "It's your job to go out and make trouble."

I felt as if he was talking directly to me.

With advice from the Chief Justice ringing in my ears, I packed up my sheepskin and went home. Sharon and I had talked about getting married. While home waiting for acceptance to graduate schools, I landed a job in Kings Canyon National Park in the mountains east of Fresno. While in the mountains, I suffered a rock-climbing accident, ripping out all the muscles in my left elbow. I lost my job and drove home down the winding mountain road popping pain pills like M&Ms. It was a good thing I was stoned on painkillers. Just after I got home, my mailbox was hit with voodoo on a single day. You can't make this stuff up.

First, there was a "Dear John" letter from Sharon. I should have seen it coming. I knew her parents didn't see me as an ideal match. I think she'd met someone else. Whoever it was, they were lucky to have her in *their* life. I felt the anguish for years thereafter. Nevertheless, she'd left me with a faith in the power of the unexplainable "right place/right time" serendipity in life.

I didn't have the luxury of indulging in the melancholy of a lost love affair. Alfred Hitchcock had taken over the movie of my life. In the heap of fateful missives on this single day were letters from the two graduate schools to which I'd applied. They'd turned me down or offered inadequate scholarships. I was definitely sweating my 1-A classification for the draft. Just to round out the curse, the feared letter from my draft board was in the mail as well. I'd been reclassified as draft-eligible. To top it all off, I didn't have any weed.

In order to stay out of the Army, I had to be in graduate school. San Francisco State had a good graduate theatre program. With its avant-garde theatres and urban buzz, San Francisco beckoned. I applied and was accepted. I'd dodged the bullet—literally.

Waiting to heal, I watched television with my arm in a sling. The big summer feature was the Democratic National

Convention in Chicago, held during the most turbulent summer since the 1930s. There had already been riots in dozens of cities following the assassination of Dr. King on April 4. A few weeks later, on June 5, the unthinkable assassination of Robert Kennedy had sent thousands into the streets again in rage and mourning. This summer was, indeed, the Killing Season. The Democratic Convention in Chicago opened in an angry mood.

Huge antiwar demonstrations were planned for Chicago. On the day before they were to be held, the cops yanked the demonstration permits. The crowds had already arrived. This premeditated tactic was engineered to create an inevitable showdown. The ranks of demonstrators had swelled to double the predicted numbers. The lack of a permit turned the demonstrations into illegal assemblies. This gave the cops a free hand. They took it.

This was civil war.

The Democratic Convention delegates did not discover what was happening in the streets outside until they turned on the news in their hotel rooms. Nevertheless, they didn't have to watch the news to get the picture. The law-abiding Convention delegates discovered that "*1984*/security state" tactics had been employed against them as well. The telephones in their hotel rooms had been rigged by law enforcement with special receivers. When a phone receiver was put down on its cradle, it opened a switch that listened in on the room. The same was true of the television sets. Turning off the set activated a microphone that listened in on the room. They now understood why there were anti-government protesters in the streets.

After the savage police response to the demonstrations, eight leaders of the Chicago events (the "Chicago Eight") were arrested on federal conspiracy charges. One of them, the Black militant Bobby Seale, was not allowed to conduct his own defense. He was gagged and tied to a chair in the courtroom. (DOCUMENT #12: Bobby Seale courtroom sketch) The whole world was watching. After finishing my theatre degree, I planned to give Amerika something else to watch.

SECTION IV

THE HARD RAIN BEGINS TO FALL

"And what did you hear, my blue-eyed son?
And what did you hear, my darling young one?

I heard the sound of a thunder that roared out a warning
I heard the roar of a wave that could drown the whole world
I heard one hundred drummers whose hands were a-blazing

[Chorus]
And it's a hard, it's a hard, it's a hard, it's a hard
It's a hard rain's a-going to fall"

"A Hard Rain's A-Gonna Fall"
(Verse 3, Bob Dylan, 1962)

DOCUMENT 1: The Red Scare was the foundation for discrediting any criticism during the Vietnam War. It was hard to avoid ostracism in this world.

DOCUMENT #2: My parents' wedding portrait, 1943. Dad was an engine mechanic in the Air Force, stationed in and around the Panama Canal. Mom waited at home for him in Tucson, Arizona. (Photographer unknown)

DOCUMENT #3: Though this 1950's milk poster was progressive for its time, I am not represented. No Jews here.

DOCUMENT #4: My Bar Mitzvah Picture, Fresno Ca, 1960.
(Photographer unknown)

Fresno Vandals Paint Swastikas On Synagogue

Continued from page 1-A

ney A. Mandel of 116 East Garland Avenue, went to the synagogue to inspect the damage.

They wiped the swastika off the front door but missed seeing those on the rear door.

An investigation revealed no other damage to the building, either inside or out.

Lieutenant Robert Saum of the sheriff's office reported the building was not entered. He said an investigation of the incident will continue today with a further examination to see if any clues to the identity of the vandals can be found.

Saum also said the neighborhood will be checked to learn if anyone noticed any unusual activity near the synagogue last night.

The symbols were left on the synagogue between 6:15 PM, when Rabbi Maurice A. Lazowick closed the building for the night, and 8:40.

Paint Still Wet

Bonn, Scherr and Mandel said the paint was still wet when they removed the swastika from the front door. Saum said he believes the painting was the work of vandals.

Rabbi Lazowick disagrees.

Otherwise the millions of soldiers who lost their lives in World War II have died in vain."

Last night's incident is the third to be reported in the San Joaquin Valley this month.

Both the other cases were in Merced. There on January 6th it was reported that anti Semitic literature was being distributed and last Sunday an anti Semitic note wrapped around a stone was thrown through a window of the Shepperd of the Valley Church.

Phony Inspector Gets Six Months As Foreflusher

PAINESVILLE, Ohio— AP—Most of Harry Lovell's dreams literally went down the drain today as he started his first day of a six month sentence for posing as an official flusher for the State of Ohio.

The 29 year old former resident of Atlanta, Ga., was sentenced here for charging unsuspecting homeowners up to $30 for flushing a so-

NAZI SYMBOLS—Deputy Sheriff James Moore inspects swastikas painted on the back door of Congregation Beth Jacob. — Bee Photo

DOCUMENT #5: Newspaper article on Synagogue Vandalism, Friday, January 29, 1960 P. 8 (Permission, Fresno Bee) There were several incidents that week.

DOCUMENT #6: The author at seventeen, Senior Class President class of '64, C. L. McLane High School in Fresno California (C. L. McLane Yearbook Photo, Photographer unknown)

DOCUMENT #7: An unexpected beginning to my summer vacation: I met Robert Moses at the desegregation action in the Memphis Greyhound Bus Station. Bob led SNCC's first voting drive in McComb, Mississippi. Pictured here during Freedom Summer training, in his signature clean, Sunday-go-to-meetin' overalls and clean "T" shirt. (Black Star Studio)

Document #8: *Lysistrata* (Aristophanes/Fitzgerald) San Jose State, 1964. (Hal Todd Directing) The author is the illustrious spear carrier just in the light downstage right. (Photo: Hal Todd personal archives. Courtesy of Joan Todd)

DOCUMENT #9: San Francisco Mime Troupe production of *Tartuffe* (adapted by Richard Sasoon, Directed by R.G. Davis/& Nina Serrano, lyrics by Saul Landau). I saw this show at San Jose State. Luis Valdez was sitting next to me. Maureen Silverstein(?) downstage front playing Colombina. Dan MacDermott is "il Dottore" (The Doctor) next to her. Upstage right in the dark glasses is John Broderick. Pantalone (upstage left) in black mask and soft felt hat) probably Joe Lomoto. (Photo is probably by Eric Webber.)

DOCUMENT #10: June Loring as my mother and me age 19, as the eldest son in Fresno Community Theatre production of *Life with Father*. My hair was dyed flaming red, enflaming a rash of "queer baiting" from my gym class pals at Fresno State College. June, already an activist in the Women's International League for Peace and Freedom at the time of this picture, was later to become my draft councilor. (Photographer unknown)

DOCUMENT #11: *Green Grow the Lilacs,* at U. C. Santa Barbara, Fall, 1966. Directed by Ted Hatlen. At left is Katherine Rindlaub (Aunt Eller), Center right is Joel Eis as the peddler, standing center, Laurie Walters as Laurey Williams. Seated at right is Nora Delaney playing Ado Annie. Laurie Walters went on to become a famous TV and film actress until the 1980s. (Photog. unknown)

DOCUMENT # 12: Bobby Seale tied and gagged at his trial for conspiracy after the Chicago Democratic Convention. (Artist unknown)

```
                                        Joel Eis
                                        520 Presidio Ave
                                        S.F. California
                                        November 10, 1968

Attention: Local Board # 68
           Rm.1306 Federal Bldg.
           1130 "O" Street
           Fresno, Calif.

Dear Sirs (re: Joel Eis, #4-68-46-1143)

        For the purposes of my personal appearance, I have herein
sumerized most of the main points of my religious convictions upon
which I base my Conscientious objection to war of any kind. please
regrd this as only a summary for the purposes of ecconimaccly using the
time of my hearing.

        The teachings of my faith revieled by god do not hold that
any human relation such as a nation has a greater claim on the "true
way of life" than any other. Rather it teaches in the Torah that any m an
who is sincere in his faith will reach his eternal wmeward.
        It was commanded to my people "Thow Shalt not kill." and this
gospel was to be preached to other nations thru the living example of
the jewish way of life. This is a rational moral law which all men of
good faith and knowledge acknowledge abd it transcendsany obligation
to participation fo any reasan to contemporary worldy national problems.
        The old teastament reminds us that "even the man outside your
gates is yout brother". I will not voluntarily or otherwise participate
or be part of an institution such as the military arm of a nation state
whose avowed purpose and reason for existance is the distruction of
life and property, at ana arbitrary command in the name of the "truth
of a single nation's contemporary way of life. There is a higher law
to wich I adhere and thi h I feel I cannot violate . I am sure that I
ca  serve my country in other was far better and in good conschence
without violating my religious teachings.
        I believe that thepremeditated or spontaneous use of "force"
(violence) by a man or a nation that is harmful and distructive in
fuhction and purpose is in absolutely no concievable situation a
rationall or neccessary course of action NO MA TTER WHAT THE MOMENT RY
OR TEMPORARY "TRUTH" IE IS USED TO ENFORCE. I cannot in good conscience
lend my physicaA or moral support to any human relation, such as the
military whose fuction and reasbn for existance is distruction of life
and property. It is against all of my religious teachings and my constence.
I can think of many more rational and constructive ways that I can serve
my contryy which will be within my conscientios practce of my faith amd
doing a constructive service for the United States.
        I will clarify this and any statemenjs which you might have
about my form or anything connected with it, butI feel that I am
and have been a sincere conscientious objector abd wish your to take
 my intrests as sincere, andin offering alternatives of service, patriotic
and constructive.
        Thankyou for your time in reviewing my correspondence.

                                        Yours truly,
                                        Joel Eis
```

DOCUMENT #13: Letter to my Draft Board requesting reclassification as a Conscientious Objector (Archival collection, Joel Eis)

DOCUMENT #14: Students of all ages and races supported the San Francisco Student Strike for a more relevant education. On a campus with less than 5% minority students, 80% of the student body honored the strike. The times were a-changin.' (Photo: Terry Schmitt)

Document #15: Iconic image was a reaction to the Neo-fascist official response to student demands as the cops kept the campus open. (Artist unknown).

WLF leader Roger Alvarado was arrested as he tried to le unday City Hall rally.

DOCUMENT #16: Roger Alvarado, leader of the BSU/Third World Liberation Front strike at San Francisco State Strike, 1968-69. I stayed in Roger's house during the late stages of planning the strike. (Source unidentified. presumed student paper, photographer unknown).

DOCUMENT #17: Bread and Puppet's Capitalist Landlord "Uncle Fatso" with his enforcer comrade the NYC police officer. (Photo, Richard Howard)

DOCUMENT #18: San Francisco State, 1968 was the first time that this kind of paramilitary police power was used on a college campus. (Terry Schmitt)

DOCUMENT #19: Student strike at SF State. A few weeks into the strike, Cops came in on horses to ride through the crowd and break us up. They began their "run" out in the neighborhood and entered the campus on the move. (Terry Schmitt)

DOCUMENT #20: Cops with guns, students with ideas. San Francisco State Student Strike, Fall, 1968. (UPI photo, David Kennerly)

DOCUMENT #21: San Francisco State Strike, Fall, 1968. Cops on the roof, many with automatic rifles and shot guns. (Photographer unknown, may be Terry Schmitt)

DOCUMENT #22: "San Francisco's Finest" show their attitude towards students and their issues. (Photo, Terry Schmitt)

DOCUMENT #23: Thomas Dunphy, AKA "General Waste-More-Land," famous one-man guerilla theatre performer showed up at countless anti-war demonstrations. This image was shot at S. F. State during the strike, mere days before our shared appearance at the head of an antiwar march in November, 1969 (Photographer William Haiwood).

GI Peace March Set for Today

The GIs and Vets March for Peace, beset by skirmishing in the courts and periled by rain, will move out from Golden Gate Park at 11 a.m. today.

The march, which signals an end to the relative lull in anti-war protest in San Francisco, is billed as a servicemen's protest to American involvement in Vietnam, but it has also raised civil liberties issues involving free speech and dissent in the military.

March organizers had predicted a turnout of as many as 50,000 for the hike from the Panhandle to a rally in Civic Center, but yesterday indicated some concern over inclement weather cutting attendance.

A sudden rash of inspections at Bay Area military installations may also thin the ranks of military personnel participating, which have been variously predicted as anywhere from 150 to 5000.

The major speaker at the rally will be retired Brigadier General Hugh Hester, 73, an outspoken critic of American policy in Vietnam.

On arrival in San Francisco yesterday, he charged the country has "unspeakably degraded itself" by the Vietnam war and termed the Johnson administration "the greatest disaster that ever happened to the United States."

Air Force Lieutenant Hugh Smith, the activated reservist who originated the march, said one of its major purposes was "to establish, possibly for the first time in history, that GIs have human rights."

Other speakers will include former special forces Sergeant Donald Duncan and possibly folk singer Pete Seeger. A small group of AWOL GIs is expected to participate and turn themselves in at the conclusion.

GEN. HUGH HESTER
Rally's main speaker

IMAGE 24: S.F Chronicle, Oct 12, 1968, P. 10. The march I joined and found myself at the head of the parade! (Photo: Permission S.F. Chronicle)

CHAPTER 12: SAN FRANCISCO AND BIG TROUBLE

After the collapse of my entire life in one day's mail delivery, I felt like a contestant on a TV quiz show where I had to choose a door with a future behind it. I'd taken Door #3: Graduate school at San Francisco State, deferment included.

I had no place to crash in San Francisco while I registered and looked for an apartment, so a friend from UCSB gave me the name of a man named Roger Alvarado who lived in the City. He agreed to let me crash in his pad for a few weeks. With no idea what I'd find, I got into my trusty 1963 Dodge Dart with the lucky license, EIS 474, and headed up to Roger's place.

Roger Alvarado was at least six-foot-four with a wild mane of black hair, a huge black beard, a voice like a radio announcer, and a distinctive vector to his life. In his apartment on 14th Street in the Castro District were two other housemates, a guy named Tom and a brooding Black kid named Nick. Nick was one-hundred-percent "street." He'd never been close to so many white people in his life. I slept on a bench in the kitchen. Nick had the couch. I smoked weed with them, picking up tips on neighborhoods to avoid. I went out to the school to get enrolled. I dug the city.

One Saturday night, I walked down the hill to the Both/And Club on the corner of Haight and Divisadero to hear some jazz. Yusef Lateef, $3 cover, two-drink minimum. Thelonius Monk showed up to sit in. I got back to the pad about 11:30. When I walked inside, it was totally dark. I heard voices. I smelled weed.

I walked into the dark kitchen. In a very soft, controlled voice, Tom said, "Hey, Joel, Nick's over in the corner. *He's got a knife…*"

Nick was freaking out on a paranoid trip. I could see Nick's profile in the lights from the house next door. I held out my hand. "Hey, Nick, how's it goin', man? Who's got the weed?"

Tom said quietly, "Yeah, Nick, put down the knife, man. Let's smoke that joint." So we did. Years of theatre improv had saved my life in a ten-second monologue.

For the next week or so, Roger, Tom, and a lot of very serious people rapped[15] in the house. I had no idea what the discussions were about. The next Saturday night, Nick got busted. There was more than a chance that Nick's bust was a setup so the cops could raid the house while everyone was gone. Tom and Roger went to bail Nick out. I was left to watch the house. While I sat out front, several cop cars slowly cruised by. The house was definitely on their radar. I discovered years later that photos had been taken of all of us in front. I soon found my own apartment on Presidio Avenue at the top of the Fillmore on the border of a Black neighborhood. This was not the last I was going to see of Roger Alvarado.

My personal concerns with the draft were getting stronger. As a full-time student, I had a student deferment. However, this could evaporate with the stroke of the president's pen. For years, on and off, I'd been having bad dreams like the battle syndrome nightmares described by soldiers coming home from the war. Yet I had never even been near such events. Like a deep inner voice, they'd convinced me that declaring myself a Conscientious Objector was profoundly important.

In order to get a C. O. classification, I'd have to prove that my objection to war was rooted in religious conviction. I'd recently talked with June Loring, my friend Mark Loring's mother, who was a draft counselor. She promised to help me begin my application process for a C. O. deferment. I was not refusing to serve but requesting to serve in a noncombatant capacity, a legal

---

[15] Archaic term for a serious, engaged, focused discussion.

alternative to combat. I would still have to serve if called up, but it could be as a noncombatant.

Getting the C. O. classification was not easy. Draft boards were older conservatives who expected every young man to die for whatever nonsense Washington came up with. I would have to prove that my religious beliefs committed me to a higher calling. It was time. I had to "out" myself as thoroughly Jewish and proud of what it meant. I felt like I was sewing a yellow star on my chest, but so be it. In my head, I could hear my dad warming up to quote Polonius…

June Loring helped me craft a letter to my draft board petitioning for a new classification. (DOCUMENT #13: My letter to the draft board) To my surprise, my rabbi, the temple cantor, and others wrote letters of support.

All I had to do now was wait. Piece of cake. Yeah, right.

<u>1968: What We Woke Up To Every Day</u>

The year I started graduate school, 1968, was already a worldwide revolutionary year. There were the demonstrations in Chicago at the Democratic National Convention and an exploding Civil Rights Movement around the country. A general strike had erupted in France. There were large anti-nuke demos in Sweden and the UK. The IRA was getting more militant for Irish independence. The movement against apartheid in South Africa was becoming more aggressive. There was unrest against dictatorships in South America. There was a massacre of more than four hundred students in Mexico City just before two American athletes, Tommie Smith and John Carlos, raised the Black Power salute from the winner's podium at the Olympics. In short, the shit was hitting the fan all over the planet. As could be expected, these events were covered in disconnected "dis-informative format" in Amerika's[16] "free press."[17] The lines

---

[16] After the summer of 1968, the Democratic Convention, the rising death counts in Vietnam, the riots in dozens of cites in America, and the murders of

connecting the dots were never drawn so that people understood our government's involvement.

The harassment of Black groups such as the Student Nonviolent Coordinating Committee (SNCC) and the Black Panther Party, along with the disproportionate numbers of Black and brown soldiers killed in Vietnam, coalesced the Black and brown communities into strong voices against the war.[18] The riots in the Black neighborhoods of "Amerika were being televised in real time. The FBI was engaged in direct disruption of progressive groups, especially Black and brown progressive activities. Their legitimate movements were being subjected to overt government frame-ups and assassinations. The planned attacks on Black Militant groups on the flimsiest of excuses resulted in boldfaced murders such as those of Fred Hampton in Chicago and Lil' Bobby Hutton, at age 17, in Oakland. Despite stories and witnesses to this COINTELPRO campaign, the American press denied or ignored the evidence of its existence.

For the first time, middle-class (white) Americans saw cops by the hundreds in their own cities in military riot gear, swinging ax-handle batons and spraying tear gas at everyone in the streets. Seeing soldiers patrolling the street corners of the ghettos with machine guns was becoming "business as usual." The end of 1968 saw the thin mask of "America, the nation in control" torn away.

In the fall of that year, the official number of American troops killed in Vietnam numbered nearly forty thousand. The body count of Vietnamese killed topped the million mark. American soldiers were getting high on heroin-laced weed and using heroin in order to deal with the syndromes that came from

---

Martin Luther King and Robert Kennedy, the radical/left press began to refer to this country as "Amerika" in a clear reference to its neo-fascist policies.

[17] Before the internet, every international news story was filtered through the State Department first. If the Feds didn't want the story out there, they just ripped it off the wire before the papers ever got it.

[18] In 1966, Muhammad Ali, the Black heavyweight champion of the world, spoke out against the war. Those in the multiracial sports community sat right up and thought about where they stood.

participating in the carnage. Huge quantities of heroin suddenly became available in the ghettos to placate and destabilize the movement—courtesy of the CIA and flown in by their "front" transport company, World Airways, based in Oakland, California.

By this time, the majority of us who'd been devastated by the murders of JFK, Robert Kennedy, and Dr. King were in our twenties. We'd had it up to our eyeballs with being told that our vision of hope was subversive, unpatriotic, and fuzzy-minded while the government took our money and our lives. Outspoken political heavyweights were joining our ranks. Elected officials, journalists, teachers, and business leaders were speaking out. They could be seen in the photos of marches and teach-ins. Our revolution was becoming mainstream.

With all of this going on around me, it was pretty hard to think about getting a theatre degree just to embrace a career as a goofy guy in TV commercials or wear funny costumes in endless musicals or Freudian dramas.

Our lives had been hijacked and our hopes derailed by Wall Street, which had hired Washington as the hit man to do the deed. But the plot had been exposed by our journalists and musicians.

This was war.

CHAPTER 13: RADICAL THEATRE AND THE STUDENT STRIKE AT SAN FRANCISCO STATE

> "Art is a weapon in the class struggle."
> (Vladimir Ilyich Lenin, 1917)

  As I registered for classes at San Francisco State, I was blissfully unaware that a major battle had been brewing on campus. For several years, the irrelevance of the curriculum had been under discussion all over the college. S. F. State served as a local commuter college for a city that was seventy-percent nonwhite and predominantly working class. The college was seen by these communities as the gateway to the American Dream.

  At the same time, S. F. State did not acknowledge the contributions of Third World people to our history and culture at all. This was a nationwide problem, but it rankled especially hard in the Bay Area. Their contributions were simply nonexistent in the textbooks, the faculty, the choice of guest lecturers, and the library acquisitions. In a city with a nonwhite majority population, the faculty at San Francisco State College was as male and lily-white as a KKK barbecue. The excuses for this situation were pathetic.

  A coalition of African American, Latinx, Asian, and Native American student and community groups led by the Black Student Union had requested a half-million dollars for an Ethnic Studies Program. It would serve thousands of current students. It would attract minority students in a variety of competitive fields. This group had been patiently working through approval committees for years. Finally, the Ethnic Studies Program was approved. It was announced to debut in the fall of 1968.

Mere weeks before the beginning of the semester, however, the Geology Department requested an expansion of the Natural Resources Exploration Program, serving the petroleum and uranium industries (total enrollment in this program: forty students). Their request for the same half-million was fast-tracked, and the Ethnic Studies Program was tabled. At the same time, the contract for a popular militant Black professor who had openly criticized this move was not renewed. This was the last straw.

I had barely gotten started in my classes when the Black Student Union and the Third World Liberation Front called for a general strike. Eighty-five percent of the students—mostly white—boycotted classes, marched through the campus, and gathered daily in the Free Speech Area, shouting, "Shut it down!" (DOCUMENT #14: Students on Strike) Iconic posters appeared as the college used the police to keep the campus open. (DOCUMENT #15: "Back to Skool" poster)

A Personal Surprise

When I walked out to attend my first strike rally in the Free Speech Area. Roger Alvarado, whose kitchen I had slept in only weeks before, was at the podium! (DOCUMENT #16: Roger Alvarado) Now I knew why the cops had been circling his house like bees around a rosebush. Roger spoke with eloquent rage against a culture that treated people without kindness and respect, thwarting their dreams when it should be forwarding them. His clear logic and impassioned call to action were undeniable. We took him up on it. After the rally, I went over to Roger. He had spotted me in the crowd and introduced me to the leadership of the Third World Liberation Front. We connected often and shared ideas. I'm sure I received the best end of these conversations.

The Theatre Department Takes up the Struggle

The Theatre Department at S. F. State was also seething with discontent over the lack of nonwhite representation on the faculty and the glaring lack of relevant plays on the season. Aside from Brendan Behan's *The Hostage,* about the IRA (in which I was cast in a small character part), the rest of the season was old chestnuts. The faculty refused to discuss relevance as a criterion in the selection of the season's plays. The curtain was about to rise on serious trouble.

In the theatre, we say, "timing is everything." Just at this moment, the Theatre Department at S. F. State, under the radical leadership of Dougald Macarthur,[19] was hosting a Radical Theatre Festival with shows and lectures by the three major radical theatre companies in America: *El Teatro Campesino,* the San Francisco Mime Troupe, and the Bread and Puppet Theatre of New York.

Starting a theatre company requires vision, genius, and unmitigated *chutzpa* under any circumstances. To conjure up a radical theatre troupe in a repressive society borders on insanity. Doing it well requires an alchemy that's defies the betting odds. Yet in those troubled times, political theatres were springing up like whirlwinds in the desert. These radical troupes went into the streets, the parks, the lecture halls, and the university campuses filling in the chasm of truth left out by the media and ignored by commercial theatre. These companies were the soothsayers of the Movement. They defined our connection to the issues. They were the insanity we needed.

Our street/political theatre companies employed a highly visual style. They used dynamic masks, burlesque characters, large puppets, and wickedly funny, outlandishly honest dialogue to *unmask* what was really going on. They acted out how events affected ordinary people. They demonstrated the moral and social implications of the Vietnam War and the racial conflict helping

---

[19] He was a man light-years ahead of his time. He was removed one year later.

this, the first media-bombarded generation, to see through the razzle-dazzle of news clips and government hokum.

These companies operated on a Brechtian model, showing the audience that new ideas could be crafted to fix what was amiss. They were therefore dangerous to the State. It's no wonder that Hitler considered Bertolt Brecht an art criminal to be apprehended.[20] The three major American radical theatres that appeared at the festival were in the FBI's crosshairs from the day they glued up their first posters. They were subjected to intense government scrutiny and police harassment meant to stop the shows. They had their performance permits pulled at the last minute and were often ensnared in trumped-up obscenity trials.

With my chosen career path, they struck the perfect note.

The San Francisco Mime Troupe

The quintessential 1960s political theatre group was the San Francisco Mime Troupe, founded by R. G. "Ronnie" Davis in 1959. Being part of the SFMT (or other companies like it) had nothing to do with seeking a show business career. Joan Holden, mainstay writer and co-director for the company, told me, "It was for the thrill of doing in-your-face theatre that told the truth. Nobody was in it for the money or fame. People came from all kinds of backgrounds. Some were even actors." The shows produced were highly effective in clarifying the contradictions in Amerika at the time.

I saw my first SFMT show in 1964 at San Jose State. I'd just returned from my trip across the country. Their work, based on the fast-paced, irreverent Italian street theatre called *Commedia dell arte,* was sharp political slapstick reminiscent of Buster Keaton or Charlie Chaplin.

As the SFMT rose in importance, they caught the attention of the authorities. The Mime Troupe was busted for "obscenity"

---

[20] Brecht eventually fled from Europe to the USA. A few years later, he was called up before the HUAC because he was a suspected German Communist even though he opposed Hitler even *before* the war.

while performing in San Francisco in 1965. You couldn't ask for better publicity for a theatre company fighting for freedom of expression than a front-page obscenity case.

The SFMT used masks, outlandish costumes, and over-the-top, cartoon-like characters. Their stock-in-trade was savagely accurate caricatures of government/corporate figures with dastardly exploitive plans. The hero who saved the day was always an "every-person" type. It was radical vaudeville, performed free in the parks and at political events. Sixty years later, their shows are still fantastic.

The Bread and Puppet Theatre of New York

The Bread and Puppet Theatre of New York was led by Peter Schumann, a scruffy, sandy-haired German sculptor and puppeteer. Peter was like the old German puppet-maker Gepetto in *Pinocchio*. He sure as hell knew who the liars were.

"The Bread and Puppet" was grounded in Gandhi-like values of community change through personal transformation. Their work featured beautiful sculptural masks and fantastical giant puppets. In a climate of fear and repression, speaking truth was a courageous, transforming act. One of their early pieces, acted out in the streets of Harlem, was about the complicity between the slumlords and the city. A giant landlord puppet named Uncle Fatso—a rod puppet some twenty feet tall with *papier-mâché* fists the size of small cars on the ends of long cloth-tube arms—chased a comedic neighborhood dweller (Chicken Little) around the street. (DOCUMENT #17: Uncle Fatso, Bread and Puppet Theatre) This show was instrumental in prompting New York City to reform its eviction laws to make them more favorable to tenants.

Along with their performances, the company baked and served loaves of hard, gritty, European black bread, hence the company's name. The loaves were passed around and shared with the crowd. As the audience chewed on the gritty, nourishing bread, we also chewed on the gritty, nourishing ideas. The Christ-sacrament reference (serving loaves to the people) was obvious.

The Bread and Puppet workshops at S. F. State showed that in order to energize action, ideas needed concrete physical expression, not abstract intellectual references. It had to be visceral yet beautiful.

El Teatro Campesino

Luis Valdez, director of *El Teatro Campesino,* moved to Delano, California, to join the Grape Strike in 1965. Luis had seen the S.F. Mime Troupe while attending SJS. He and I had sat together on the day he saw their performance. Upon graduation, he joined them.

When the Farmworkers' Strike exploded in the news, Luis went down to Delano with the idea of using political theatre to organize for the strike. Luis brought his experience as a *commedia* actor and his skill as a comedic playwright into the mix. By the time *El Teatro* appeared at the Radical Theatre Festival at S. F. State in 1968, the company's star was rising. *El Teatro* had recently won a special Obie Award in New York for socially relevant theatre. *El Teatro* was now a company with an international reputation.

****

The student strike continued to escalate outside the Radical Theatre Festival. The appearance of these groups in the festival ratcheted up the heat on the ideological battle lines of the strike, especially among the theatre department students. The lectures, bull sessions, and press conferences with the three companies reflected on the rightness of the student struggle outside. Then, without warning, the leaders of these theatre companies staged a walkout from their own press conference in solidarity with the strike.

Amid the rising tensions over educational relevance (the focus of the student strike), the Drama Club met a few days later. The irrelevance of the production season had been highlighted by both the strike and the Radical Theatre Festival. The Drama students voted to support the strike by boycotting the auditions for the season's plays. The Drama Club would soon vote to use their talents to go even further. Once again, with no intention and no idea of how it happened, I'd landed in the right place at the right time to put my ideas into action.

CHAPTER 14: BILLY CLUBS, NOT BOOKS

The students at S. F. State were not spoiled kids from the suburbs taking classes in surfing and sociology. The average age was twenty-seven. They were interesting in professional training courses in teaching, social services, the sciences, and medicine. Many students were working parents, Vietnam vets, or single mothers. Some were Latinx, African American, or Asian.

What was fundamentally revolutionary about the student strike at S. F. State was that the white students accepted the Third World students as our leadership. At a time in America when there was only one Black tennis star, no Black football coaches or quarterbacks, a handful of Black people in government, and almost all of the Black people on television and in movies played thugs, whores, or buffoons, we recognized the Third World Liberation Front as the vanguard of the Movement.

With the simple but radical gesture of stepping back and following their lead into the police lines, the cop vans, the tear gas, and the streets, we turned a clean page in the history books. For the first time, tokenism in our fundamentally racist society was wiped away. The idea that thousands of white people embraced this fundamental paradigm shift sent the American Establishment into cluster-fuck. Our "Power to the People!" salute was a fist of five clinched fingers. The joined digits stood for Black, brown, yellow, red, *and white*. Our slogan was, "A PEOPLE UNITED CAN NEVER BE DEFEATED!"

The college's response to the students' demands and the subsequent strike changed the face of American political dissent.

Until that moment, America had only seen newsreel footage of paramilitary police and military force called out against dissenting citizens in other countries. In America, we'd only seen cops in the South with billy clubs and shotguns being called out in fairly large numbers to intimidate and break up civil rights demonstrations. Images of cops breaking up union pickets at factories were never shown. Even these cops appeared only in khaki, short-sleeved shirts, and slacks, perhaps wearing motorcycle cops' helmets. All of that changed with S. F. State.

When we arrived on campus on the first day of the strike, we were greeted by an army of jackbooted Blue Meanies. More than six hundred officers invaded the college. In a meta-theatrical display of control, they were "costumed" in intimidating midnight-blue riot gear, bullet-shaped helmets with Plexiglas face shields, combat boots, ax-handle-sized billy clubs, gas masks, shotguns, machine guns, and thug-like black gloves on their fists. (DOCUMENT #18: S. F. State riot cops phalanx) Nowhere in Amerika had this kind of paramilitary Gestapo response been employed before. This was war declared against a future that threatened milk-poster Amerika's comfortable perception of control.

Even this army of booted goons was not enough. Within days, they trotted out riot cops on horseback to thump us at a gallop. (DOCUMENT #19: Cops on horses) Nothing like this response had ever occurred in a demonstration since the labor strikes of the 1930s.[21] I cannot emphasize strongly enough the shocking importance of this tectonic shift in American politics. Today we see these kinds of robocops called out as "business as usual" to deal with hostage situations or a terrorist threat.

At the time, however, this was utterly shattering. You never forget your first time with Fascism in your face. As we ran from these phalanxes, it was unavoidably clear that the government was willing to gun down its own citizens for exercising their First Amendment rights. (DOCUMENT #20: Cop with gun drawn)

---

[21] Such as the Bloody Thursday massacre on the docks in San Francisco in 1934.

Each day, at some point in the gathering in the Free Speech Area (ha!), came a muddled announcement on a bullhorn from a rooftop that the rally was an illegal assembly. Usually, we never heard it. Before the crowd could even try to disperse, tight little squadrons of riot cops appeared and began to march toward the crowd. The PIGs (Prejudiced Ignorant Gestapo) broke into groups of about thirty and began to trot toward us in a solid flying wedge, holding their batons in a "ready to thrust" position.

    Without any warning, a dozen or more cops would split off at ninety degrees, mowing down people who thought they'd escaped the forward march of the larger group. There was no warning when they would do this or to get out of the way. All of this was to punish us for trying to get a relevant education. We'd committed THOUGHT CRIME.[22] Unannounced, they would break into a run, charging us in close formation, mowing down anyone in their path. When they got close, the ax handle was thrust into your kidneys or slammed against your head, your collarbone, or your back. If you fell, you were dragged to the side, beaten, and arrested.

    Professors, women with kids, even old people were all pushed and prodded. People were randomly dragged off and arrested. I must have been chased by a dozen of these cop groups while trying to leave the campus. This was the official version of "Jew Boy." I was very lucky. I never got clobbered or busted.

    The cops kept slicing up the crowds, crisscrossing the open lawn area. Groups were cornered between buildings, chased into the trees, even chased into moving traffic. No one knew where they could stand. The cops hooked the tips of their clubs or their gloved hands into hoop earrings worn by Black and Latin women and ripped them out. Ambulances arrived all day like pizza-delivery trucks to take away people injured by the cops. Watching all of this from the rooftops of the surrounding buildings were cops

---

[22] It is noteworthy that after the S. F. State Strike, all California college and university campuses were designed to make outdoor gatherings of large groups on campus difficult, if not impossible. The Establishment was not going to risk any more central quads or "free speech" areas.

with shotguns, M-16 automatic rifles or Thompson submachine guns. (DOCUMENT #21: Cops on the roof)

This was war.

We started improvising self-defense gear. Some of us took to stuffing a heavy magazine into the rear of our pants to protect our kidneys. *Cosmopolitan* or *Glamour* were the best. Others carried a magazine rolled up to be held against one's forearm to protect against billy club blows. The best body protection was a thick navy pea coat, already "hip" urban gear. We started to carry a wet cloth in a plastic bag to cover our faces against tear gas. The women stopped wearing hoop earrings. No women wore high heels, not even the office secretaries caught in the cop runs. Some of us wore motorcycle helmets or two wool caps to protect our heads. We'd pioneered the People's Defense Gear *tres chic*. We carried the phone numbers of lawyers and bail bondsmen in our wallets or inked on our hands.

There were also moments of simple but profound street theatre. A group of Black students formed a line. A Black student playing the "teacher" in clown-white face makeup (the reverse of minstrel show actors) went down the line, slapping his hands with the others in the line in an old-style "Gimme five," with the hand-to-hand slap at waist level. The "students'" hands were now covered in white paint.

The action of making their hands "white" was shocking. What happened next was even more so. Each of the grim white-handed actors looked at their hands then ran their fingers down their faces, turning the white pigment into African-style war paint. Then, as a group, they made the Black Power salute and marched off in close order, Black Panther-style. If you didn't understand that the effort to "make them white" was turning them into angry warriors, you were an idiot.

Strikers also engaged the cops as they stood in formation. We would walk directly up to the white cops holding the big billy clubs and say, "You know what Abraham Lincoln, the *bearded* founder of the *Republican* Party, said? *'The bigger the stick, the smaller the man!'*" You could see the anger on their faces and the cluster-fuck in their minds. Sweat poured down their foreheads, burning their eyes. We immediately got the fuck out of there, melting into the crowd.

The next day, there would be another rally in the Free Speech Area, and the cops began to break it up again. Sometimes there were scenes of real combat. I watched a student confronted in the middle of the wet, muddy lawn by a single cop. The cop was about to wail on him with his ax-handle club. The young man picked up a handful of mud and smeared it on the cop's Plexiglas facemask. The cop was now blind. The blind cop reached for his gun holster as he was trying to get his facemask off. Before he pulled out his gun, the kid grabbed a metal lawn chair and hit the cop across the back; he laid the officer out cold. The student ran into the waiting crowd.

Everybody now knew you could blind the cops with a handful of mud, but we also saw that the cops wouldn't hold back on pulling out their weapons. Great. Blind, frightened, trigger-happy cops. Now, in addition to the magazine in the back of our pants, the magazine we held to protect our forearm, the wet bandana in a bag to protect against tear gas, and heavy wool caps to protect our heads, we had a baggie of mud in case we were cornered. We were carrying as much shit as the cops.

College administrators could have simply sat down with the Third World Liberation Front leadership. Instead, reinforcements of white cops from the suburbs, who resented students as "spoiled hippie draft dodgers" or "commie, nigger-lovin' troublemakers" arrived by the busload. (DOCUMENT #22: Cops with attitude) They'd called out the dogs to teach us a lesson.

The lesson we learned was how far the power structure would go to repress a democratic movement. They pulled their guns on students armed with nothing more than a different idea of their own future. We endured four months of this.

The college administration colluded with the Federal Government to punish strikers. The administration turned in the names of male students to the draft board who were prematurely failed by anti-strike teachers. These young men would lose their student deferment and be immediately eligible for the draft.

One of the drama students caught up in this premature failure scheme was my Nigerian friend, Paul Okpokom. Paul's father had been involved in an unsuccessful democratic uprising in his country. He and his son Paul were on the "wanted list" of that dictator's government. Paul received early fail notices for two classes, lost his student visa, and was summarily deported back to his country. Six months later, Paul was arrested by the dictator and hanged.

Drama Students Get the Governor's Attention

The solidarity from the theatre companies for the Radical Theatre Festival radicalized the students in the Theatre Department. Three weeks into the strike, the Drama Students Club held a meeting. We'd already decided to support the strike, but we wanted to do more. I remembered that in high school, I'd written and performed many short, satirical, five-to-ten-minute pep rally skits. I thought, *what the fuck?* At the next Drama Club meeting, I raised my hand. "Why don't we put together agitprop political skits? We could show up in unexpected places and gain support for the strike."

I volunteered to write, direct, and organize the appearances of these "hit and run" troupes. In the next few days, I quickly wrote a few short skits for groups of two or three actors. These little squads went out all over the city and then all over the state. They appeared in the adjacent Stonestown Mall, downtown at Union Square, and at City Hall. The strikers were soon getting support letters in the newspapers from every place we played.

The Theatre Department chair Dougald Macarthur allowed me to use the Department's office to book the agitprop appearances. One afternoon, in about the eighth week of the strike, I was on the phone in Dougald's office. Suddenly, from inside the office, I saw the secretary throw herself up against the frosted-glass partition like a bug on a windshield. I could see the blurred outline of four SFPD "Blue Meanies" with ax-handle nightsticks surrounding her.

Alice said, "If you want to arrest him, you'll have to take me first!" They were not prepared to handle a blonde secretary with big hair and real attitude, so they left to find a female officer to move her out of the way.

She stuck her head into the office. "The campus has a closed phone system. The only way these guys could know you're in here is if the administration let them set up a wiretap. You've gotta go someplace else. I guess I won't be telling any more dirty jokes on the phone for a while."

Our little theatre troupes went to other campuses to gain support for the strike. These performances were more successful than anyone imagined, encouraging sympathy walkouts and agitating for Ethnic Studies programs on other campuses. In his television appearances, Governor Reagan started referring to us as "off-campus agitators" spreading revolution and unrest.[23] You can't beat free publicity like that. ... And six-hundred cops with billy clubs, tear gas, and machine guns—not to mention fifty Cossacks on horseback—aren't "off-campus agitators?"

I think the wiretap on the Drama Department's campus phone marked the beginning of my security file. Perhaps they matched me up with photos taken in front of Roger Alvarado's house. Maybe my speech at the State Capitol two years before was also recorded. Police cars started following me home and to school. I was often stopped for no reason and thrown up against these squad cars. There was never an arrest. This was just Gestapo-style intimidation.

Then, suddenly there were new players in the game. The American Federation of Teachers (AFT), a bonafide AFL/CIO union,[24] voted to support the strike. They staged a walkout that made the TV news. AFT member professors held classes in their

---

[23] We were now twice as much in demand than before. Never be afraid of critical press.
[24] American Federation of Labor/Congress of Industrial Organizations, the official support group to which most labor groups belonged.

apartments, in cafes, in bars, and in parks. All of our exams became take-home papers. We continued school without violating the strike. Mom would have approved.

Next, the full A. F. of L. (American Federation of Labor), along with the CIO (Congress of Industrial Organizations), officially recognized the faculty strike. This meant that no union would violate the strike line. Teamsters no longer delivered food to the cafeteria. No laundry was picked up at the gym or dorms. No paper was delivered to the offices. Garbage was left to rot. The Black Police Officers Association refused to accept duty on the strikebreaking line.

The strike was costing millions in police overtime. Salaries for scab delivery drivers were also costing millions. At some point, you'd think that the college administration might have figured out that they should have just voted the half-million dollars to the Ethnic Studies Department. But there was more at stake. This was a power struggle with deep roots in institutional racism. It was a single battle in a cultural war.

My Charlie Chaplin Moment

Political activism began to wash over my life. One Wednesday afternoon during the strike, a guy showed up dressed in a pseudo-military costume with toy airplanes sticking out of his hat and phony medals on his chest. Thomas Dunfey, AKA "General Waste-More-Land"—a caricature of General Westmoreland, commander in chief of the forces in Vietnam (DOCUMENT #23: General Waste-More-Land)—was a famous one-man street theatre performance artist who appeared at demonstrations around the country. "The General" was handing out leaflets for an antiwar march to be held the following Saturday.

This march was organized by the Bay Area Veterans for Peace, an antiwar vets group. They'd invited active and past servicemen and women to show their opposition to the war. A real retired general was going to head up the march. I resolved to attend. On Saturday morning, I went down to the march. We were to meet at the McKinley statue at the corner of Baker and Fell Streets in the Panhandle and march to the Federal Building in Civic Center Plaza. I sat with a book at the base of the statue, waiting for the march to begin. I was so absorbed in the book, I didn't notice that the entire gathering had formed behind me. As someone with a bullhorn announced the beginning of the event, I found myself exactly like Charlie Chaplin, unintentionally at the head of a march in the film *Modern Times*. Marching alongside me at the head of thousands of current military and their supporters was the retired general (DOCUMENT #24: Antiwar march in San Francisco with real general), the reporter Robert Scheer, and the one-man political theatre activist, General Waste-More-Land.

I am sure the FBI has shots of me at that march that they put together with the ones from the anti-tuition rally in Sacramento and Roger Alvarado's house. I was becoming a poster boy for the Revolution.

Eldridge Cleaver and Me

Other events in this intense period brought me to a dangerous edge. My apartment on Presidio Avenue was just west of the Fillmore District, a highly concentrated Black neighborhood. One evening in November, I got a phone call from my friend Mark Loring. Mark's uncle was Charles Gary, the lawyer for Eldridge Cleaver, Minister of Information for the Oakland Chapter of the Black Panther Party. Mr. Cleavers was a hunted man.

Mark's uncle had called Mark because he needed help with a little chore that evening. Eldridge Cleaver was one of the most inflammatory leaders of the Black Power Movement advocating an armed response to police brutality in Black neighborhoods. The FBI and local police were gunning for him, literally. Eldridge was hiding in a house on Bush Street, about three blocks down the hill from my place. Eldridge planned to leave the country for Havana that night.

If Eldridge was seen leaving, he and anyone in the house would be gunned down as the cops had done to Fred Hampton in

Chicago and Bobby Hutton in Oakland. Mark explained that in about an hour, a gaggle of Black women was going to come out of the house laughing, yelling, and "loud-talkin'." They would all climb into a big car and drive off. This was the cover for Eldridge's escape.

They needed someone unknown to the cops to stand on the corner at the top of the hill where Presidio and Bush Streets made a "T" and watch for police cars or SWAT vans heading down the hill. If I saw any cops coming, I was to light up a cigarette. The people in the house would see the flare from the matches and the cigarette glow. I felt like I was in a bad noir movie. I told Mark about my own surveillance worries for activities at S. F. State. He said there was no one else.

I went out, bought a pack of cigarettes at the corner store, and hung out on the corner as if I had nothing to do but watch the fog roll in. Soon a posse of women came out of the house carrying on loudly. They got into a Yellow Cab and rolled away. One of these women was Eldridge Cleaver in a dress, heels, and cloche hat with a thick veil. The brother had become a sister to get out of the country. No cops showed up.

A Short Trip Home

In the middle of this madness, I was ordered by mail to take my physical at the Armed Forces Induction Center in Fresno. I packed up my laundry and my fear for a short trip home. My parents were glad to see me but not happy about why I was in town. My mom dealt with her nerves by overfeeding me.

My memory of that day at the building on H Street in Fresno is hazy. The experience was kaleidoscopic and unreal. I stood in line under cold fluorescent lights in a cold stone hallway with farm boys and Mexican kids. We sat in school desks. We filled out papers. I got a five-minute physical and a stamp on my papers. The aroma of a dozen aftershaves and the smell of fear filled the air.

I was handed a paper label and a pen and told to write my name on the label. Then all of us boys-about-to-be-men were given a plastic cup with a cap. We trooped into the lavatory. Amid nervous jokes in English and Spanish, we each filled a cup, snapped down the lid, stuck on the label, put the warm cup on a tray, and got dressed.

Aside from maybe one of the doctors who gave the physicals, I think I was the only Jew in the building. Lastly, we stood crowded in a room for a pep talk and a swearing-in. I looked around me at the other boys in the room. *How many of these kids like me would be dead in less than a year? What carnage would they be asked to inflict in the meantime?*

There was probably a picture of Nixon hanging on the wall somewhere. After the procedure, we were out of there. I went home for one of Mom's dinners.

I was now fully focused on getting my C. O. reclassification. I was sure that my concept of serving my country by ending the war was not going to fly. If I didn't get my C. O., I would refuse induction or leave the country.

They didn't even let us keep the pen.

****

I returned to San Francisco and the struggle the next day. The strike at S. F. State lasted for more than four months. It was the longest student strike in American history. It exposed the System's hardball playbook to everyone. The strike forced the issues of racism and relevance into the content of every discipline in higher education. It exposed the covert machinery of the university system structured to serve corporate interests, which included resisting hiring Black and brown people for good-paying jobs. However, after the strike, it was no longer possible for any institution to automatically pass over Black, brown, Asian-American, or female candidates for promotion or hiring. Most importantly, the power of student protest was given its full voice. The whole world was watching.

My personal transformation was more profound than I fully understood. Writing and directing the agitprop projects during the strike taught me about hitting an audience's hot buttons. Taking charge of this project sharpened my organizational and problem-solving skills better than any classes I could have taken. Risking my own safety had transformed my sense of self. My priorities had been clarified. I was closer to that voice that Sharon and I had heard inside my head only a few short months before.

CHAPTER 15: I MAKE A CIRCLE

While the strike at S. F. State ground on, I awaited the determination of my Conscientious Objector's status. I was depressed and very scared. Then my C. O. classification came through! I would still have to serve, but I could choose a social service agency stateside. I cannot tell you what a relief this was.

On one of the later days of the strike, I'd dodged the cops a few times already that day. I watched them busting some guy out of the middle of the crowd. As they cuffed him and stuffed him into a cop car, he lifted his head. Somehow, we made eye contact. It was Frank Verges, my former philosophy professor from Fresno State! I had no idea he was now teaching at S. F. State. Before they pushed him into the police car, he smiled and yelled, "I see you got the point of the philosophy lectures, Mr. Eis!"

This encounter with Professor Verges was when the decision to devote my life to taking apart a power structure profiting from unfairness became visceral. I didn't become radicalized in a single moment. It didn't happen by taking a college class, reading a single book, or hearing a single speech. It happened by answering my heart. It happened while running from the cops who were chasing me for trying to make this a fair country. It caught me like a tidal wave. I'd seen people "get it" watching an agitprop performance, connecting their own lives to the bigger picture. The people in power were relentlessly driving the Juggernaut that crushed the poor and disadvantaged. As Mario Savio had said, this was never going to change unless we decided to stop the machine. We had to throw ourselves on the gears. It was my turn.

I knew what I wanted to do, what I had to do. My personal switches slammed closed. During the Radical Theatre Festival, I helped *El Teatro* with the tech on their show and rapped with Luis Valdez's younger brother Daniel, an actor in the company. Danny and Luis invited me to join *El Teatro*. I told them I'd think about it.

The widely supported strike at San Francisco State to establish an Ethnic Studies Program ended in March of 1969. Millions of dollars had been spent on police. Hundreds of people were jailed, and many were bloodied in body and wounded in spirit, but in the end, we won by "doing it in the road." The Ethnic Studies program—now the College of Ethnic Studies—has been at San Francisco State for fifty years.

Months of upheaval during the strike had outed racist, anti-progressive professors and administrators. Several of my own professors had made it very clear that due to my politics, getting a degree at S. F. State would be impossible. I needed to get away from what was destined to be a very bad scene for years to come, particularly in my own department. I decided to transfer home to Fresno State. I took a drop from classes taught by anti-strike teachers and got passing grades in the others. I would transfer home to Fresno State and join *El Teatro*.

****

I was on my way to Fresno. Through my friend Mark's mother, June Loring, I made a connection to live and organize in the Draft Resistance community, a small colony of old wooden farmhouses a few miles north of Fresno State at First Street and Herndon Avenue.

When my family moved to Fresno in the sweltering San Joaquin Valley in 1959, no one had any idea that in five years, Fresno was to be the epicenter of political upheavals that far outweighed its reputation as a town where people said, "Fresno? Oh, yeah, I stopped off for gas there once."

Split by Highway 99, the spine of the valley, it's a place of glaring social contrasts. Sprawling ranch houses are within sight of tarpaper labor shacks for workers who toil like landless serfs to pay for their palm trees and their pools. The large factory farms would soon become the battlefields for farm labor unionization and a spawning ground for the Brown Power Movement. The farmworkers' struggle would mushroom into the anti-pesticide movement waged for the health of the entire nation.

The Vietnam War would bring special attention to Fresno. Fresno is the location of one of only three Army Induction Centers in California. Fresno would become Ground Zero for demonstrations, draft card burnings, marches, and more. Fresno would soon be the front line of History. I would be in the middle of it all.

It washed over me just after I passed a new motel on the barren stretch of Interstate 5, rounded the cloverleaf, and headed east on Highway 152 (called Blood Alley for its dangerous passage in the fog) toward Highway 99. I was listening to the radio. I was a little buzzed on sticky Mexican dirt weed. The pieces had fit themselves together.

In the Strike at S. F. State that I had just left behind, I realized that my theatrical work would be political, and my political work would be to show others how much they could do. There would be public intention to all of it. Theatre is a weapon, but not the only one I had to wield. My public political acts would be "meta-theatrical." In the act of bearing witness, the timing would be everything. I grokked that the power in demonstrating is that someone is watching, someone who you want to step out of the sidelines and join the struggle, to become more than a passive observer, to "take arms against a sea of troubles."

I was an artist, but I was also a citizen who could join a march or … organize one. For an actor, the true "moment" on stage is about fully committing to an honest action. The same is true when you take off your costume and get out in the street. I had to be a good actor *in society*. The stars had turned. Mine would be a life of "any means necessary." It would all be part of a single exercise, a mantra of self-discovery acted out.

As I tooled down toward Fresno, somewhere near Los Banos, the song, "Goin' Up the Country," by Canned Heat, came on the radio:
"I'm going, I'm going where the water tastes like wine.
Well, I'm going where the water tastes like wine.
We can jump in the water, stay drunk all the time."

This was more than mere poetry. Fresno, with its water system fed by seven deep artesian wells, was, in fact, known for the sweetness of its natural water supply.

Next, they played Dylan's "Maggie's Farm"—"I ain't gonna work on Maggie's farm no more..."—an anthem for not serving The Establishment. The radio station was playing the soundtrack for my new life.

I had heard my own voice. I had volunteered for the revolution, full-time.

Fresno was the right place and the right time. The antiwar Resistance group held weekly demonstrations on the steps of the Induction Center, handing out leaflets before the cops chased them off. (DOCUMENT #25: Resisters handing out fliers by the bus) *El Teatro Campesino* was moving to Fresno. Fresno was a dry political field ready to catch fire. I'd come home to drop a little lightning around.

I pulled in to the Draft Resistance community nestled in the middle of an old fig orchard. The Resistance community was made up of draft counselors, labor organizers, pacifists, church group dropouts, even an activist from the Japanese anti-nuke movement. I found the house offered to me, met my housemates, and unpacked my shit. Our little compound was in a beautiful, rustic setting. The four small wood-frame farmhouses were in the middle of an orchard of ancient gnarled fig trees that stretched out around the houses for more than a quarter-mile in all directions. An irrigation canal with a bridge ran through the orchard. It was picturesque and peaceful.

My small Russian-style farmhouse at 6545 North First Street had one bedroom on the ground floor with walls that beveled up to the bedroom above it. (DOCUMENT #26: My house at the Resistance Community) The trellised roses around the house were glorious in the summer. One of the lease stipulations was keeping up the rosebushes. There was nothing but farms and orchards north of our location all the way to the San Joaquin River. We could see the snow-capped Sierra Nevada Mountains every morning. Occasionally, on summer evenings, spectacular lightning storms lit up the foothills.

When the rain came, it drummed on the sheet metal roof of the house and on the broad, heavy fig leaves all around. The deafening cacophony sounded like a band of crazed drummers. Conversation was impossible in a real downpour. Hearing the TV or radio was out of the question. On stormy evenings, I'd fire up a joint, read, or just sit and listen to the mantric pounding rain all around me.

In the fall, when it was quiet in the morning, I stood motionless on the frost-covered ground, I could hear a clean "click' from each of the millions of dry, brittle fig leaves snapping randomly off the trees that disappeared into the mist like a Japanese watercolor. The silences were part of the very essence of its unpredictability. It is impossible to capture this experience in any medium.

It was a Zen koan.

This was the outpost from which we made revolution. It was run-down but sublime. There were no gates or fences to keep out our detractors or enemies, yet we felt safe ... for the time being.

In a few weeks, I got acquainted with the tight squad of half a dozen who were at the center of a cadre of perhaps a dozen men and women. It consisted of my housemates, Patrick Conroy, a tall, thin Irishman from Brooklyn in rimless glasses, who was the levelheaded one, and Paul Dunham, tall and athletic, who was flamboyant and adventuresome. There was Don Teeter, barrel-chested with a handlebar mustache, the good-natured tactician. There was big Doug Rippey, a singer, banjo player, and another actor with *El Teatro*. Doug was always ready for anything. Dozens of others gave us strength, advice, and good vibes.

Gail and Dale Klemm lived in the house across the dirt road. Dale was sandy-voiced and baby-faced. He was the patient planner. His grounded yet ethereal wife could say more with a quiet sidelong look than any of us could with ten minutes of blather. Gail and Dale, both blonde and freckle-faced, wore rimless "granny" glasses and overalls. They looked as if they'd stepped out of a Norman Rockwell painting...except for the peace buttons. Gail became my secret confidant. Dale had been kicked out of Lutheran divinity school because of his strident antiwar stance. Gail was a Christian-raised girl with views that extended beyond traditional religion.

Their place was also the office and the print shop for the Draft Resistance community. (DOCUMENT #27: The Resistance House, Fresno, CA) Their place smelled like printer's ink, coffee, and Gail's apple pie. Dale printed all of the Draft Resistance leaflets and newsletters on a Multilith 1250, a press that two people could lift into a Volkswagen van if they had to, which we did on at least one occasion. Patrick Conroy, my housemate, was also a printer. He and I spared Dale on the press runs, especially after Dale and Gail's baby, Matthew, was born. After Matthew arrived, the aroma of baby oil was added to the mix.

We had a lot going on for a small operation. Volunteers ran the office, taking phone calls, handing out literature to visitors, making appointments for draft counseling, and speaking at events. Central to our activities was the recruiting and training of draft counselors. A bookshelf at a local bookshop required regular stocking. There were demonstrations to plan, organize, advertise, supervise, and attend.

The Monday night organizing potluck dinners were held in Dale and Gail's place. Characters of all ages came to the potlucks—everyone from an eighty-year-old IWW (Industrial

Workers of the World) member from the World War I era[25] to an eighth-grade girl who became one of our best weekend leafleters.

The potlucks required supplies, housecleaning, greeting visitors, and dishwashing. Everyone took their turn at these tasks; even Joan Baez pitched in when she came to dinner. (DOCUMENT #28: David and Joan in the kitchen at the Resistance House). David and Joan appeared at several events that we organized in Fresno.

Liaison meetings with Chicano, Black, and other political groups, as well as various church groups, were required. Legal challenges directed at the draft law often had to be reported in the newsletter. Occasionally, there were guerilla actions like going down to the Induction Center on H Street before dawn and running the Draft Resistance banner up the government's flagpole. (DOCUMENT #29: Resistance Flag over the Induction Center, Fresno, CA) As if this was not enough, we began a guerilla theatre group. Finally, there was the pay dirt from all of this—saving young men from killing or dying in the war.

All of these activities were covered in the newsletter, printed monthly, along with endless leaflets distributed by volunteers at the state and community college, high schools, and the Induction Center downtown. Marches alone wouldn't have changed things. Each of these activities had to support the other.

Between my work with *El Teatro Campesino*, my schoolwork at Fresno State, my draft counseling, and Movement organizing duties, I felt like I was smashing the State full-time.

---

[25] In 2018, I was to learn that Fresno had been the site in 1910-12 of a large IWW movement and a series of demonstrations and arrests on issues of free speech and the right to organize. One fiery old man had been there when he was my age. Over fifty years later, we were following in his footsteps.

SECTION V

QUE VIVA LA HUELGA! QUE VIVA LA REVOLUCION!

"And what did you hear, my blue-eyed son?
And what did you hear, my darling young one?

I heard ten-thousand whispering and nobody listening
I heard one person starve, I heard many people laughing
I heard the song of a poet who died in the gutter
I heard the sound of a clown who cried in the alley

[Chorus]
And it's a hard, it's a hard, it's a hard, it's a hard
It's a hard rain's a-going to fall"

"A Hard Rain's A-Gonna Fall"
(Verse 3, Bob Dylan, 1962*)*

CHAPTER 16: 1969—*EL TEATRO CAMPESINO*

> "Art is not a mirror held up to reality.
> It is a hammer with which to shape it."
> (Bertolt Brecht, German playwright, 1936)

As soon as I got to Fresno in January 1969, I settled in with the Draft Resistance then connected immediately with *El Teatro Campesino*. These two activities filled my life in two parallel stories best told separately. The tale weaves together in good time.

The Chicano community's cry for inclusion and dignity resonated with me as if I were one of them. The Latinx population in America was misunderstood, exploited, and maligned. Jew Boys *con huaraches*.[26] Political theatre work was a calling for me based on the fact of my otherness in Amerika. The Black militant, Stokely Carmichael, said that white folks in the Movement could blend in, but Blacks wear their target status on their skin. They wore their politics in their faces. The same is true for the Latinx population in Amerika.

Jews might look white to most other people, but to the forces of repression, our Semitic faces and distinct culture make us worthy targets as well. The same people hate us just for being ourselves. We are wounded and segregated by them, reminded that we are decidedly "other" in their eyes. The experience of the early Jewish immigrants to America more than a hundred years ago was exactly parallel to that of Latinx people, and we have that in our collective memories. When the riots happened in Charlottesville, Virginia, and at the Capitol on January 6, anti-Jewish slogans were

---

[26] Mexican peasant sandals.

shouted and Jewish senators and members of congress were singled out. This is not to say that our experience in America has been anything like that of African Americans in Diaspora or the Latinx community.

The situation for the migrant farmworkers and the Latinx community in general moved me in a way that I could not have predicted. Something in Jewish culture and history—at least in my generation—opened us up to the slings and arrows of their suffering. In my case, it defined much of who I am.

I have been a very real victim of racism and anti-Semitism myself on several occasions, including very real threats of violence, even in Fresno. Black people understand where we are coming from. I once had a Black dude say to me, "You're Jewish, ain't you?"

"Yes, I am," I said.

"Shit, the way The Man treats you, you might as well be Black."

This perverse "outsider equality" grounded my commitment to *la Causa*. These hardworking people were paid substandard wages. They lived in the poorest areas and were constantly subjected to police intimidation and harassment from Immigration authorities, even if they were born here or naturalized.

Those who worked on the large fruit ranches lived in appalling conditions. They were housed in labor shacks on the ranchers' land. Exorbitant rent for these tarpaper and plywood hovels was deducted from their substandard wages. They were forced to buy cheap, unhealthy food at shocking prices from the on-site company stores. Most of their pay was taken back in food purchases and rent.

Many lived in their cars as they moved from farm to farm as the temperature soared over a hundred degrees for weeks at a time. They had no medical care or coverage. There were no schools or care facilities for their children. Farmworkers' children were getting rickets while the ranchers hosed down mountains of oranges with gasoline, right in front of hungry families, just to keep the prices high.

Workers who protested these conditions were evicted from their meager living quarters on the ranchers' compounds and then blackballed from work on other ranches. They were beaten by company goons or county sheriffs. Then they were fired. The life of farmworkers was slavery with another name. Virtually the entire local political, police, and justice systems were controlled by white ranchers who had intermarried with the cops' and judges' families. The cops and the companies were literally in bed with each other.

The ranchers brought in Mexican or Philippine nationals on temporary work visas, complicating the situation for resident Mexican-American workers seeking to unionize. These even poorer "guest workers" toiled for less money and had no rights at all. If one of them was robbed and murdered, the cops removed the identification papers from the body to save themselves the job of finding the family. The body was dumped in a pauper's grave, and the family never heard from them again. Cops hate paperwork.

On September 8, 1965, the Filipino farmworkers around Delano, led by Larry Itliong, went on strike. Two weeks later, the Mexican workers, led by Cesar Chavez and Dolores Huerta, joined them. Together they called a general strike in the grape fields. A short time later, Luis Valdez, barely twenty-four years old, arrived at the union hall in Delano. With Agustín Lira already working with farmworkers as a singer and musician, Luis worked up some skits to take out to the fields to support the strike.

Their fast-paced, physical *commedia* skits were the perfect artistic weapon for the struggle. One of the skits that was wildly successful was an *"acto"* called *Las Dos Caras del Patroncito* (The Two Faces of the Boss), featuring Luis and either Felipe Cantú or Augie Lira.

In this simple, *commedia*-like skit, the *patron* (boss) tries to talk the *campesino* (farmworker) out of going on strike because he has all the benefits of life: sunshine, fresh air, etc. The *campesino* has none of the "problems" of being rich. In a Tom Sawyer-like reversal, the boss talks himself into switching places with the farmworker, who then begins to lord it over him. After about five minutes of the *campesino* ordering the boss to do the things expected of a farmworker, the boss begins to cry, "*Huelga! Huelga!*" ("Strike! Strike!") (DOCUMENT #30: *El Teatro, Dos Caras del Patroncito*)

The guerilla theatre company took their pungent *actos* out to the picket lines in the fields and to the meeting halls. When the farmworkers saw themselves on stage, they became stronger, larger, more welded to the struggle. On Sundays, the little company performed the *actos* for the *campesino* families relaxing in the parks on the ground or on the back of a flatbed truck. Soon the cops started coming to break up the shows. If we heard someone yell, "*¡Ahí viene la placa!*" ("Here comes the cops!"), we barely got all our props into the van and drove away, still in our costumes, before they got out of their squad cars.

El Teatro began making headlines. After going on the march to Sacramento,[27] they were invited to perform on college campuses. Before I joined the company, Robert F. Kennedy came to Delano and sat on the grass with the *campesino* families to watch them. They took their show to New York and received a special Obie Award for creating an activist theatre.

When I joined the company, they were just moving from the small farming hamlet of Del Rey to a rehearsal hall, scene shop, and office in Fresno. As I helped them clear out their storefront space and load their scenery into a truck, I noticed that the set pieces were all stamped, "SJS." I'd seen them before. This was one of those serendipitous "déjà vu" moments in my life. When I was a freshman at San Jose State, I'd done lab hours in the scene shop. I'd struck these very set pieces after the premier of *The Shrunken Head of Pancho Villa* in January of 1965 and loaded them into the scene shop storage bays. I was probably the last person to handle the scenery before it showed up in Del Rey. Sometime between 1964 and 1968, Luis—probably with the help of Jim Bertholf and Eddie Emanuel—had "liberated" the wall pieces, furniture, puppet heads, and cockroach puppets from the

---

[27] On March 17, 1966, Cesar Chavez embarked on a three-hundred-mile pilgrimage from Delano, California, to Sacramento. Robert F. Kennedy and other notables joined them for parts of the march.

college while the tech director, Dave Purdy, also a notorious outlaw, opened up the shop for them then looked the other way. Such are the ways of a pirate theatre company.

Shortly after moving to Fresno, we visited the union hall in Delano. There I met Cesar Chavez for the first time. The union hall was a pale, gray-green cinder-block building lit with partly blown-out fluorescent fixtures. It had a worn linoleum floor. On the walls were photos of FDR, JFK, and Martin Luther King; the Mexican revolutionaries Pancho Villa and Emiliano Zapata; and an image of the Virgin of Guadalupe. There were also notices and strike posters.[28]

In that meeting hall, I witnessed one of the most moving acts of dedication to a cause I have ever seen. We ate lunch with the workers before we did a show in the local park. Lunch was rice and beans, tortillas, and *carnitas*.[29] There was also a big bowl of canned fruit salad. Everybody served themselves. As I sat down, I noticed that every person in the room was carefully spooning out the non-union-picked grapes from their fruit salad before they ate the rest.

Yes, the grapes had already been purchased. However, this personal *acto* mattered to them. This simple action—almost Zen in its profoundness—caused me to think about everything I did and their effects in the world. These laborers understood political action. They had to change their own lives. No one else was going to do it for them.

No one else was going to do it for me.

When entering a new situation, it's wise to hang back and check out how things are done. However, I joined *El Teatro* in the middle of their productions. I had to gain my chops while producing the plays. At the time I came on board, the company was still doing shows in the parks in the small towns around

---

[28] Cesar would go to a house on Sunday morning and walk the *abuelita*, the matriarch, to church. After the Sunday supper, she would tell her family, "That Cesar Chavez is a good man. We should listen to what he has to say." You cannot organize a community that you don't understand.

[29] Cooked, shredded pork.

Fresno. The Chicano community loved them. The cops, under the control of the local ranchers and racist city governments, did not.

To form a radical theatre company was a crazy enough idea. To organize a bilingual theatre company took a special kind of "*loco*." The moment was quintessential for a desperate struggle and a people in need of a voice for their depression and rage. It had to be something like *molé*'[30], conjured up like chili and chocolate. *El Teatro Campesino* was pungent and unexpected. It was "a theatre of survival."

We moved to our new digs in an old church in the Fresno *barrio*, an area with a lot of Mexican families in small houses and apartments, and turned the old church into a *centro cultural*. We were near material supplies, volunteer help, and most of all a large Latinx *and* Anglo community. Luis gambled on launching *El Teatro* as a second front for *la Huelga* to bridge the access to a progressive Anglo base in a college town. As one of a series of Anglo *compañeros* in the company, I was actually an unexpected but important part of that transition. I soon formed a strong personal and artistic bond with Luis Valdez. We were a solid team. Cesar Chavez was an occasional visitor to our *centro* in Fresno. (DOCUMENT #31: Cesar Chavez at our *Centro*)

The presence of white people like Don Teeter, Doug Rippey, Donna Haber, and me in the company sent a powerful message to the *gringos* in the audiences that this was their struggle as well. *El Teatro*'s efforts continually brought a harvest. Church and college groups added their voices to *la Causa*. College fraternities, sororities, and student unions pressured their colleges not to buy table grapes until contracts were signed with the union. *La Huelga* (The Strike) was gaining momentum everywhere. Ranchers, banks, and racist-supported institutions were on the run. *El Teatro* would soon move on to bigger *chingasos* (fights).

El Teatro worked very much on "Chicano time." This is the idea that it's more important to arrive in a good spirit than to keep

---

[30] An unbelievably rich, exotic sauce of chili and chocolate invented by the Aztecs.

to a regimented schedule. It's Mexican Zen. On a Sunday in the park, we could take our time while the *campesino* families hung out, sipped beer, ate *Gallina en Mole,* and played with their kids. It has nothing to do with being backward or lazy. Working-class communities of all races take their off time with a spirit of ease. In the case of *la Raza,* it was a part of *Chicanismo.*

I learned about Chicano time and *Chicanismo* just after I joined the company. *El Teatro* was on a tour to L. A. City College. An audience member came backstage to tell us that his *abuelita* (grandmother) was late. She'd been a field worker most of her life. Our performance was very important to her. She'd been talking about it for weeks. Could we wait for her to arrive?

Danny Valdez smiled. "*Simòn, ese*" ("Sure, man"), he said. "I'll just go out and let *la gente* (the people) know what's going on." Danny took the mic and made the announcement. Everybody was cool about waiting except me. I was used to Anglo audiences who expected a show to start on time. Ruben Rodriguez, a company member who'd become a good friend, took me aside. "Look, man, this is not about us, it's about *them*," he said, pointing to the audience. "They've been waiting five-hundred years to get their lives back. Thirty minutes don't mean shit."

When the proud old lady came in and sat down, the entire audience gave her a standing ovation. She said, "If I had known, I would have worn a nicer dress!" *¡Que viva la Raza!* It was a great show.

There were many levels of education happening at the shows—not only for me but for the Anglos who were now a large part of the audiences. Daniel would come out on stage and begin by saying, "¡*Bienvenidos a Mexico ocupado!*" ("Welcome to occupied Mexico!") He would then begin speaking Spanish. After a few sentences, he'd stop and say, "You all didn't understand a word I said, did you? Well, that's how we all felt in the first grade."

I soon felt well integrated. They called me "the token *gringo*" (white guy). (DOCUMENT #32: *El Teatro*, family-style) I acted in the company, served as tech director and road manager, built and painted props and scenery. I even drove the company van, named *Siete Leguas* (Seven Leagues) after Pancho Villa's favorite horse. I was using everything I had learned at university and beyond.

    I still had a lot to learn. At that time, most of the company members were from the *barrio* (the deep Chicano community). To them, Anglos were always overseers, ranchers, schoolteachers, or cops. They'd never worked closely with an Anglo as an equal before. Therefore, I was in a learning situation in terms of proper behavior within their community. Even though I dressed like a hippie, I have never been good at the "laid-back" thing. And I was, after all, the road manager for the company, though under Luis. I was in charge of getting the show up and ready to run by the time the rest of the company arrived. I was definitely in the middle. Most of the time, Luis had my back, and he was the boss.

    It wasn't just me. Luis could see that things were changing for the company. As the *rasquache* company became more successful, starting at the announced time became something of a sore point. They found themselves at something of a cultural crossroads. Getting the shows set up on time was driven by the host theatre that paid its staff an hourly wage as well as the expectations of the Anglo audience. This put me in the position of occasionally having to push the rest of the company. This comes with the territory of road manager. Nevertheless, this caused both personal and cultural friction. Ultimately, the need for changing how the company operated was Luis's responsibility. It was a problem not of my making. Our growing success soon proved that my perspective was justified.

CHAPTER 17: BREAKING IN

Hey Joel, how to make a Thief's Omelet?"
"I don't know."
"First, you steal two eggs…"
("Guerito" [Whitey], seventeen-year-old Mexican farmworker
and actor with El Teatro Campesino,
quoting Lenin's parable on the need to break the rules
in a revolutionary struggle)

Because of the years as a hit-and-run guerilla theatre company, *El Teatro* toured like a garage rock band. Our simple stage setup for the *actos*—a folding rear screen, small props, masks, etc.—traveled in a small van. We were ready to go on in less than an hour after we rolled up to the theatre load-in door. Sometimes we played on a real stage with lights and curtains. Most often, it was just a raised platform at one end of a church or community center auditorium. Pre-show tech was a cinch—sound check on the PA and lights up. The costumes and musical instruments always traveled with the actors. This assured that if the van with the props broke down, at least there were characters to do the show.

On those occasions when we performed so far out of town that we needed to stay over, the Chicano community and their supporters, teachers, single mothers, labor organizers, construction workers, *huelgistas* (strikers), and students in the *movemiento* opened their homes to us. They fed us at potlucks organized in our honor. We slept on their couches, in spare rooms, on living room floors, and yes, sometimes in their beds. Friendships and connections were made with open hearts. Sacrifice was part of the joy. We were a community of mutual support.

Touring Luis's full-length play, *The Shrunken Head of Pancho Villa,* was more involved. It required a full box set including furniture; a beat-up couch, monstrous easy chair, coffee table, rocking chair, specially rigged TV set, costumes, and weapons, as well as three large "shrunken-head" puppets and papier-mâché cockroaches in various sizes and degrees of ugly. The stuff for this show had to be packed just so, and it filled the entire van.

This was where my road-show experience helped professionalize what had been, up to then, a skit company performing on flatbed trucks in the fields. Even with the bigger show, we went in and did our greetings. I sent my cue book to the booth, and we began a polished, practiced routine. Two hours for the setup, the same for the breakdown after the show.

When there was a hitch, my *gringo* attitude turned out to be a mixed curse. In the early fall of 1969, *El Teatro* was booked for a Saturday show of *actos* at the University of the Pacific in Stockton, two hours north of Fresno. We'd packed up *Siete Leguas* (the company van) the night before. I picked up Antonio Bernal, Ruben Rodriguez, and *"Guerito"* (Whitey), our young, baby-faced actor. We headed north. The others came later.

Antonio had assured me that all the arrangements had been made. However, I had an itch of a doubt. On the way up to the gig, I questioned him as delicately as I could on an important point concerning shows arranged by community groups not familiar with the needs of a theatre company. "Did you talk *to the actual* person with the keys who is supposed to let us in, or did you talk to someone not working in the theatre itself?"

This pushed his buttons. He thought I had an attitude about Chicanos. That was not where I was coming from.

"No, man, I talked to the student group. They have their shit together."

I still had that funny feeling. "Sometimes people who don't work in the theatre don't nail down this kind of detail. The message falls through the cracks."

I could tell that he thought I doubted *la gente's* ability to take care of business. Actually, I was just doing my job.

"Why are you always so uptight, man?"

Ruben Rodriquez, usually my sidekick, decided to give me some *pedo* (trouble) too. "Yeah, why are you so always so *white* about everything?"

"Because I'm always the guy who has to solve the problem when we get there after I'd suggested how to avoid it in the first place."

We listened to Santana. Nobody said anything else.

We rolled up to the back door of the auditorium. Sure as a tortilla's flat, there was nobody there to open up. The place was locked up tighter than a bank on Sunday. The message had never gotten past the secretary's desk. Campus security couldn't be found either. Antonio wouldn't look at me.

Finally, Antonio said, "What now?"

"Get the tire iron from the toolbox."

"What are you going to do?"

"Don't ask." I went over to the padlocked load-in door. I slipped the tire iron behind the lock and twisted. It popped right out of the sheet-metal steel door. "Oh, look!" I said. "Somebody's opened up for us."

Antonio said, "You're gonna get us in a whole lot a trouble, man."

"Don't think so, *carnal* (brother). We have an invitation from a campus group and a contract signed by the Dean of Students. The Chicano community will burn the fucking administration building down if the show is canceled. Somebody did them a favor. Let's unload and set up for the show."

We rolled aside the big load-in door, found the switch for the auditorium lights, and began to set up. It was a large lecture hall with minimal theatrical gear. That was okay. Our shows were designed to be performed in spaces like this. Zero light cues were required. The three-hundred-seat auditorium was loud and "ringy." The musicians might be pissed that nobody had set up microphones. They could talk to Antonio about it.

The bigger problem was the lack of heat. It was a real icebox in there. I turned on the thermostats around the room but got nothing.

Antonio said, "They probably turn off the boilers for the weekend. This sucks."

I looked up at the balcony front rail. There were about a dozen old, five-hundred-watt theatrical spotlights pointed at the stage.

"See if we can find a ladder."

"Why?"

"I've got an idea."

I found the custodian's ladder and climbed to the balcony. "You guys finish setting up on stage. I'll be down in a minute."

I checked out the lighting setup. As I'd hoped, the cables from the lights on the balcony rail were plugged directly into an ancient resistance dimmer pack controlled by large handles. I turned on the dimmer switches then slowly raised the big handles on the old light board. All twelve lights came on.

"We don't really need those," said Anthony.

"Oh yeah, we do." I focused most of them down onto the backs of the seats in the first ten rows of the audience.

"What's that for?"

"The Lord's heating system. It should keep everybody warm in at least the first ten rows. The rest will warm up too."

"That's great. I could kiss you."

"I bet you say that to all the uptight white guys you work with."

The show went well. Everybody sang their loudest and their best. Nobody from the administration, the police, or the theatre staff ever showed up.

We packed up and rolled away. From then on, Anthony made sure he talked *directly* to the auditorium supervisor. Being an uptight white guy has its advantages.

CHAPTER 18: BACK TO SCHOOL AND INTO THE WORLD

I reentered graduate school at Fresno State and began organizing for the Draft Resistance and working for *El Teatro*. The company had been invited to perform at the *Festival Mondial du Théâtre* in Nancy, France, and then on to Paris, all expenses paid. This meant that I would need to take a three-week leave from my classes.

I announced to my family that we were going to this prestigious festival. I expected my folks to be supportive. However, there was a small rift instead. Actually, it was more like the Grand Canyon. This was a scene in the movie of my future that I had not written for myself. Dad just couldn't wrap his head around it.

Dad: "Why do you want to quit school?"
Me: I'm not *quitting* school. I'm taking three weeks' leave.
Dad: There's no money in it.
Me: The group is world-renowned. It's an investment in my professional future.
Dad: This isn't what we planned.
Me: I didn't know *we'd* planned anything.
Dad: If you stay in school, I'll buy you a car.
Me: Great. I'll be back to school in three weeks.
Dad: How about I buy you a used VW bug.
Me: Jesus, Dad. If you're gonna bribe me to give up my values, don't insult yourself. Make it a Mercedes.

He was not entertained by my comeback. I left the house.

Dad's admonition, "To thine own self be true," had come home to roost. We didn't talk for almost a year.

CHAPTER 19: THE JEW BOY *CON LOS CHICANOS* IN FRANCE

This was going to be one hell of a trip.

We rehearsed the shows, gathered the props, and made final arrangements. It helped that I spoke some French. Everything was packed and labeled for Customs. We were booked to do some of the *actos* in Nancy and *The Shrunken Head of Pancho Villa* in Paris. (DOCUMENT #33: Performance of *Shrunken Head of Pancho Villa,* Paris, 1969) This show included three "shrunken-head" puppets. Everything was *rasquatche* (broken down, secondhand, cast off). *El Teatro*'s signature style was jokingly referred to as "*Rasquatchismo*." We'd pick up the furniture for the set when we got there.

All of our stuff went into two steamer trunk-sized containers. The real steamer trunk held costumes, masks, hand props, and the surreal, oversized cockroach puppets that moved across the walls on strings pulled from behind. The other crate was a hand-built packing crate that turned into a specially rigged TV set. It held the rifles, pistols, and cartridge belts as well as the three head puppets for *Shrunken Head*.

These brutish, cartoon-like heads with archetypical, mustachioed "Mexican faces" were very funny. There was one regular-sized head to toss around and another regular-sized head that sat on top of the TV set. Its eyes and mouth moved by strings operated by an actor sitting inside the TV set. At one point in the play, this puppet head was replaced by an actor (Luis) who sat inside the TV. He spoke only to Joaquin, the rebellious teenage son. The third head was a monstrosity more than two feet in diameter. (DOCUMENT #34: Big head puppet in *Shrunken Head of Pancho Villa,* Paris, 1969) It sat on the couch. Its working eyes and mouth were manipulated through the back of the couch by ropes and levers. All of this gear was neatly packed and duly recorded for Customs. Everything was ready to go.

There were some changes in personnel before the trip. Augie Lira left the company and was replaced by Antonio Bernal. We'd recently added another Anglo member to the company, Donald Teeter, also from the Draft Resisters community, to play the cop in this show and several parts in the *actos* and to sing. We packed up and headed to Los Angeles International Airport (LAX).

Our company of ten *revolucionarios* walked through the airport dressed in black or brown berets, fatigues, ponchos, and dark glasses. The crowd parted in front of us like the Red Sea. We looked *muy malo* (badass), a true revolutionary cadre on our way to get French support for *la Huelga* (the Grape Workers Strike).[31] We were cool. We were bad. We were going somewhere.

However, just as Luis and Ricardo Duran, our backstage crewmember, approached the boarding area, they suddenly realized they were headed for trouble. In the early 1960s, they'd both travelled to Cuba illegally. Their trip had been interdicted by the State Department. They went anyway. They were photographed with Fidel Castro. If they tried to leave the country now, their passports would be confiscated. They had to think fast.

With an impish grin, Ricardo, the quintessential pirate, grabbed Luis by the arm. They disappeared into the crowd. We'd no idea where they had gone. Our flight was called. The rest of us climbed the gangway onto the Air France plane. The engines started up. The plane was about to leave. *How the hell are we going to do the show without Luis?* Just before the cabin doors closed, Luis and Ricardo appeared in the plane and sat down quietly. Both had their tickets and boarding passes stamped.

Ricardo and Luis had gone through a side door to the baggage handling area. They talked with the workers, who were all

---

[31] Little did we realize what a political firestorm we were going to leave in our wake. The French wine grape industry was scared shitless that the idea of a strike would spread to their workers after we left.

Chicanos. They dug the Grape Workers Strike. They found a baggage stamp and stamped the two passports. Then Luis and Ricardo were ferried with theatrical flare to the gangway in a jeep like VIPs. As the plane left the ground with everybody on board, we all said, "*Adios, pendejos*" ("Goodbye, fools").

We drank a lot of wine and ate the best airline food, compliments of Air France. Joints were smoked in the bathroom as we flew over the North Pole. Ten hours later, we touched down in Paris.

True to our M. O., we started raising *"pedo"* (trouble) as soon as we hit the ground. While waiting for the train, the musicians in the company pulled out their guitars and started singing revolutionary songs. Within minutes, a crowd of French people had gathered, singing along. I returned from the Customs office just in time to see Gestapo-style troopers from the CRS (Committee for the Safety of the Republic) breaking up the spontaneous Unity celebration. The cops were breaking up the show again, just like at home.

Between myself and Antonio, who also spoke French, we got everyone and the luggage to the train headed for the festival in Nancy, France, on the German border.

Traveling *au le Paissage Française*

We rode through the French watercolor countryside in a train that was like the ones in the movies. It had windowed cabin compartments on one side and a corridor on the other. As Luis and I passed in the corridor, he said, "Excuse me, I'm looking for Marlene Dietrich," and smiled as he lit up one of his signature cigars. He even offered me one. We smoked outside in the rear of the train car. As we watched the fields of wheat and cattle roll by, Luis shared his concerns with me about an unavoidable confrontation that had been brewing for several weeks.

Luis was still with his current ol' lady, Donna Haber. Donna was his lead/opposite as the mother/wife in *The Shrunken Head of Pancho Villa*. However, Luis was now head-over-heels with Lupe Trujillo, a smart, very pretty Mexican college student who would play the Latina in the *actos* (skits) and the wisecracking daughter in *Shrunken Head*. Donna knew Luis was carrying on with Lupe. When we got to our hotel in Nancy that night, Luis wouldn't be sleeping with Donna ever again.

However, Donna was the business manager for the company. She was carrying the money. I imagined an Agatha Christie plot, finding Luis and Lupe stabbed in the hotel room and Donna headed south to Marseilles with our bread.

The *mierdre* finally hit *el ventilador* when we got to the hotel in Nancy. Donna was not very "French" about the new situation. After much yelling, a few doors slammed. Lupe left the room she shared with Donna and moved in with Luis. Donna had her own room. Antonio was in with me. Musical beds in a French hotel. It was so very continental. We still had to finish the tour. The angry yelling scenes in the play were going to be particularly good.

As I said, this trip was going to be anything but dull.

****

We were an American radical theatre company invited to perform at a political theatre festival in a country with a Socialist government. The French General Strike of 1968, in which the progressive faction spearheaded by students had prevailed mere months before.

Touted as *the* working-class theatre *par excellence*,[32] we were to perform twice in Nancy, once on a weeknight and as the main event of the final Saturday closing the festival. This was top billing. Our shows were in a big circus tent that could hold about four hundred people. It was the perfect place for our raw, direct shows. It was *Rasquachismo au Françias*. "Groovy" doesn't even begin to cover it.

---

[32] Even as recently as 2017, after nearly fifty years, the World Theatre Festival website still features this event as the signature performance of its mission.

There were at least eight or ten languages represented at the festival. Nevertheless, the work was so physical and the ideas so clear that everyone understood what was expressed. The university found student volunteers to be our guides around town. I found myself attached to a terrific French girl named Marie-France. Boisterous and high-spirited, Marie-France looked like the actor Cybil Shepherd but with a stockier, country girl figure. I was smitten. That was my kind of *bienvenue*. We connected with theatre people from around the world. Tales of revolutionary experiences, arrests, police brutality, governments spying on leftist groups, etc., confirmed the universality of our struggle. For all of us speaking out against oppression, this was Hamlet's question answered.

Because we were from the most militarist superpower in the Western world, *El Teatro* and Bread and Puppet Theatre of New York—also at the festival—were the focus of extra attention. We learned that little of radical theatre's contributions to protest in America were covered in the press. Only the French leftist papers reported anything of our reputation. Nevertheless, the word was out with great anticipation. Several of the *Journal du Festival* issues were devoted in whole or in part to interviews and commentary on our work. (DOCUMENTS #35, #36: *Journal du Festival*) We were as important to the *Festival Mondial* as the festival was to us.

Luis, Peter Schumann (of Bread and Puppet), and I were on a press panel about making revolutionary theatre in Amerika, where racial violence and the Anti-war movement were generating worldwide headlines. We responded that it was typical in a repressive society for official Amerikan sources not to fully report the wide opposition to the war and racial injustice that was growing every day.

The reporters then grilled us about our reaction to the French grape workers also organizing a strike in support of a union. We'd been told that instant deportation would result if we commented on this situation. Luis demurred on the matter. Our shows would be comment enough.

A journalist then asked about our productions. "Is it true that you tour your shows with one steamer trunk?"

I said, "No, that's not true. We have greatly expanded. We now have *two* steamer trunks."

Needless to say, with such a festive atmosphere and so many young people from around the world, there were plenty of parties. My comrade and fellow "token *gringo*" in *El Teatro*, Don Teeter, was a particularly enthusiastic partier. At one heavily saturated party, Don—pretty well saturated himself—threw himself into singing the Italian Communist anthem, "*Avanti Popolo*" (People Forward). Don was a little fuzzy in the pronunciation. I distinctly heard him singing, "I am a buffalo!"

****

The festival was a rare opportunity to enrich our work with ideas from around the world. As directors/designers/writers, Luis and I went to see every show and rehearsal that we could. By far the most revelatory experience for me was the Bread and Puppet Theatre's show, *The Cry of the People for Meat*. This ritual/processional piece performed in the circus tent was about the hunger for "blood violence" that fed the frenzy for the mass bombings in Vietnam.

After stylized dialogue and choreographic movement by masked actors, the piece ended with the cacophonous clang of bells made of one-gallon gasoline cans filled with heavy rocks and metal junk. This horrific, deafening *anti-overture* climaxed with the shocking, unexpected arrival of a *deus ex machina,* a puppet with a fifteen-foot wingspan that looked like something between a B-52 bomber and a pterodactyl. (DOCUMENT #37: Bread and Puppet, *Angel of Death*) It swept over the performance area and the audience alike, leaving the characters on stage posed in a horrific tableau before making its terrifying, cacophonous, cathartic exit.

After this Dante's *Inferno*/Armageddon-like puppet left the stage, the entire audience of several hundred, myself included, found ourselves lying on our backs, gently stacked on top of each other like disaster victims. It was as if the flash of a bomb had washed over us all. *We had spontaneously performed the same reaction as the characters on stage.* I had no memory of how or when we'd fallen down. No one was injured. In that visceral instant, the audience was transformed from observers into participants. I have never experienced anything like this epiphany in the theatre before or since. The profound feeling of communal transcendence was unforgettable. I imagine this was the effect of the Living Theatre's *Dionysus in '69* when the entire audience joined the cast to walk naked out the back door of the theatre into the streets of New York.

****

The younger generation in France had found itself fed up with a ruling clique that had run the country since World War II. Resistance to change had reached neo-fascist proportions. In the spring of 1968, months of violent demonstrations in virtually every French city led to a general strike and the call for a national election.

The plebiscite was held while we were there, and the party of the future—the party of labor and the young—had shown that the nation had changed. Though he narrowly prevailed, it was clear that De Gaulle was on his way out. The celebration in the streets went on for three nights. Every café, every bistro, and every bar was packed. We were there when our leftist generation had won.

It could be done.

****

After Nancy, we were booked at the University of Paris to perform *Shrunken Head* in an auditorium that seated well over a thousand people.

On the second day in Paris, I returned to our dorm room to discover Marie-France and a few other girls from Nancy sitting on our beds. The girls had hitchhiked two hundred miles to follow us to Paris. We had French, socialist, college-girl groupies who broke the rules. Cool.

From Marie-France, I learned that if you saturate a poster with condensed milk and spread it on a concrete wall, it bonds chemically with the concrete. Unless you sandblast it, the poster can't be removed. When we got back to the USA, we used this technique thereafter on late-night postering sorties.

Because we were obviously Americans, we sometimes experienced a marked coolness from waiters in the cafés. Waiters in Paris are famous for attitude, but this was different. In one café, they refused to serve us at all. I asked why. They said: "Because you are Americans. You made the war in Vietnam."

In my brutalized French, I said to them, "*Mais, non! Nous sommes les gauchistes, avec un théâtre Mexicain-Americain, en grève contra les capitalistes, contre la guerre, contra le class droitist.*" ("But no! We are leftists with a Mexican-American theatre of farmworkers, against the capitalists, against the war, against the right wing.") After that, we drank and ate at that café *gratis*.

The shows went well, the press was good, and we left a few broken hearts behind. The minute we were finished with the last performance of *Shrunken Head,* Donna gave Antonio the rest of the bread along with our tickets and returned to the States. We never heard from her again.

CHAPTER 20: COMING HOME … AGAIN

At the World Theatre Festival, we'd been strengthened by the shared struggle. We brought home many ideas. It was a rewarding tour. Everything was cool until we got to Customs at LAX. When the Customs Officer cracked open the hinged TV set/packing case and the huge, papier-mâché Mexican head stared back, the poor guy jumped. When the weapons and cartridge belts fell out, he pushed a button and suddenly we had a half-dozen armed federal officers around us in a nervous circle. Slowly and calmly, I explained who we were and where we'd been. I showed them that the weapons were fakes and the cartridges were only shell casings, not live ammo. Because the Customs manifest matched the contents of the cases, despite our badass *revolucionario* outfits, they let us go with all our weird shit. I bet we were the employee break room story for at least a week.

A few days after returning from France, we were booked to film the *acto*, *Los Vendidos* (The Sell-Outs), for a NET (National Education Television) program at KQED Studios in San Francisco. The show was to be aired across the USA. In *Los Vendidos,* I played Honest Harry, the seller of Mexican stereotypes to the governor's secretary. It used to be called *Honest Sancho's Used Mexicans*, but with an Anglo playing the purveyor of stereotypes, he was given a "white bread" name. (DOCUMENTS #38-39: Performance of *Los Vendidos*)

I had a lot of fun with this part. Honest Harry was the oiliest, smiling-est, smoothest-talking salesman you could imagine. Sometimes I did the character too well. After one performance in the Chicano *barrio* (community), the local Brown Berets almost took me outside for a little chat. Danny Valdez showed up in the nick of time and reminded them that I was with *la causa*, just playing a character. Instead of beating the crap out of me, we all got stoned.

Lupe Trujillo played the Mexican-American secretary. She was excellent in this part. She made sure to emphasize "*American*" when she spoke of herself and noted that her character's name was Martin, *not* Martinez. Danny Valdez played the greasy-haired, knife-wielding *pachuco* (juvenile delinquent). Big, warm-hearted Ruben Rodriquez played the *Zapatista* revolutionary in *sombrero, pistola, bandaleros,* and *rifle*. Antonio Bernal, tall and naturally suave, played the smooth-talking, whitewashed, anti-Chicano Mexican-American in whiteface who made racist remarks about his own people.

The only time that the KQED studio was available for the shoot was at night. We drove up to San Francisco in the afternoon, got into costumes, stood for the light tests, and walked through the scene for our marks. It was a one-take shoot with three cameras rolling. It would all be live sound. They would make their own intercuts in the edit.

We were too much into just doing it to think about which camera was picking up the segment that would be saved. We just worked them like it was a live house. Sometimes I noticed which camera had the red light on over the lens turret, so I played to that one. We did it in one take, then a short retake of the beginning and the end with close-ups of the three "used Mexicans" while Lupe and I talked downstage. It was a four-hour drive back to Fresno. I got home just after dawn.

The shoot went very well. It was sold to National Education Television and shown all over the country. *El Teatro* would invade the living rooms of America. Radical theatre was going big-time. We landed a lot of bookings from that filming.

Not long after the *Los Vendidos* filming, Luis and Lupe got married.

The Traditional/Revolutionary Wedding of Luis Valdez and Lupe Trujillo

Luis and Lupe were married a few months after we got back from the trip to France. The ceremony and reception were held at our *centro* in the Mexican *barrio* in Fresno. The spirit of *Chicanismo* was center stage in the wedding preparations. Weeks before the wedding, a summit occurred in the *Teatro* office between Luis, Lupe, and the priest who was to do the honors. For some reason, I was in the room. The mood was electric. Luis sat in his chair near Lupe in a "laid-back" pose. Lupe was running the show. The short, balding Latino priest had expectations of a traditional Catholic ceremony. He had no idea who he was dealing with. He said something like, "What's wrong with a traditional ceremony?"

Lupe said, "Nothing. We want a traditional ceremony, a traditional *Mayan* ceremony."

Luis gave me a sidelong "this is not going to be good" look. There were daggers in Lupe's eyes. Very slowly, she said, "We could do the whole ceremony the Mayan way. We could tie you to an altar stone and cut your heart out."

As the well-meaning padre turned red and broke into a sweat, I left the room. They worked it out.

****

Theirs was to be a Chicano hippie wedding. The ceremony was held in the basement of the center. It was easily fifteen degrees cooler than the main hall in midsummer, filled with copal incense and flowers, and festooned with decorative Mexican paper cutouts. The priest kept a low profile in a brown Franciscan robe, not a white ceremonial chasuble. There was no image of Christ or a crucifix on the altar, only flowers and feathers in a Oaxacan vase reminiscent of the ceremonial decorations in Central American murals. The only cross in the room was worn by the priest.

The bride and groom didn't kneel and take communion. After the vows and the ring exchange, the priest stepped aside. Ricardo Duran stepped forward in a white, highly decorated poncho and headband. He recited a benediction, perhaps from an ancient *Nahuatl* text. This went over with the priest about as well as pork ribs at an Orthodox Bar Mitzvah.

Luis was in his usual black field boots (polished for the occasion), dark pants, and a cream-colored embroidered shirt. Lupe was in a creamy lace "layer cake" dress from Veracruz that harked back to Aztec engravings. If memory serves (I was pretty stoned), both of them wore banded and feathered *penachos*, the simple but elegant Indian-design headbands. The nervous priest said his congratulations to the family matriarchs, picked up his check, and left.

I was the only white person at the wedding. I wore my best blue jeans and a blue embroidered Mexican wedding shirt. Because I was tight with the *Teatro*, I was treated like *familia*. There was a small *banda* performing music, with Danny Valdez and Ruben Rodriguez on guitars. Small knots of young men occasionally went out to the cars to pass around joints and bottles of tequila. Little clusters of laughing young women did the same with joints and wine. Soon everybody between sixteen and thirty was high on something.

As I tried samples of the platters of *gallina en molé*, a spicy chicken barbecue sauce made of chili and chocolate, I was shamelessly scrutinized by the *abuelitas* who'd cooked the dishes. If I went back for seconds, they found a reason to send their eligible granddaughters over and tell me it was their grandmother's recipe. This was a hard sell that had its strong points. I left about midnight, stoned, full of great food, and danced out. It was a great wedding no matter what your tradition.

After the wedding, we were back to the business of *la Causa*. Everything in our lives was about a revolutionary future. There would soon be important victories.

A Racist Incident Breeds Great Political Theatre

In October 1969, an incident occurred that highlighted the constant humiliation faced by the Latinx community in Amerika. A call came to the *Teatro* office from Kerman, a farm town twenty miles west of Fresno. Someone out there knew of the company's history of political action. Kerman was at least seventy-five percent Mexican-American (Chicano), but the power structure was all white. In many of these towns, students caught speaking Spanish in the halls of the public schools were subjected to suspension, arrest, and/or incarceration in Juvenile Hall.

This seemed like an official variation of the "Jew Boy" game to me.

Kerman High School administrators decided to make an example of one high school boy caught breaking the rule. He was pulled out of class, cuffed by the County Sheriff, and hauled off to Juvenile Hall. His parents were called. This same school offered Spanish as a language acceptable for university admission. You figure it out.

The next day, the entire Chicano population of the school walked out on strike. Cops came from all over. This was when somebody called *El Teatro*. Luis grabbed some costumes and two other actors. I jumped into the driver's seat of *Siete Leguas* and headed to the school as the actors rehearsed an improvised *acto* in the van.

Young Guerito was to play the student/farmworker in peasant whites and a straw field hat. Big Ruben Rodriguez was to play the "Enforcer," dressed in a brown shirt, brown slacks, a cowboy hat, dark glasses, and a badge. Luis was to play the big *Chingon* (administrator/official) in a sport coat, tie, white shirt, and dark glasses. On the way to the site, they made cardboard identification signs with strings.

The skit was simple. The Enforcer made the farmworker say the "Pledge of Allegiance." Sometimes the hapless *campesino* forgot the English word and said it in Spanish. Each time he uttered a Spanish word, the Enforcer pummeled the poor innocent *campesino*.

Suddenly, the *Chingon* (authority figure) came over to see "what the trouble is." The Enforcer told the *Chingon* that the kid was not "speakin' Amur-can." At one point, the Enforcer said the word "Fresno [the county name], California," and other Spanish words now in the English language. The authority figure (*chingon*) began to beat the crap out of the Enforcer each time one of these "*Spanglish*" words slipped out. Pretty soon it wasn't clear who was speaking what. The crowd loved it.

An angry pack of ACLU lawyers convinced the school that the rule was unenforceable as well as more than slightly illegal. The kid went home and the rule disappeared. Luis came away from this action with the idea for a new *acto* about the school system's contribution to cultural apartheid. It was called *"No Saco nada de la Escuela"* ("I don't get anything out of school").

This is how it went: At the end of a series of biting comic scenes[33] including the Pledge of Allegiance *acto*, the kids on stage could graduate because they'd "stopped being Mexican." They turned away and bowed their heads. As the graduation march was hummed, they turned around. Each was wearing a white paper lunch bag over their head (a pun on the Spanish word *saco*, "to take away," the equivalent of the word "satchel" in English). Shocking in its visual simplicity, this climax reminded me of the white-paint *acto* performed by the Black students during the San Francisco State Strike.

The audience could feel the humiliating sense of "otherness" and shame from the official apartheid forced on the now headless student characters. The sack looked eerily like the bags put over the heads of prisoners to be executed.

El Teatro performed *No Saco* for more than a year. It was very powerful theatre. Much like the simple experience of Daniel Valdez speaking Spanish to a white audience, the lesson was unmistakable. They *got it*. This was a battle fought and won with theatre as a weapon in the war at home.

---

[33] In one wickedly powerful little scene, the kids try to hide their tamales and brag about having peanut butter and jelly sandwiches, a real American lunch. It was a heartrending moment from real life for every Mexican-American in the audience.

My Father Joins *la Huelga*!

My father was a printer and large-volume producer of printed envelopes. Around this time, he was invited to attend a lobbying conference on postal legislation in Washington, D. C. I was still not speaking to him. Perhaps my silence, along with the changing face of politics in Amerika, was working on him.

While in Washington, Dad attended the special dinner for volume postal customer businesses. The lunar astronauts Neil Armstrong and "Buzz" Aldrin were there and gave out souvenir sheets of postage stamps canceled on the moon. Also at the dinner was Vice-President Spiro Agnew. Agnew had recently posed in a photo with Nixon shoving non-union table grapes into their grinning faces, insulting the striking workers and trying to derail their struggle for decent wages, health care, and schooling for their children.

On the banquet tables were piles of scab-picked grapes from non-union farms. Someone from the podium noticed the placard in front of my dad with his hometown of Fresno, California, and called out to him, "Hey there, Mr. Eis! What do you think of those table grapes?"

Ever mindful of the theatrical moment, my father (an ex-labor theatre member) stood up. In his best New York baseball park voice, he riposted, "I'm not eatin' those grapes, and if you call yourself an American, you won't eat 'em either!"

Upon returning home from the conference, Dad put a "BOYCOTT GRAPES" bumper sticker on his big Mercedes. He proudly commenced to collect parking tickets and cop stops as if his car was a broken-down labor truck.

Que Viva La Huelga!

CHAPTER 21: PARTING MORE SORROW THAN SWEET

Several months after the trip to France and the NET shoot, *El Teatro* was at a crossroads. The company was now attracting politically inclined Chicano students instead of farmworkers as new members. Additionally, the subject matter of our plays moved to broader concerns for Chicano rights and full dignity. Phil Esparza, Felix Alvarez, Olivia Chumacero, Juan Gomez, and others joined the company. These new *compañeros* were specifically recruited as actors. They did not expect to participate in the technical areas. They didn't come in with a full "cadre mindset." This didn't bode well.

At the same time, Luis's richer ideas demanded more time and energy for the technical side of the company. That was me. It became so time-consuming that I no longer acted with the company. Occasionally they found help, but it was inconsistent. As technical director, designer, and road manager, I put in long days. I opened the theatre in the morning. I did the building or painting before the company rehearsals. I watched rehearsals, took notes, then locked up the theatre and went home. In addition to working with *El Teatro*, I was organizing with the Draft Resistance. I also had schoolwork. I was getting stretched thin.

At my request, a work call was announced for the entire company the next day. It was to build an entire stage with a backdrop, side wings, working traps, and cabled light pipes before the opening of a new play. This work needed more hands to get finished on time.

The next morning, I showed up at nine o'clock with my Danish and coffee, opened the doors, turned on the lights, and pulled out the tools. I waited until after ten. No one else showed up. This was not the first time this happened. *Ya Basta!* (Enough!) I'd had it. I tossed my empty paper cup into the trash, locked up the space, and drove away. About 11:00, my phone rang.

It was Luis. "Hey man, I thought you were building today."

"You made a company call last night. No one showed up. So I did like everybody else. I left to do something else with my day."

"Nobody showed up?"

"*Que nuevas*? [What's new?] This is not the first time."

"What are you gonna do, man?"

I was really mad. "You tell me! *Sabes que* [You know what], right now you got a lot of 'token *gringo*' manpower[34] driving this Chicano theatre company."

He was truly wounded by my words, but it was the truth.

"Okay. I'll call the others and meet you there in an hour."

Some of the company showed, but they weren't happy. In the end, I built the stage almost entirely myself.

Unless Luis did something about this situation, I was heading for burnout.

Additionally, *rasquachismo* (funkiness) was quickly becoming an outmoded approach. It was hampering the professionalism of the company. We had booked *Shrunken Head* at U. C. Berkeley's Zellerbach Auditorium, a state-of-the-art theatre with a spit-and-polish crew. Their people were miffed before we even arrived because we hadn't provided a light plot in advance. I assured them that all we needed was general lighting and the unplugging of a few instruments that lit beyond the acting area. They'd never worked in such a seat-of-the-pants way, doing theatre with a rough-and-tumble polish.

Rasquachismo also extended to the live calling of the light cues. With the loose vaudevillian way the actors played, it was

---

[34] There had always been important Anglos with the company. Doug Rippey played in *actos* in 1967. Dave Purdy built the sets and props for *Shrunken Head*. Luis's old girlfriend, Donna Haber, was Jewish. Don Teeter and our photographer, George Ballis, were also white.

impossible to prepare a cue book for exactly when the actors would leave the stage. I had to call each cue on the fly to a very hostile board operator. I was "professional" in that I knew the actors and the show. I knew how to use the theatre equipment to do our style. It was more like jazz than classical. However, despite my clear control of the situation, the mood simmered through the entire show. The show went well, but the house crew was glad to see our truck roll off the loading dock.

It was clear that both the lack of support for the technical end of things and our current methodology needed serious reassessment. Even rock 'n' roll shows now used sophisticated light plots provided in advance and programmed with exact cueing. It was clear that something had to give. I talked with Luis about this situation. He could see it, but he was not ready to do what had to be done.

Things finally reached a breaking point during our next undertaking. After the festival in France, Luis wanted to organize the First Annual TENAZ (*Teatro Nacional de Aztlan*)[35] Festival. He also wanted to debut his new play, *Bernabé,* for this event. The company went ahead with both of these ambitious projects. In the interim, we'd moved to a building of our own on Van Ness Avenue in the Fresno Tower District. (DOCUMENT #40: *El Teatro* building, Maroa Avenue, Fresno, CA)

Luis's writing had fully blossomed into the magical realism hinted at by the surrealist elements in *Shrunken Head*. In his lyrical play, *Bernabé,* a mentally retarded farmworker lives at the edges of his community. The local young men taunt him. One night, some of them take the poor unfortunate out to the fields, taunt him about women, get him drunk, and leave him. He falls asleep abandoned in the field. In his dream, he falls in love with the moon, and they are married. The next morning, he is found frozen to death in the field.

With this script, Luis entered into a full articulation of his skill and his style. Characters drift in and out of reality and a

---

[35] The Aztec name for their holdings, which included California.

magical place. The miraculous is here and now. Creating a setting for such an important new American play would be a payoff for me for all the schlepping and the hassles. The practical aspects of this show needed to contribute to the dreamlike quality as well. The show would tour, so everything had to fit into the van to be set up by a small crew in less than an hour. This set also had to look good in professional venues. Most importantly, the shifting of the scenes had to be smoothly choreographed to contribute to the dreamlike atmosphere.

Piece of cake.

Luis's surreal, Lorca-like play was set in four locations. I designed a set of richly painted panels on three *perioktoi* (small, rotating, triangular platforms) that, if handled properly with rehearsal, would allow a graceful simultaneous rotation to show the setting. Because there were four locations but *perioktoi* have only three sides, one of the panels on each triangle had to be switched out on the unseen side during the performance. They had to be three-sided because when they finished each rotation, they had to block off the rear stage area. Four-sided squares would not rotate past each other and nest close together. The smooth operation of the set required the same crew to perform it for each show. If rehearsed, it wouldn't be any harder than any of the stage blocking required in any ordinary play.

The set pieces were clearly marked. I showed Luis and the actors how to do the shifts and watched them do it several times. There wasn't anything I had to do for a week or so. I decided to take a break before heading into the production and the festival. I left the project in the director's hands. I was confident Luis was motivated to see his show done well.

I took off to the mountains for a break with my girlfriend.

A Fateful Interlude

I packed my tent, my weed, and my girlfriend, Elsie Hannel, into my car for the Sweet's Mill Folk Festival, an annual music event in the foothills outside of Fresno. That year, the performance on the last Saturday night was by the Floating Lotus Magic Opera Company, a "Transformation Theatre" collective. Floating Lotus was a poetic/sacred folk theatre created and directed by Daniel Moore. This kind of ritual-based theatre generated an experience of opening up the compassionate side of humanity. It didn't expostulate a dogmatic political line. It was *inherently* political.

The Floating Lotus's dance/ritual performance, *Bliss Apocalypse,* was very much a Dionysian event. (DOCUMENT #41: The Floating Lotus Magic Opera Company) The wildly costumed principal male and female performers danced around three large fires while a troupe of dancer/drummers performed a tribal, orchestral score under the chanted dialogue. It was a gypsy morality play in which the devil was the good guy. Soon everyone was up and dancing. This kind of theatre found its way into the mainstream in *the* signature theatrical product of the entire decade, the Broadway musical *Hair: The American Tribal Love-Rock Musical*. It was a wildly refreshing weekend.

When I returned, *El Teatro* was on a tight schedule getting ready for the TENAZ Festival as well as our own show. Groups from as far away as Mexico City were coming to perform. The Festival would open amid international Latinx press.

To my sad surprise, I discovered that the rehearsal of the scene shifts had been neglected by the director in rehearsing the show. This was a disastrous choice. Instead, on the day of the performance, Luis provided me with two "*vato locos*" (ordinary street dudes) from the *barrio* for a backstage crew. These guys had never done anything like this in their lives. One of them didn't speak English, the other was a heroin user, and they were both high on something. The show was headed for real *pedo* (trouble).

Silhouetted in dim "shift light," they (and I) frantically tried to arrange the panels as the audience laughed. Luis came backstage to help. After one disastrous shift, I kicked them all off the stage and did the rest myself. We managed to get through the show but without the dreamlike choreography under the music that could have made it magical.

Needless to say, some bridges had been badly burned. I didn't come out for the company bow, nor did I go to the party.

After I dutifully helped with the rest of the festival, I cleaned the shop, loaded up my tools, and left the company. In the two years I'd been with the company, I'd acted in or designed the sets, lights, and props for every show in the company's repertoire. I'd facilitated the company's evolution from a back-of-the-truck guerilla theatre to a professional company ready for bigger things. At this juncture, I felt like Moses at the River Jordan. I needed to move on.

The *Bernabé* incident pointed out in undeniable terms that more attention was now required to improve on technical elements to fulfill Luis's vision. *El Teatro* was cursed with success. *Rasquachismo* was a thing of the past. Shortly thereafter, *Teatro* moved to San Juan Bautista, a tiny farming hamlet near Salinas, California. This move gave Luis the opportunity to start anew. Luis asked me to move with them. I don't think he really understood how badly I felt about having my sincere (and correct) advice ignored. I declined. Luis however, must have learned something from the *Bernabé* debacle. When they settled in San Juan, they began hiring professional actors, Los Angeles designers, and a trained technical staff.

Feelings between Luis and I eventually healed. Two years later, I went to visit him in San Juan Bautista while he was working on the script for *Zoot Suit*.[36] Even with his writing deadline, Luis came out to chat. To Lupe's surprise, he asked for some advice on the script! As Luis said his goodbyes and headed back to his office, Lupe gave me a complex look that I will never forget. I got the opportunity to work with Luis and *El Teatro* again ten years later.[37]

---

[36] *Zoot Suit*, the story of racism around the Sleepy Lagoon murders in Los Angeles in the 1940s, became a major motion picture and a Broadway musical, both directed by Luis and starring his brother Danny and at least one of his younger sisters.

[37] In 1981, I worked with *El Teatro* again as a builder and painter for *Bandito,* a play about the bandit Tiburcio Vasquez. It felt really good.

The experience with *Bernabé*, as well as other events at that time, left me with a heavy case of "Movement burnout." The need to pay attention to good advice from one's cohorts in the struggle is important. However, despite the personal setback, I wasn't ready to quit the Movement or stop doing political theatre. This life was not an easy road to follow, but it was my calling. These things happen in all theatre companies.

Political theatres worked in cold lofts, church basements, and recreation halls. We performed on street corners, in the backs of trucks, in public parks, in storefronts, in picket lines, and every now and then, in real theatres. We warmed heatless spaces with our passion and our ideas. We wore our own clothes with masks or slogan signs over our necks. We dumpster-dove for props and shopped thrift stores for outlandish costumes. Furniture for the plays came out of our own homes. Many times, music was made with junk—orchestral *gamelans* of castoff materials. Political theatres survive on *rasquachismo*. Making everything with our bare hands was part of the message: "If you have to, make a new world from the castoffs of the old one."

We lived on survival salaries paid from passing the hat or weren't paid at all. Sometimes we found food stamps in the hat instead of cash. World-famous directors including R. G. Davis, Peter Schumann, Allan Mann, and Joseph Chaikin slept on people's couches or the hard floors of rehearsal spaces. Nevertheless, the work needed to be done. The urgency of the times overshadowed careerism. Our dedication was propelled by daily Vietnam body counts in the news. Stories of African American and Latinx brothers and sisters jailed, beaten, or killed every day heightened our resolve. It was our show against Big Brother, and we couldn't afford to fail. As Luis Valdez correctly said, "Ours is a theatre of survival." Every artist working in a political theatre company was fighting in a war at home.

However, something was happening. As radical theatre companies made better theatre and the movement grew in numbers, audiences were getting bigger. We performed in more university theatres. We were written up in theatre journals, even reviewed in *Time* magazine. Increased commitments stretched the balance between theatre work and straight gigs to pay our bills. Except for Bread and Puppet, whose handmade puppets were an enduring hallmark, *rasquachismo* was waning as a modus. More sophisticated properties, sets, music scores, lighting designs, and company structures were part of an evolution absorbing us all.

The more successful the radical theatre groups became, the more we were on the government's radar. There was never a performance of political theatre that wasn't photographed by the FBI. This included *El Teatro*. The government's files probably contain the most complete record of this entire theatrical period. I could spot the government photographer at almost every performance. Usually, he was the only person in a collared shirt in the crowd. At least in order to blend in, he bought a ticket or put some bread in the hat. Occasionally, he even caught himself laughing. I just hope he got shots of my good side.

****

After I left *El Teatro*, I was very much at loose ends. Other things in my life were also changing. Unexpectedly, Luis's brother, Danny—who *was* the true star of the company[38]—drove out to rap with me about how things had gone down with the TENAZ Festival. Danny told me that the Bobby Seale and Soledad Brothers Defense Committees[39] up in San Jose had called *El Teatro* looking for a director for an anti-draft, antiwar play. He encouraged me to give them a call.

The gig in San Jose had tangible support, a designer, a rehearsal hall. The show was booked into a real theatre. It offered a

---

[38] Danny later starred in the play and film *Zoot Suit* and was in the film *Stir Crazy* with Richard Pryor and Gene Wilder. Danny also toured with Linda Ronstadt for her hit album, *Cancionies de mi Padre*.

[39] Bobby Seale was being railroaded as part of a trumped-up conspiracy charge resulting from the Chicago Democratic Convention riots. The Soledad Brothers were three Black prisoners in Soledad prison who were persecuted for becoming radicalized and speaking out about conditions in the California prisons.

director's fee, housing, meals, and a per diem. The play they wanted to perform, *Say 'Uncle' Sam!* was by a prominent screenwriter, and playwright, Lester Cole,. Lester was one of the infamous Hollywood Ten screenwriters who had been blacklisted during the McCarthy Era. Lester's script on the recruiting process exposed the thin mask of rationalizations for a war without anything to say for itself. I took the gig in San Jose. It would be exciting to bring this project to life.

    Now the story needs to be told of my antiwar work in Fresno simultaneous with the work at *El Teatro*. Both of these activities hit a kind of breakdown transition at the same time. So, now we roll back to January 1969 to look at the other half of my life.

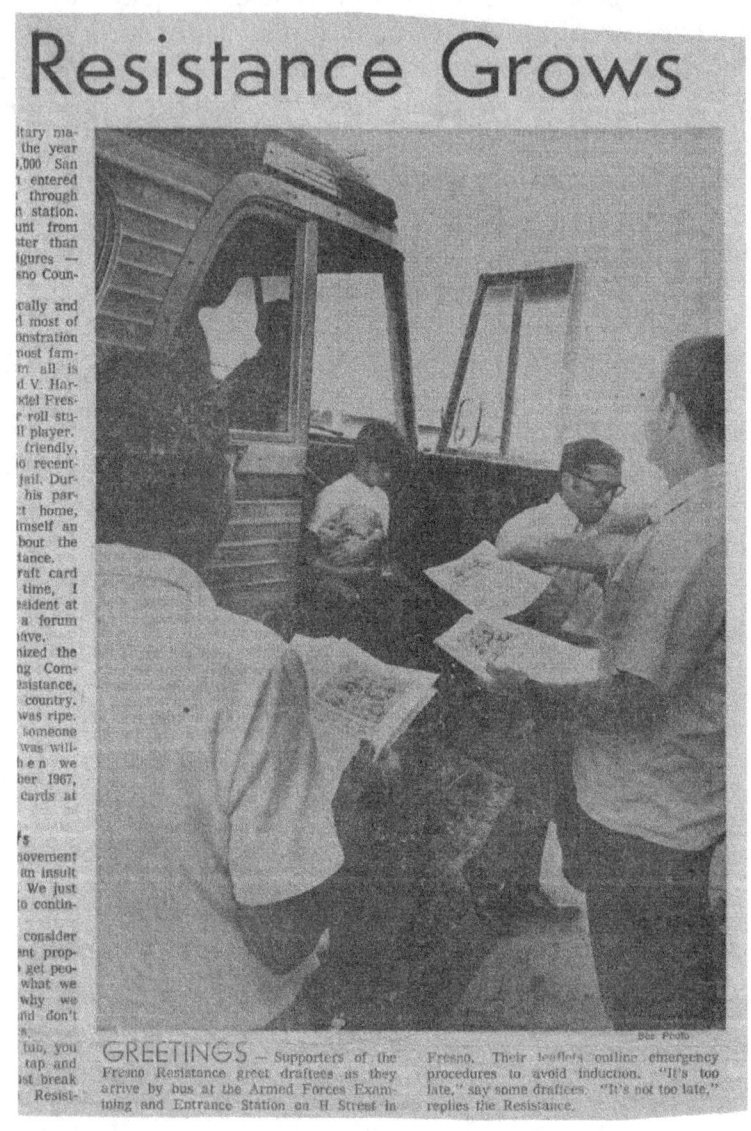

DOCUMENT #25: Resistance organizers leaflet new draftees coming off the bus in front of Fresno Induction Center, 1969. (Photo: Courtesy Fresno Bee,)

DOCUMENT #26: My house at the Resistance Community. Note upper bedroom window with access out to the roof. 1969. Person on the roof is Joyce Beach. (Photo Paul Dunham)

DOCUMENT #27: The front of the Resistance House in 1971, several months after it was vacated. (Note small Resistance Movement symbol on the wall, at center.) Photo: Gail Erwin (Klemm)

DOCUMENT #28: Joan Baez and David Harris visit Fresno Resistance Community, 1969 At left: Byron Black, Professor of Linguistics and Draft Resister, Center, Joan Baez, Resistance supporter, at right, Joyce Beach. (Photo: Gail Erwin (Klemm)

Joan Baez and David Harris visit Fresno Resistance Community, 1969 at left Gail and Dale Klemm. At center, Joel Eis,, at right center/background Mimi McMath and unidentified draft Resistance Community member. At far right foreground, David Harris, founder, Draft Resisters. (Photo: Gail Erwin (Klemm)

DOCUMENT #29: Guerilla action: The Draft Resistance banner flying over the Armed Forces Induction Center, October, 1969. (Photog.: Dale Klemm)

DOCUMENT #30: Luis Valdez (left) and Augustin Lira, co-founders of El Teatro in, *Dos Caras del Patroncito*, performed in a union hall. (Photo George Balis) (Permission UCSB CEMA /El Teatro Campesino Archives)

DOCUMENT #31: Cesar Chavez with Lupe Valdez in a private moment at an *El Teatro* art party. I am somewhere in the room. (Image Courtesy CEMA Archives, Univ. of CA, Santa Barbara)

DOCUMENT #32: El Teatro, Family style. From left, Luis Valdez, Teresa Gomez, Juan Gomez, Phil Esparza, Ricardo Duran, woman unknown, and the author at a party in late 1969. The company was much like a large family with all its blessings and curses. (Photo, courtesy CEMA Archives, Univ. of California Santa Barbara)

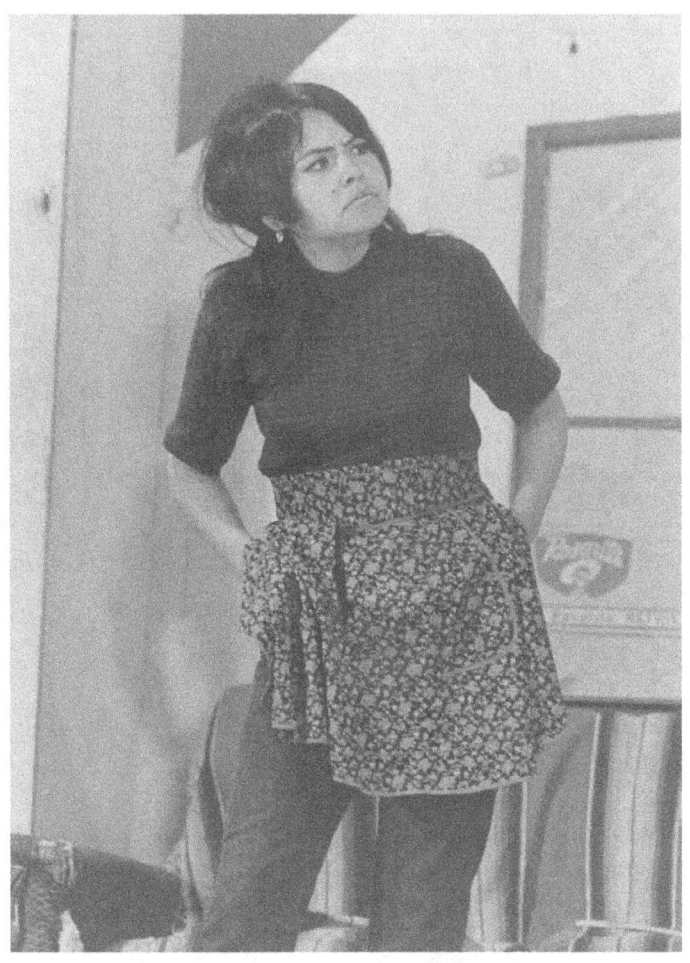

DOCUMENT #33: Lupe Trijillo (later, Valdez) as the smart-aleck daughter in, *The Shrunken Head of Pancho Villa*, (1968). Note the funky couch and little cockroaches on the wall, telling examples of the El Teatro's signature "*Rasquachismo*" (Run down and funky) style, (Image courtesy of CEMA Archives, Univ. of Ca., Santa Barbara Library)

DOCUMENT #34: Donna Haber as the Wife in *The Shrunken Head of Pancho Villa*, (1968). This big head sat on the couch. It talked and moved its eyes. Note the image of JFK on the set wall behind Donna. (Image courtesy of CEMA Archives. University of California, Santa Barbara)

DOCUMENT #35: *El Teatro* at the Festival in France. The festival devoted an entire issue of their journal to *El Teatro* as well as this one to radical theatre in the U. S. (Permission *Festival Mondial* Archives, Nancy, France Photographer unknown).

Numéro 6

LE JOURNAL DU FESTIVAL

Samedi 26 Avril 1969   30 centimes

Théâtre politique ou théâtre humain

La troupe colombienne de Cali tient dans les colloques quotidiens du Festival une place importante. Les lignes qui suivent témoignent du sérieux de la réflexion à laquelle les membres de la troupe soumettent leur pratique théâtrale. Ce texte est une contribution à la discussion d'ensemble.

Document #36: El Theato in France. (Note: The caption is wrong. It describes a group from Columbia.) This *acto* is "*Los Hulegistas*" (The Strikers). Left to right, Ruben Rodriguez, Lupe Trujillo, (later Valdez), "Wuedito" (Whitey), Ricardo Duran, Daniel Valdez and Don Teeter, as the white land owner. The character signs have been translated into French for the festival. (Permission *Festival Mondial* Archives, Nancy, France Photographer unknown).

DOCUMENT# 37: Angel of Death puppet from, *Cry of the People for Meat*. Wings are folded back to less than ½ their wing span during performance. This was a truly frightening puppet in performance as it was carried over our heads. (Photo, Carter Tomassi)

DOCUMENT #38: *Los Vendidos* performance, 1968, (Left to Right) The author (Honest Harry) praises the Mexican-American who denies his culture, speaks no Spanish, and puts down his own race. *Guerito* "Whitey" (last name unknown) the stereotypical "lazy Mexican." Antonio Bernal the sell-out. Danny Valdez is the *pachuco* (hoodlum). Lupe Trujillo (later Valdez) plays the Governor's representative, looking for an acceptable stereotype. (Image courtesy of CEMA Archives, U. C. Santa Barbara)

DOCUMENT #39: Performance of *Los Vendidos,* 1968. (Left to Right) Danny Valdez as the *pachuco* (hoodlum), the author as Honest Harry, (seller of Mexican stereotypes), and Lupe Valdez (ne Trujillo), as the Governor's representative, looking for an acceptable stereotype. The simple signs are a hold over from street theatre and our signature style, "*Rasquachismo.*" (Photo courtesy CEMA Archives, Univ of Ca. Santa Barbara)

DOCUMENT #40: El Teatro building, (1969) on Maroa Avenue in Fresno, later to become "The Building," Movement headquarters after El Teatro moved to San Juan Bautista. (Photo Courtesy of CEMA Archives, University of California, Santa Barbara)

DOCUMENT #41: Transformation Theatre: Floating Lotus Opera Company orgiastic performance. (Photographer unknown)

SECTION VI

COLORING IN THE FULL PICTURE

"Oh, who did you meet, my blue-eyed son?
And who did you meet, my darling young one?

I met a young child beside a dead pony
I met a white man who walked a black dog
I met a young woman who her body was burning

[Chorus]
And it's a hard, it's a hard, it's a hard, it's a hard
It's a hard rain's a-going to fall"

"A Hard Rain's A-Gonna Fall"
(Verse 4, Bob Dylan, 1962)

CHAPTER 22: THE FRESNO DRAFT RESISTANCE MOVEMENT

> "If I had a hammer, I'd hammer in the morning,
> I'd hammer in the evening, all over this land."
> (Peter, Paul and Mary, 1964)

    I returned to Fresno after the San Francisco State Strike and the Radical Theatre Festival. Simultaneous with my beginning with *El Teatro*, I began to work with the Fresno Draft Resistance. Again, I was in the right place at the right time. Though Fresno was not much more than a glorified farm town, as previously mentioned, it was actually a major outpost in the struggle to end the draft and the war because it had one of the three induction centers in California. In any war, geographic position can determine strategic importance.

    Much of the antiwar organizing work was on the Fresno State College campus. Young college men were on the cusp of deciding to enlist, seek a deferment, or resist the draft. Most of them had no clue about their legal rights under the draft law. We counseled these young men one-on-one and made speeches to large gatherings. We passed out leaflets to crowds or in front of schools. We confronted the young men lined up at the Induction Center to take their physicals. Often we had to hop-skip away from the cops or guys wanting to beat us up.

    Every Friday afternoon, we made speeches in the Free Speech Area at Fresno State. (DOCUMENT #42: Free Speech Area, Fresno State College) Before this gathering, one of us would sometimes jump up on a table in the cafeteria and say, "If any of you want to hear about the Draft Resistance, come out to the Free Speech Area!"

A successful leaflet might read:
If you DON'T WANT TO DIE for Standard Oil and The Bank of America, come to the Draft Resistance House and hear about the dozen _legal ways_ you can get a deferment from military service (and still serve your country)!

Because guerilla theatre was part of the arsenal of confrontational communication tools, I encouraged the Draft Resistance to employ theatricality into our political presentations. (DOCUMENT #43: Agitprop political theatre at Fresno State: Byron Black eats his draft card) This was quite successful. It's amazing what you can get away with in a funny hat. Nevertheless, our battle to end the Vietnam War and the oppression of large segments of the population was not a game, a hobby, or an academic exercise. It was a very real insurrection against deeply entrenched forces. Every activity, whether it was a march, a sit-in, a teach-in, a small guerilla action, or a public appearance, was part of this campaign. There was a lot at stake and a lot to lose.

This was war.

During the speeches, several guys were taking pictures. They were not journalists or talent scouts. Our audiences were regularly peppered with local undercover cops and the FBI. It was my personal mission to see to it that the FBI lost as much sleep as possible knowing what I did with my time. I went to towns around Fresno such as Bakersfield, Clearlake, and Modesto to help set up Anti-war movement/peace centers. It was during this time that the nightmares of the screaming and battle sounds in my head were the strongest. The visitation could be a five-second flash in the middle of the day or a disturbing moment in my asleep. I told my girlfriend Elsie about them. This helped.

I'm sorry to reveal to the conspiracy buffs out there that although several of us were SDS-affiliated, none who I knew were card-carrying members of anything. We didn't know any secret passwords.[40] Amerika did unspeakable things in Vietnam in our

---

[40] There was, however, a specific Black Panther handshake with a minor, almost invisible variation that informed both parties to the shake that one or both of them was carrying a weapon.

name. Amerika's troops burned villages without provocation and chased their populations into undefended refugee camps. Commanders in the field condoned gang rape and the murder of children and old people. We belonged to the human race. That was enough.

All of the organizers in the Fresno Resistance Community did share one important thing. Each of us began our journey toward radical activism with a defection from a traditional religion because it failed to act on its rhetoric. My roommate Paul was a lapsed Lutheran. Patrick had been a Catholic. Don Teeter was a Lutheran kicked out of the church for challenging them on their silence on the war. Dale and Gail Klemm, residents of the Resistance office, were a lapsed Lutheran and a lapsed Presbyterian. I was the Jew-in-Residence.

All of us walked out because the Sabbath palaver wasn't backed up with weekday action. We were viscerally revolted by the image of the holy men of our faiths blessing pilots who were about to kill innocent people from five miles up. We had no choice but to be part of the solution and not the problem.

Our college-educated generation was expected to become custodians of this system that deliberately exploited our Black and brown neighbors and held the Atom Bomb over the whole world. We were expected to fight and die for this arrangement. Our repugnance was personal.

We were opposed to the draft as a tool of this policy for one simple reason: If the government couldn't gain the voluntary support of its citizens to defend their policies, how was it that this government was enfranchised to carry out such wars? Drafting young people with a campaign of lies inferred totalitarianism. Gaining personal profit from their sacrifice was corrupt.

In a clear violation of the Geneva Accords against chemical warfare, the U. S. Military used napalm and Agent Orange, an herbicide and defoliant chemical. Up to four million people in Vietnam were exposed to Agent Orange. Nearly one million suffered serious health issues resulting in horrible, crippling deformities to thousands of children born to exposed mothers.

Agent Orange also caused enormous environmental damage. More than twelve thousand square miles of forest were defoliated, eroding tree cover and poisoning the soil, making reforestation or farming impossible. There were high numbers of cases of leukemia, Hodgkin's lymphoma, and other cancers inflicted *on our own soldiers* who were exposed to the stuff.

The military draft was essential to a corrupt and wrongful war effort. We were out to end it. Americans were never told about this human and ecological holocaust until very late in the war. It was our duty to counsel others about what they would be part of if they put on a uniform. This included the hidden hazards to their own health.

From the standpoint of the Federal Government, the existence of the Draft Resistance (along with the Grape Strike/Chicano Movement) made Fresno "ground zero" for FBI surveillance, infiltration, and sabotage. The FBI was not content with mere surveillance of legitimate political protest activity. Using secret slush-fund money, they engaged in a program called COINTELPRO (Coercion, Intelligence, Provocation) in which they turned peaceful demonstrations into riots and infiltrated legitimate groups and encouraged them to take illegal actions. Their main target was the Black Panthers, but the Anti-war movement was also high on their hit list.

Would you fight to defend a government that does things like that?

Being a Draft Resister and Resistance Counselor

Many of the Resistance counselors in Fresno had destroyed or returned their draft cards. This was usually orchestrated as an act of political theatre that happened at the end of a well-attended demonstration, complete with FBI and police photographers. Among the thousands of young men who carried out this act were local resisters Paul Dunham, Doug Rippey, Steve Price, and others. (DOCUMENT #44: Paul Dunham burns his draft card) In a stunning piece of political performance art, Professor Byron Black of the Linguistics Department at Fresno State did us one better. He ate his draft card. (See DOCUMENTS #43.)

The profound devastation that the Vietnam War perpetrated on the social fabric of this country was unimaginable. Working in the Draft Resistance Movement often put us on the outs with our families and former friends. The fact that Amerika was committing genocide and environmental devastation in the name of "fighting communism" just couldn't break through the thick fog of bumper-sticker brainwashing. I don't remember a single male member of the Movement who was not told by his father, "If you burn your draft card, you're no son of mine." This included me. When the Big Lie of the war—along with the facts of who was benefiting from it—finally broke through the doublethink, there were apologies at dinner tables all over Amerika. However, for most of us who'd been abandoned when we were in this plight, this was a war wound that never healed.

The Check from The Kremlin Was Always Late

While living at the Resistance Community appeared idyllic, we were all dirt poor. Work for the Movement was a task of sacrifice. For organizers in other places, there may have been financial support, but for us, the check from the Kremlin never came. Most of us lived on food stamps and part-time jobs. The steadiest source of employment was café work at Café Midi, Fresno's bohemian social center not far from the college. Mort Bennett (AKA Vitae Bergman) gave Draft Resisters under-the-table jobs at the Midi. Sympathetic college professors helped by paying us for house painting or yard work. Our farmhouses were rundown, and the plumbing was iffy. Keeping warm in the winter required extra sweaters, space heaters used sparingly, and a lot of cheap red wine.

I stretched my student loan with my meager salary from *El Teatro*. Our rent on the farmhouse was sixty dollars a month, a real bargain even by the standards of the day. My share was twenty dollars a month plus utilities. Everybody lived on food stamps. We never took Movement money for personal expenses, not even for rent. We got turned on to weed by friends who grew their own. Leftover food from the potlucks helped Dale and Gail get by.

Most of us were educated enough to get good-paying "straight" jobs if we wanted them. But who would expose the lies and speak truth to power? Who would bring home the men and women who'd been duped into a terrible, mistaken war? Like a soldier in any war, we made the choice of accepting a short-term personal sacrifice to achieve long-term gains. From his grave, we could still hear JFK: "Ask not what your country can do for you..."

Draft counselors were not allowed to advocate resistance. We could only inform someone of the options and the personal cost of that choice. Advocating resistance was an act of treason. But then again, so was recruiting without informing the young man of his full options. You could call the way they got their cannon fodder "shanghaied lite." They didn't hit the kid over the head or drug them. They just lied to them all the way to the grave.

In my high school days, we all filed into the gym to hear some guy in a flattop haircut and a pressed uniform give a talk to the senior boys. He said, "Every boy has to register for the draft, and there's no way out of it." Technically, this was true. However, not informing us of all of our legal options under the Selective Service Act was a premeditated sin of omission. The fact that there were legal deferments available for a long list of valid circumstances never came out of his mouth. Most importantly, the legal option of Conscientious Objector on religious grounds was never spoken of, *and it did not appear on the handouts*. His obligation, under the law, was to *explain fully* the Selective Service Act. Nothing like that ever happened for me or for millions of other young men.

Sure, some guys were gung-ho to join up. We respected their desire to serve our country. Serving our country was why we were doing what we were doing as well. That was their right, but not under premeditated government mendacity. Poor whites, Blacks, and Latinos joined to escape poverty, almost inevitable gang involvement, and future prison. "Regular Guys" had their *machismo* pushing them into uniform. However, not informing them of their legal alternatives amounted to coercion under false pretenses.[41] We considered it our patriotic duty, therefore, to fill in the missing information for as many young men as we could. (DOCUMENT #45: Dale Klemm and Ron Thiesen counseling young men)

Finally, among the full list of choices was the *right to refuse induction entirely*. This choice involved stiff penalties. However, compared to death in a fabricated war, it was a real choice. As the bloodbath claimed more and more men, three to five years in jail and then being alive for all the birthdays thereafter became a more and more viable option. According to the National Lawyers Guild and the National Draft Resistance, by 1971, almost half of the men of draft age never registered or refused induction. It had become an unenforceable infraction.

Draft counseling did what it was supposed to do. Many young men were gung-ho at the beginning of our "rap" but changed their opinions soon after. Truth is a powerful weapon. That's why the government was after us. However, to avoid a charge of treason, draft counselors followed a specific script. We were allowed to say, "Have you considered all your options *under the law,* including the alternatives to registering for the draft?"

We could then hand them a pamphlet and explain *in an informational way* the result of all the choices available to them. These included various legal deferments, Conscientious Objector status, refusing to register entirely, and emigrating to another country. The boys had a right to know their choices before they chose to kill or die. They could then make an *informed* choice ... like in a real democracy.

The FBI sometimes sent undercover agents to draw us into advocating resistance, which would lead to arrest and federal prison. These people were usually young FBI or law-enforcement

---

[41] There were numerous lawsuits by families claiming that their sons were inducted under illegal circumstances.

recruits or young men already in the military. They showed up in twos or threes because a witness was required. Sometimes they came with a "girlfriend." We also always had a witness as well. These shills would say, "What do you think about resisting the draft, maybe going to Canada?" The answer had to be, "You have a range of choices. It's all in the pamphlet. We aren't counseling you to choose any of these options."

Occasionally, when we were pretty sure the young man was genuine, we related a "story" to him. We might say, "I've heard about a guy who went into the Induction Center with a small straight pin in the band of his underwear. When he went into the bathroom to pee in the cup for drug testing, he took out the pin, poked his finger, and let a few drops of blood fall into the cup. This made him appear to be either diabetic or kidney diseased. This got him a 4-F deferment." This was not related as advice but simply as an anecdote. We probably saved a few dozen lives with that kind of "story."

However, sometimes we had a bona fide FBI ringer. We'd get his name and a description—even a picture if we could—and pass this on to other counseling centers. On one occasion, a young couple set off real alarm bells. He had a GI haircut. She was a nondescript "girl next door" type. They said they were planning to get married, but she was not wearing an engagement ring. Other things about this pair didn't ring true. He claimed he'd gone AWOL from the naval base in San Diego and wanted information about resisting. So what was he doing on our doorstep in Fresno, three hundred miles north?

I suggested he see a lawyer familiar with the UCMJ (Universal Code of Military Justice) and request reassignment from combat duty under military procedures. I then mentioned that the Resistance in San Francisco regularly dealt with young men from the Presidio and Moffett Field. We warned the group in San Francisco that this dubious pair was coming. This couple was counseled at the San Francisco Resistance Office and then disappeared. About a week later, the FBI raided that office with a warrant for counseling draft resistance and aiding and abetting a deserter. One of the staff there must have overstepped the script. The general conclusion was that this couple were plants.

Agents provocateurs sent to incite illegal activity were occasionally exposed. The young man on the right in DOCUMENT #25 (Resisters handing out fliers by the bus) passing out leaflets to recruits at the Fresno Induction Center was suspected of being a government plant. He would never take on a project or action himself, but always showed up to "help." No one knew where he lived, and though he appeared to be of student age, he was not in anybody's classes. Another guy came around offering us weapons. Shortly after several of us were arrested in 1970, a longhaired young man often seen at our gatherings offered $3,000 to a Draft Resister to report to him what was said at our meetings.

Aside from the wiretaps and the photographing of our speeches and interactions, I am sure we were followed to and from meetings and demonstrations. There were often people in the Café Midi, our usual hangout, taking notes on whomever we spoke with.

David Harris tells the story of how he finally got tired of the same guy in the same car following him even when he went out for a beer. Finally, David suddenly pulled over. The guy had to pull over right behind David's car. David got out of his car and walked back to the FBI agent.

"Listen," David said, "this is ridiculous. Why don't you just get in the car with me and save the gas?"

The poor factotum was so chagrinned that he just took off.

The Buddhist and the Cowboys

There was a price to be paid for living as we did, believing what we did, looking like we did. Fresno County was populated by racist descendants of the Oklahoma Dust Bowl. They hated hippies. Some of these peckerwoods decided to "teach one of them a lesson." Our longhaired friend Larry Sheehy had previously done a hitch in the Green Berets but was now vehemently against the war. Larry was a Buddhist and a vegetarian. One evening, Larry was riding his bicycle along Shaw Avenue in North Fresno. A pickup truck with three cowboys pulled over. They taunted him as a "peacenik" and told him they were "gonna cut off your faggot hair and teach you a lesson."

This was not the smartest thing the Good Ol' Boys might have done. Before they got started, Larry calmly informed them that he was registered as a black belt in karate and a former Green Beret. They laughed and moved in.

Larry left all three of them lying beside the road. He then pedaled across to the shopping mall and called the hospital to send ambulances. He came out to the Resistance House, recounted the event then sat in the orchard with a cup of tea to mellow out.

Big Demonstrations, Little Marches, and One-on-One

The government continued to drive an ideological wedge between the Anti-war movement and the men and women in uniform. The government couldn't allow them to discover that we had their real interests at heart, that the war was a hoax, and that people's loved ones served and died for a craven, criminal fabrication.

The mainstream media actively contributed to this dangerous cultural rift. They never quoted us in print to make our position clear. We were branded as unpatriotic, giving aid and comfort to the enemy. We simply wanted to bring our soldiers home. However, as more real information about the war and its motives surfaced, the great majority shifted to embrace our position. The times were a-changin'.

On October 15, 1969, the first National Moratorium to End the War in Vietnam took place. Two million people of every shape, size, color, and occupation marched all over Amerika to end the war. As an organizer, I went to observe the march in San Luis Obispo, a small beach town and the home of the California Polytechnic State College Institute, a technical/agricultural school with big ROTC and space training programs. The town was filled with ex-military retirees. My mission was to observe the antiwar sentiment in such a place.

To my surprise, even in this remote conservative hamlet, more than four hundred people marched. Young mothers, white-haired grandmas, truckers, hippies, surfers, and students filled the street. Instead of the usual wild-eyed hippie appearing next to the article in the local paper, there was a photo of a young mother with a baby in a stroller holding a "Bring My Daddy Home" sign. This was tangible progress.

This nationwide moratorium was followed one month later on November 15 by two massive moratorium marches, one in Washington, D. C., and another in San Francisco. The estimated two million demonstrators in Washington made it the largest demonstration in U. S. history until that time. The sister event that day in San Francisco drew more than three-hundred thousand. I joined a contingent from Fresno to attend the event in San Francisco. As we drove north in the early morning hours, we passed uncountable cars and VW vans heading north, festooned with antiwar slogans and peace signs.

In the march, I reached the crest of a hill and looked forward and back. I was part of an endless carpet of people chanting in a mix of joy and anger. These were our troops on the move. The feeling of marching among so many people with a single ideal was overwhelming. We felt joy at the outpouring of kindred souls yet anger that such an extraordinary effort was needed for us to be heard.

Essentially, this event amounted to a one-day general plebiscite and strike. The government estimated that for every person in the marches, there were a hundred who could not attend. This meant that there were countless millions opposed to the war. After this incredible day, President Richard Nixon—born a Quaker and therefore theoretically a Conscientious Objector—said, "Under no circumstances will I be affected by it." In the face of the numbers, he sounded like a kid denying he'd been caught with his hand in the cookie jar.

Pretty damned soon, he was gone.

Famous and Not-So-Famous Folks at the Draft Resistance House

Our little enclave in the fig orchard was an unofficial Counterculture Center. Anyone could and did show up there to learn, to help, and to seek community. We lived public lives. On several occasions, David Harris, originator of the Draft Resistance, or his then-girlfriend (and eventual wife) Joan Baez, would come down to Fresno to do a teach-in or perform at fundraising concerts. David grew up in Fresno, so they were there often. (DOCUMENTS #46: David Harris, Joan Baez, and Paul Dunham at Fresno State, 1969; DOCUMENT #47: Newspaper article announcing concert, 1969)

When Joan was at the Resistance House, she helped with the potlucks and washed dishes. She and David sat around drinking wine and talking after the other guests had gone. She would sometimes dig out her guitar or sing a cappella. Though this added a bit of glamour, the work of ending the war was the same with or without such luminaries.

At any time, we could be snagged to do draft counseling. One Sunday morning after a big blowout the night before, I was entertaining company in my room. A car rolled up in front of the house. The car radio was playing AM "easy listening" music. It had to be a visitor. I apologized to my guest, slipped into my clothes, and went out to greet them. A big station wagon occupied by a mother and her son had pulled up in front of our house.

I stepped out to the front yard and glanced down to discover my two revolutionary housemates were passed out naked on the lawn. One of my comrades had a significant member pointing skyward. The other was facedown with his "personality" smiling up at the morning sun. The visitors in the car had already spied them in the grass. This was not putting a good face on the Movement to say the least.

The mother was genuinely concerned for her son's safety. Coming from a straight-laced American household seeking advice from treasonous hippies was stepping way out of her comfort zone.

The *tableau naturale* on the lawn must have pushed her trust to the limit. I steered the mother and son-in-need across the road to the Resistance office and gave them the necessary literature. After they drove off, I turned on the garden sprinklers. I ignored the screams as I returned to my company inside.

****

In the spring of 1970, my work as a draft counselor and my work with the Chicano Movement intersected in an unexpected way. I was out in front of the house performing the revolutionary duty of watering the rosebushes when a big sedan rolled up the dry dirt road and stopped. Out of the driver's seat rose one of the biggest men I'd ever seen. He was solidly built and close to seven feet tall. He had piercing black eyes, curly hair, and a face like an old shoe. He walked around and opened the door for the young man in the back seat.

The young man from the back seat had straight black hair. He was wearing overalls and work boots. Deep dimples were etched into his warm, kind face. As he walked over, the giant stood by the car. The young man held out his hand. "Hello, I'm Fernando Chavez. I heard about you over at the *Teatro* office. I've refused induction. My dad suggested I talk to you guys about my case."

"Sure, come on in the house."

He called back to the other man waiting by the car, "*Tiny, soy en la oficina allá, treinta minutos. Tu quieres un agua?*" ("Do you want some water?")

"*No señor, 'ta bueno.*" ("No sir, that's okay.")

On the way into the office, Fernando explained. "Tiny's my bodyguard. My dad's Cesàr Chavez."

We talked and I gave Fernando brochures and leaflets. The men got back into the big car and drove away. With his family's history of professed nonviolence, he had a good chance of proving he had no business in the Army. When César was at the *Teatro* for the soft opening of *Bernabé,* he thanked me for helping his son.

Fernando won his case and didn't do any jail time.[42]

The Phone Company Helps Out

As far as the FBI was concerned, anyone who didn't vote Republican was a "Commie nigger-lover," probably a Jew, and maybe even a queer. In my case, it was three out of four. The FBI was sure we were working for an evil empire even if we didn't know it. Their job was to save us from ourselves. They couldn't embrace the idea that we had a right to object to the course our government was taking and that all the facts showed we were right. On second thought, that's probably what pissed them off.

Tapping phone conversations was—and still is—one of their primary tools hoping to connect you to the Big Conspiracy in the Sky. Hence the invention of the wiretap court order. For this permission, lawmen need "probable cause." This chicken-or-egg situation means that there has to be some kind of surveillance before the invasive process can legally begin. Early computers were used to record repeated contact with specific phone numbers that were already on their list. This record supposedly gave the G-men probable cause. *How those people got on the list in the first place was never questioned.* The number of "associated individuals" ran into the hundreds of thousands.

The process works like a comedy written by Franz Kafka. If a suspected person calls the same phone number several times, the computer assumes this number is linked to nefarious activities. The fun fact about the Official Enemies List is that once you're on the list, you never drop off.

One of the obvious problems with this system is that the content of the call is not considered. There was a Me-n-Ed's pizza place on Blackstone Avenue we called nearly every week. They're

---

[42] According to Draft Resister Doug Rippey: "Fernando refused induction, was indicted, and tried in the Fresno U. S. District Court. The prosecutor made a fool of himself, saying that Catholics couldn't be COs. Fernando's lawyer buried him in quotes from scripture and encyclicals." (Doug Rippey, email to the author, Nov. 20, 2017)

probably still on the Enemies List even though their Four-Meat Special is fantastic. Does anyone ever check to see why the first call was ever recorded? Don't be silly! (That job security thing.)

Once a phone number shows up some magic number of times, the Feds listen in on calls. This requires that they install equipment in the line. That used to be the guy with the headphones in the basement of your apartment building or in a phony utility truck outside. Between my Draft Resistance work, *El Teatro Campesino*, calls with Civil Rights and Black Power groups, and my family—who had leftist leanings as far back as the Great Depression—my phone was overflowing with red-hot numbers, and I do mean *Red*. There was often a utility company truck at the end of our street "working on the wires." (Soooo clever!)

With the equipment back then, when we dialed out or answered a call, there were so many audible clicks on the line that we had to wait until they all finished hooking up before we could begin a conversation. There was a small power drop caused by each wiretap. Sometimes the power draw from the multiple devices was so strong that the call faded in and out or disconnected entirely.

One night, my fellow counselor Ron Thiesen was so angry at all this that he telephoned the phone company. I was sitting across from him. The following exchange took place.

Ron: Is this the phone company's Repair Department?

Voice on the other end: Yes. How can we help you?

Ron: You can disconnect all the damned wiretaps! There are so many clicks on the line, I have to wait to start talking. Sometimes our calls even disconnect.

Voice: I don't know what you're talking about.

Ron: Oh, give me a break. I see the trucks out here all the time with leads running down from the connection box.

Voice: *Oh, you must be out at the Resistance House. Our technician says not to worry. The taps shouldn't interfere with your calls...*

One might consider that the amount of surveillance is a backhanded barometer of one's radical effectiveness. In a perverse way, showing up on their list might be proof that you're doing something worth their attention. As the Dalai Lama has said, "If you think that you can't make a difference with continual individual activism—that a small, insistent voice is not important—try sleeping in a dark room with one mosquito."

The Post Office Caper

Sometimes you even have to protect yourself from well-meaning good friends.
One Saturday morning in the winter of 1970, Ron Thiesen and I were hanging around my place. The phone rang.

The guy on the other end said, "This is the Main Post Office on E Street. There's a package here for you. We'd like you to pick it up."

Ron asked about the call. "Who was that?"

I put the phone to my chest. "It's the Post Office downtown. There's a package for me."

"Why didn't they just send one of those postcards you take back to get your package?"

"Because they want to be sure they know when I'm coming. They looked up my phone number and called … on a Saturday."

"What do you think it is?"

"I don't *think*, I know what it is. It's a package of hashish candy from my friend in the Peace Corps in Afghanistan."

Ron looked like I'd just told him that Christmas was coming six months early.

Back in early 1968, while I was still a student at UCSB, my friend Allen Garner had received his draft physical notice. Scared shitless, Allen immediately signed up for the Peace Corps to go to Afghanistan.

He was accepted and went.

Allen had alluded to sending me some *bhang*, a confection of hashish pollen candy. This miraculous treat is made by children wearing leather aprons covered in butter. As they run through the cannabis fields, beating the plants, to raise the pollen, it sticks to the aprons. The pollen and butter are scraped off the aprons onto trays that are warmed until the liquid is gone. The gummy confection that's left is unbelievably stony stuff. It was very hard to get stateside. I didn't think Allen was ditsy enough to send it, but there it was, stinking up the post office in downtown Fresno. The Feds had known it was coming ever since Allen wrote to say he was sending it.

"What the hell?" Ron said. "Let's go down to see."

"If I put my hands on that package, we're busted for drugs through the mail. When we get out of federal prison, we do California prison time for possession of a saleable quantity. After we get out of jail, we don't have to worry about getting drafted or voting or getting a job, ever."

"Let's go anyway."

"Okay," I said, "but let me handle the whole thing."

We got into my Dodge Dart with the monogram license plates (easy for the cops to spot) and headed for the Main Post Office. We pulled up in front of the imposing, Depression-Era monolith. There were two "dead giveaway" powder-blue Fords parked across the street. So much for low-profile surveillance.

We went in.

There was nobody inside except for a guy in a dark suit and a thin tie looking at a newspaper as if that's what you do in a post office on a Saturday morning. Another guy in a cheap suit was around the corner by the P. O. boxes.

I went up to the window. I said, "I got a call to pick up a package." I gave my name and showed my ID. As soon as I spoke, the guy with the newspaper began to put it away.

The postal clerk returned with a beat-up, string-and-paper-bag-wrapped, sorry-ass excuse for a sealed package. There it was, right in front of us, the Holy Grail of counterculture goodies. More than two pounds of Grade-A hashish resin candy.

As the postal clerk stepped back, Ron tried to reach over and pick it up. I body-blocked Ron to the side. Feigning indignation, very loudly, I said, "I am not claiming that package! I don't know where it came from, and I don't want it!"

I grabbed Ron and headed out the door. Ron was close to tears. The Feds were so bummed out that we weren't even followed.

My last letter from Allen was from Quebec. He'd emigrated after his Peace Corps hitch. I didn't have the heart to tell him I had to refuse his gift.

CHAPTER 23: 1969—THE BATTLE OF PEOPLE'S PARK, BERKELEY, CA

Events became more provocative and more violent. In the summer of 1969, the battle for People's Park in Berkeley, California, was a terrible sign of the tragic disconnect between the government and the people. People's Park is still a ragged scar of memory and a political flash point sixty years later.[43]

The Battle of People's Park was about everything we held sacred.

People's Park is a large vacant lot near the corner of Haste Street and Telegraph Avenue. It belongs to the University of California. Community volunteers cleaned up this neglected, junk-filled empty lot, seeded it with lawn, and planted it with donated trees, transforming it into something of value to the community. The people of Berkeley believed that those who cared for the land should own it. It had become *The People's* park. (DOCUMENT #48: People's Park, Berkeley today)

In the late spring of 1969, the university announced plans to develop the site into apartments and retail shops. This was a total miscalculation of the park's social importance. By threatening to take the park away, the university lit a fuse under a powder keg. People's Park represented far more than a symbolic issue. This was a concrete battle over land turned useful by the work of a politicized community. You can't get any more *American* than a fight over land. You can't get any more revolutionary than planting something that grows.

---

[43] In January 2021, the State of California again attempted to develop the property into a profitable investment.

For weeks after the university's announcement, there were daily demonstrations on nearby Telegraph Avenue. The university tried to put up a fence around the park. It was immediately torn down. Cops surrounded the park and marched through it, chasing homeless people off. There were so many demonstrations that the people in apartments near Telegraph Avenue moved out to get away from the endless tear gas inundating their homes.

The Fresno Resistance Community (or "The Conspiracy Farm" as we jokingly called it) followed the People's Park story with growing fear and anger. It was clear that the university backed by Ronald "Gunslinger" Reagan, was hell-bent on a showdown. After weeks of sham negotiations, the university called in the National Guard. They specifically chose Guard units from outside the area who, though they were men working at jobs in order to send their own kids to college, regarded university students as spoiled rich kids!

These enforcers wanted to kick some ass, and trigger-happy they were. As they energetically broke up the demonstrations, everyone in their path—even old women—were prodded with rifle butts. (You never know what a septuagenarian might be carrying in her wire laundry cart.) The news cameras were rolling. The world was watching. The enforcers were not ignoring the cameras. *They were performing for them.*[44]

James Rector was on the roof of his three-story apartment building on Telegraph Avenue. He was probably flipping the bird at the cops on the street below. One of the cops took aim and shot him dead. (DOCUMENT #49: James Rector, shot on the roof, Berkeley, CA) There were claims by the police that James had thrown a chair off the roof. *The cameras rolling at the time did not show any chair being tossed down.* Nobody saw a chair. Nothing. A chair was never found on the street. There were never charges against the officer or an investigation into the shooting. After this brutal act, the demonstrations turned into a running battle.

---

[44] It was rumored—and I believe confirmed—that a Hollywood film crew had come up to shoot the event in order to acquire stock footage for future movies.

Berkeley looked like Beirut. The Battle of People's Park became part of the war at home.

It was reported that the guardsmen who fired their weapons on the unarmed crowd were only using birdshot. However, medics who treated the victims found that all of it was "00" buckshot, a kind of small shrapnel that can be lethal at close range.[45] *The ammunition had to have been distributed to the troops by their quartermasters.* This was a planned and ordered decision, destined to become a bloodbath if it escalated in the hands of the trigger-itchy soldiers.

Two days after May 15, now known as Bloody Thursday, most of the Resistance Community and others from Fresno traveled to Berkeley. Don Teeter, Patrick Conroy, and Paul Dunham and I were there.[46] (DOCUMENT #50: Paul and Patrick at People's Park, 1969) Thousands filled the streets around Telegraph Avenue. I marched behind a piece of brilliant direct action. A large stake-sided truck loaded with rolls of sod appeared. The truck stopped, and sod was handed down to those of us who were directly behind the truck and laid over the street, creating another park. (DOCUMENT #51: Stake-sided truck at the front of the parade.) Bill Haigwood, the photographer for the image for this story, was a participant in the sod maneuver and attests to my account of this unique action.

As we got to Telegraph Avenue, we confronted rows of National Guardsmen with their rifles out, Plexiglas riot masks in place. Then the order came for them to fix bayonets. *Jesus Fucking Christ, they are going to charge the crowd with bayonets!*

---

[45] Each pellet of 00 buckshot is half again as large as a .22 caliber bullet. It's flesh-ripping shrapnel, a brutal, vicious munitions choice.

[46] On November 20, 2020, Showtime$_{TM}$ released a four-part documentary series, *The Reagans*, on Ronald Reagan, who was the governor of California in 1969. In Episode 2 is a segment on his handling of the student movements, including Berkeley and People's Park. At exactly 30:44 into the film, a two-second clip caught my Fresno Resistance comrades Patrick and Paul in the frame. (Image #50A: Paul and Patrick at People's Park, 1969) I was most assuredly somewhere nearby.

(DOCUMENT #52: National Guard and the people, People's Park demonstration)

After the murder of James Rector, we didn't know what to think, but we didn't back down. We advanced to within four feet of the guardsmen. They were told to take one step forward. The guardsman directly in front of me advanced. He put his bayonet to my throat, resting it on my chest, just below my Adam's apple. Then he looked at me. This weekend soldier was Chuck Hess, part of a National Guard unit from Fresno. Chuck and I had been in junior high school together back in 1960. Chuck and I held eye contact, poised on the personal knifepoint of this dangerous moment. He had sweat pouring down his face under his helmet. Sure as shit, this felt like civil war. As I looked into the blue of his eyes, I knew that History was where you put your body. Mine would be on the front line.

Some of the guys in uniform on either side of him were also from Fresno. Some recognized me. I saw eyes waver. They were having trouble keeping a grip on their rifles. Eventually, they were ordered to stand down. Chuck stepped back with his rifle held across his chest. We moved away and continued our march to the park.

Nobody died that day.

In a nearly *Twilight Zone* coincidence one year later, Chuck and I crossed paths again.

CHAPTER 24: SECURITY DETAIL AND THE BRASS WORKERS' STRIKE, 1969

"You must be at one with the people and serve the people.
Share their struggles. Serve their needs.
This is the only way to make a genuine revolution."
(Mao Tse Tung, *Little Red Book*)

In the early autumn of 1969, I was contacted at *El Teatro*'s office by the United Farmworkers Union to participate in the security detail for an event at Fresno City College. Dolores Huerta and labor organizer Saul Alinsky were speaking, and they needed security. I'd never done such a thing, but they wanted me.

Dolores Huerta, courageous cofounder of the United Farmworkers Union, was a great organizer and a powerful speaker. Saul Alinsky was also a major figure in the American Labor Movement. Alinsky encouraged and advocated the powerful tactic in other industries of bringing wives and families to the strike lines to deescalate brutal responses by the factory bosses and to bring attention to who was affected by low wages and unsafe working conditions. In the case of the Farmworkers' strike, *campesino* women and families belonged on the strike lines because they *were* the workers.

Alinsky was also the mastermind behind the rolling consumer boycott—aimed at one company at a time that sold scab-made (strikebreakers') products. In the farmworkers' struggle, store chains would have to sign a contract and buy only union-picked grapes in order to avoid a crushing boycott of their stores by thousands of grape strike supporters. This nonviolent, direct-action guerrilla tactic by moms with shopping carts was highly effective against the Lucky and Safeway grocery store chains.[47]

The need for security at the Fresno City College event in the heart of the agribusiness empire was not an empty pose or a publicity stunt. To the corporate farm owners in the San Joaquin Valley, Alinsky and Huerta were very bad news. Before the audience came in, we checked all the side rooms, the balconies, the basement, and around the building. We made sure that the fire hoses were secure. Someone checked the bathrooms every fifteen minutes to be sure that no one flooded the toilets by stuffing toilet paper in them to break up the meeting. As the crowd came in, I sat on the stage and scanned the audience, watching for people who didn't look like they belonged.

In his presentation, Saul alluded to the strike going on at the Fresno Brass Works in southwest Fresno. Alinsky noted that the grape strikers and the student Anti-war movement needed to show unity with the brass workers' struggle to defuse Labor's prejudice against "spoiled college kids who never did an honest day's work." We needed to grok the brass workers' double bind of either working for an oppressive corporation or dying to defend it overseas.

Brass is crucial to agribusiness and to war. The large irrigation systems that watered the endless fields required brass fittings by the millions. Artillery shells and cartridge casings are also made of brass. The industry appealed to patriotic support for the war to keep the brass workers from taking action against unsafe workplaces and cut-rate wages while the shareholders made millions.

Coming from a pro-labor family, this immediately attracted my interest. Don Teeter, along with myself and a few others, went out to the Brass Works to see what was going on. This was a real eye-opener. The Fresno Brass Works was a very old factory. "Safety inspections" were probably done in a downtown restaurant

---

[47] This tactic was also used with success in stopping the production of napalm by Dow Chemical.

over a fat steak dinner, a bottle of good whiskey, and possibly a "friendly female companion" who left with the inspector to seal the deal.[48]

On the upper floor of the factory, the brass ingots were melted in firebrick-lined vats. The molten brass was then poured down ceramic channels to the casting operation on the next floor. After the roughcast fittings cooled, they were ground and buffed to take off dangerous, razor-sharp edges. They were then shelved as stock or shipped out.

Every step of this process is dangerous and backbreaking. There were tiny, razor-sharp shards of brass everywhere. A worker goes through a pair of heavy leather gloves every few days. Face and arm lacerations were common. Infections from brass splinters were normal. Highly toxic fumes were emitted through the entire process. Ventilation in the factory was primitive and inadequate. Workers did not wear respirators. None were issued to them.

The heat in the factory in the Fresno summer—where it is a hundred degrees outside by noon—was hellish. When it rained, water dripped from the leaky roof into the open brass pots, causing molten brass to spit and scar the workers. Plastic goggles were useless against hot brass. Partial blindness was common. The firebrick brass pots and ceramic channels were old. A break in the brick lining of a brass pot could cause a pour-out of molten brass, instantly cutting off a man's legs at the knees. If he survived the searing pain, he could bleed to death before the ambulance arrived. We were told that it was such an incident that caused the walkout and the strike.

When we showed up, the strike had been going on for about two months. We'd done a food drive on the college campus and arrived with a carload of stuff. We sat down for coffee and

---

[48] A few years later, my landlord was a Bureau of Land Management forestlands inspector. He told me that occasionally he was asked to meet for "inspections" with lumber company executives. The meetings were always in pricey San Francisco restaurants or on private yachts. Expensive whiskey was given away and sufficient young female "party favors" were available to cast a Broadway chorus line.

sweet rolls with the picketers on the tailgates of old pickups and on rickety lawn chairs at the picket line. We were truly moved by their struggle to survive.

Don Teeter jumped up on the back of a pickup and talked about his days in the Navy. I made a short speech about how I'd grown up in a labor family, working in my dad's shop when I was nine years old to help the family get by. Then I said, "A guy who goes to work in a suit and tie is still a worker. It don't matter if you want to buy chorizo, chitterlings, or a hamburger. If you're paid shit wages, you can't afford to feed your kids. We're all the same…" Don finished up with how much we'd learned from them and the importance of unity. Grape Boycott literature was passed out on the picket line.

Soon after, the press ran a big story about our support for the strikers on page two, not as a small article on page ten. Ten long, hard months later, the factory signed with the union. The company installed new brass pots and exhaust fans. They fixed the dangerous leaking roof. They hiked wages by a fraction and gave out respirators. By joining together, we'd helped to win a victory for the brass workers in the war at home.

CHAPTER 25: NOT SEX—SEX AND THE REVOLUTION

One springtime weekend in those crazy days, I was at that wild, kaleidoscopic experience called the Haight-Ashbury Street Fair. I was standing right next to a small blues combo wailing away on the corner of Haight and Cole. Suddenly, near the music, a beautiful African American woman strolled towards me. She planted an incredible open-mouthed kiss and said, "That's mah *guit*-tar solo, honey!" then walked off into the crowd, leaving me dumbfounded, accompanied by cheers and laughter.

Women were now renegotiating their entire contract with society by any means necessary. In the early 1960s, the media bombarded us with goddesses simmering with sexually self-aware, predatory expressions. The inference from these frankly presented images was that women were no longer waiting to be approached for sex. However, Madison Avenue had badly miscalculated. This new image of women also introduced the idea—to the women themselves—that they also had the right *not to offer themselves at all* and instead to define every encounter on their own terms.

Years before, I'd been treated early to a lesson from a woman who was no longer going to accept a sexually-defined subservient role.

Four Pounds of Bacon = A Feminist Leaflet

In the summer of 1965, I scored a job in Yosemite National Park. I soon met red-headed, green-eyed Gina, who had a job in the café at Tuolumne Meadows in the high country. The supervisor there had a reputation for hiring pretty young women and then making it clear that if they wanted to keep their jobs, they needed to be really nice to him.

Gina politely declined, but her boss continued to harass her. She put in for a transfer. On the evening of her last shift at "TM," her coworkers were quaffing beers around the campfire. No one invited the *jerk du jour* to Gina's going away party. He had already gone to bed in his tent.

It was the height of bear season. This is when the big furry critters are extra hungry and brazenly approach human habitations. Gina came out of the kitchen with four pounds of raw, fresh bacon, or as we called it, "bear candy."

She snuck over to her boss's canvas tent and smeared the canvas sides with the greasy meat. She then tossed the bacon under the wooden floor of the tent cabin, turning it into a ten- foot-square bear bon-bon. Not long after, a quarter-ton bruin smelled the meaty treat and came out of the forest. The sound of splitting wood and canvas accompanied by roaring from both the bear and the boss was the soundtrack for Gina's exit. I can't think of a more socially relevant use for four pounds of bacon.

Between Gina and the Revlon Girl, whom I'd met a few months before, I was beginning to get the message on refocusing my views on women.

The Feminist Movement began at least five thousand years ago. The literature of every culture and in every age is replete with stories of girls running away from dominating fathers to marry who they pleased or striking out on lives of their own choosing. Exploitation in the factories owned by men in the Industrial Age was only a massive variation of this very old theme.

The twentieth-century commercialization of women's bodies added a new twist. With very few exceptions, images of women in earlier periods displayed them posing with ethereal, almost mindless expressions—statuesque and removed from the world. Beginning in the 1920s, advertising images of fashion models showed them with simmering, sexually predatory expressions as if these "liberated" women were already thinking of themselves as sexual even before we had come into the room.

However, in vitalizing the women, The Madison Avenue suits had tossed Eve the apple. By introducing images of women actively think about *something*, the admen miscalculated the result. If women believed they were supposed to be thinking of themselves as sexual beings before the fact, they also had the right to say "no" about going to bed with someone ... *or doing anything else*. The high heel was on the other foot.

By the early 1960s, women were becoming more forthright about everything on their minds. The first major sign of the cultural dynamite that was about to blow was when counterculture women began to suggest—and then insist—that they had the right to keep their own names after marriage. Clearly, there was something unfair, disrespectful, and *fundamentally unequal* in the assumption that a woman had to give up her name to join in a relationship with a man. We didn't smell the fuse burning when that one rolled out. We weren't paying attention.

Women in the Movement: Hard Lessons Learned

This account would not be accurate or complete without some disclosure about our successes and failures with the women who were part of the Movement.

Forthright, interesting women have always been attracted to rebellious men. Being leaders of a movement about humanizing our culture said a lot about the kind of men we were. There was even a slogan on posters, lapel buttons, and bumper stickers: GIRLS SAY "YES" TO BOYS WHO SAY "NO." Progressive women such as Jane Fonda, Gloria Steinem, and Joan Baez included this slogan in their speeches. (DOCUMENT #53: Girls who say "yes," Joan Baez, Mimi and Pauline Farina)

While the young men in the Anti-war movement generally held many of the same social/sexual attitudes about women as our non-activist peers, we saw the women in the Movement as comrades. The activist community had neither the time nor the patience for "groupies" or hangers-on. We called them "Movement chicks." Though this is admittedly a pejorative label, it meant that they were more than social decoration.

However, just as in the society around us, it was assumed that women were fitted for subsidiary roles that followed "traditional" patterns. This was the world we lived in. Grown women were not even allowed to hold a credit card in their own name. Neither a First Lady nor a working single mother with two jobs could buy a house, a car, or a washing machine in her own name until 1974.

It was inevitable that although we afforded a good deal of respect for the women in the Movement, our prejudices still ran deep. Bettina Aptheker, major labor and feminist organizer, describes a typical scenario during the work on the Angela Davis Defense Committee. "Out front, organizer Fred Hirsh has center stage. ... Ginny (Fred Hirsh's wife) was in charge of the research on the jury pool in the Angela Davis trial. Some 300 people in the original pool before computers, etc. ... She put together detailed information on potential jurors." Usually this kind of crucial, thankless background work, out of the limelight, fell to the women in the Movement. The issue here is whether this division of labor was a matter of real choice or roles assigned by cultural assumptions. Did Ginny want to grab the soapbox, or did Fred hanker to get his hands on the paper work?

The women who joined our circle marched, gave speeches, handed out leaflets, and ran from the cops with us. They were tear-gassed, beat up, and busted along with us. (DOCUMENTS #62: Women Comrades Busted with the Men) This led to bonding that expressed itself in many ways. Yes, there was a lot of sex, but there was genuine respect as well. We were well aware that through the death of sons and lovers, husbands, brothers, fathers, and friends, women suffered in the war as much as we did.

Then as now, women had their own battles here at home. They didn't have to put on a uniform. Domestic violence against women was not even considered a crime, not to mention the backward attitudes toward rape. More women died from illegal abortions during the period of the Vietnam War than men killed in combat. I am sad to admit that what was missing was that our voices in support of their struggle did not measure up to their sacrifices in support of ours.

There were plenty of dedicated women who were national leaders of the Anti-war movement, such as Joan Baez, Jane Fonda, Bella Abzug, Shirley Chisholm, Angela Davis, and Dolores Huerta. The Women's International League for Peace and Freedom (WILPF) were a major force against the war. And the leadership and the spokespeople in the Soledad Brother's Defense committee were entirely women.

As young women, including my sister, sat on the street blocking traffic or marching, they looked around and said to themselves, "I have a right to be here. Nobody can say my opinion and my voice do not matter." From this grew the confidence to speak up in their own behalf within the sexist confines of the Movement.

While we were busy saving our own asses from the war, we did not recognize the growing women's movement within our own ranks. Mistakes were made, feelings were hurt, painful disappointment and bitterness was felt by women resulting from our self-centered attitude. Who's to say what battles were lost for them because we did not stand with them when the call was there? As I recall, however, when the Women's Movement got rolling, there were no putdowns from us. No one was shut out of speaking their mind. It was their movement, and they wanted and deserved to run it from the front office to the back room. We did childcare, housework, taxi duty, and marched alongside.

In the clearer vision of hindsight, we were not as revolutionary a counterculture as we could have been. This is an important lesson to be learned for future struggles. It is crucial not only to listen to the voices of those who speak up but to look around the room at the faces of the people who are not speaking up. *They* are the troops. They *are* the movement.

CHAPTER 26: ABOUT DRUGS AND REVOLUTION, FOR THE RECORD

> "Excuse me while I kiss the sky"
> (Jimi Hendrix, musician and poet, 1967)

> "You only live once.
> If you work it right, once is enough."
> (Mark Twain)

There is no mystery why the drug culture arose. It was a direct result of the failure of Western religion to address our spiritual needs. Western religions had dry-cleaned themselves into such desiccated, ineffective dogmas that a hunger grew for something else, *something that worked*. Drugs were not a religion, but they opened the window to finding a new perspective. They opened us up to ourselves and our connection to the world around us. We quoted the 3M company's slogan, "Better things for better living through chemistry."

We were always aware that our activities were being closely watched.[49] Movement folks indulged in mild social drug use; serious drug dealing or heavy habitual use was not only against our ethics but made us more vulnerable to official scrutiny. There was a schism between the drug culture and political activists.

Some found politics and did a little weed on the side. Some found drugs and did a little politics on the side. Our official policy

---

[49] I carried my passport and about $400 on me all the time. Ask any field agent working in hostile territory. This was standard procedure.

was that the bread spent on dope to relieve your stress could be used to do something about the reasons for it in the first place. "If you're bummed out about getting drafted, then help end the war."

To my knowledge, no one involved with Movement activities was ever on drugs when they were doing political work. There were never any drugs at the weekly potlucks. These informational/social dinners were serious business. Drugs get in the way of business.

Nevertheless, there was a larger political implication behind the drug culture. The practice of getting high was an anti-Establishment ritual. Rolling and smoking a joint was a deliberate, in-your-face, "I'm going to do this, fuck you!" towards "square culture." The act of sharing it in a circle was an anti-Capitalist exercise. It was a ritual of *our* tribe.

Stronger psychedelics such as LSD, mescaline, and peyote offered an entirely different experience that never really interested me. Heavier drugs require that the "tripper" relinquish complete control and be comfortable with that. I was not. I was after *finding* myself, not losing myself. Except for one time…

1970: Me and LSD

The joke about the Sixties is that if you can remember them, you weren't really there. Despite the joke, I remember it all very clearly.

I did LSD once. That one time changed the rest of my life. On a cool February evening, I came home to my pad out in the fig orchard. When I pulled back the Mexican blanket that was my door, I discovered a young woman sitting on my bed. Her army surplus backpack was on the floor. I'd never seen her before.

"Hi. What's up?"

"The chick in the other house said you might be home soon."

She'd probably talked to Gail. "How come you're here?"

She shrugged her shoulders. "The people I rapped with said you guys were cool."

Not an actual answer to the question. "Okay. What's your name?"

"Jennifer, Jenny."

"Are you running away?"

She shrugged and looked away. "My dad's an asshole, and he's home right now."

Again, not a real answer, but it was clear there was probably sexual or physical abuse at home.

"Do your folks know where you are?"

"I told them I'm staying at a friend's house. Can I stay here tonight?"

Many young people found us to be a refuge when their situation put them in danger. It was obvious that she was probably underage. If I asked, she would have told me what I wanted to hear anyway. I wasn't going to ask to see an ID. I didn't know any guys who hadn't sleep with forthright young women who'd lied about their age or never brought it up. There were girls her age who were married to men my age with their parents' permission. The bottom line was that it seemed wrong to send her back into her home situation, and I wasn't going to send her alone out into the night. "You can sleep out in the living room or have my bed, and I'll sleep out there."

She took off her boots. "I've got some weed." She took a joint out of her backpack.

"Are you hungry?"

"We had some brown rice and veggies."

"If you change your mind, I'll drive you home."

"Okay."

Then she dropped an unexpected offer.

"I've got two hits of acid. It's good stuff, blue dot.[50] We can trip together."

What the fuck, I thought. "OK, let's do the acid."

"Far out. Can I take a shower?"

---

[50] This was the Dom Perignon of LSD. It was hard for anyone to get. I wondered who her connection was.

"Sure. My robe's on the hook behind the bathroom door."

She dug into her pack and fished out a metal screw-top film canister. "Here's the acid. Let's do it now. You'll be tripping when I come out of the shower."

On two postage-stamp-sized paper tabs were blue smears like small Japanese brush marks. If she hadn't been ripped off and it was just food coloring, she had hard-to-get, primo-grade LSD. I put the paper on my tongue, chewed it up, and swallowed it with a sip of tea. She headed for the shower. The aroma of shampoo made my room smell like bottled springtime.

I waited on my bed. Five minutes later, I *really noticed* that the walls of my room were leaning inward. My room *did* actually have beveled walls because of its construction as a Russian-style farmhouse, but now I was really noticing them. Not only that, the walls *knew* they were leaning inward. Now *that* was interesting.

My disk-shaped space heater on the floor morphed into a hot flower, but I knew it was a heater. I took my heavy shirt off. The air rushed around my skin. I thought, *For the next few hours, everything is going to be very important…*

My room was lit with a soft-yellow light from my small, amber, paper-covered lamp. The whole room appeared to be filled with honey. Jenny came out of the shower in my robe. Crystals flew off her head as she shook her wet hair. The aroma of her body and the soap filled the room like wine. She seemed to move as if she was swimming in oil. We closed the Mexican blanket curtain over my doorway. She slipped off the robe.

Jesus, God Almighty, she was beautiful. The idea of sleeping out in the living room was off the program. Her idea.

She went to the kitchen and brought back a glass of water. Every sip seemed three times more refreshing than normal. We lay down.

"You can take off your clothes too."

What a great idea that was! She helped me because I was tripping so heavily that I couldn't perform the mysterious task of undoing the buttons on my Levi jeans. All I could do was laugh and keep saying, "Oh, wow! Oh, wow!" like a useless, disconnected idiot.

Jenny stretched out on the bed, warm and relaxed. She was obviously inviting me. As I watched her move, she turned into every famous nude painting and every *Playboy* model photo I'd ever seen.

"Oh, wow! Oh, wow!"

She rolled over slowly.

I thought, *She is wise beyond her years.* This thought triggered a new cerebral cascade. Like hot wax, her face and body transmuted itself. She seemed to melt slowly into herself as thirty, forty, fifty, and sixty, then seventy years old. This is called "tripping" for good reason, believe me.

"Oh, wow! Oh, wow!"

Then she was back to looking like a perfect young woman. I began to run my hands over her body. Every curve, every texture, every aroma triggered an infinite reverberation. There were so many sensations that I couldn't get it together to focus on making love with her. I couldn't *do* anything. I began to see red crystals in the air. "Oh, man! There's crystals everywhere!"

"Oh, yeah, I see 'em!"

Despite her obvious interest, sex was something from a different lifetime.

She reached over and took my sex in her hands. The touch of her hand on my body sent waves of unbelievable sensation, but I didn't get hard.

"What's the matter? Don't you think I'm pretty?"

"Oh, man, you're incredible! You're turning into every beautiful woman I've ever seen. It's too much. I can't … focus."

She was obviously disappointed. "That's cool, maybe later."

"Yeah, maybe later… Oh, wow!"

"Is this the first time you've tripped?"

"Yeah, it is."

I curled up in a ball beside her on the bed. For the next few hours, I felt myself *existing* inside my own head. In my dreams, I was in other bodies, on other planets.

In the morning, we had tea and some food. I apologized for not making love. I think if I'd made love with her, my head would have exploded.

She didn't want a ride. She shouldered her backpack and headed out toward the main road. She didn't leave me her phone number. She was clearly disappointed in my lack of performance, but it was beyond my control. When you are tripping, the trip takes *you* where it wants to go. At least she'd spent a night in a safe place.

I took my tea out into the chilly, silver dawn of the fig orchard. The morning was cool and infinitely quiet. The surreal, gnarled branches of the rows of fig trees disappeared off into the mist. I was still tripping. The peaks of the Sierra Nevada were just barely visible, dreamlike above the softly outlined trees. I felt as if I was standing in a Japanese ink-brush painting. Dew was forming on the branches like trillions of diamonds as far as I could see.

Slowly, I turned my head to the sound of wind chimes on somebody's porch. Maybe I'd only conjured them up inside my head. I panned my gaze to the postcard view beyond the rough farmhouses to the snow-capped mountains beyond. I knew that there were experiences all around me, inside my head and beyond, of which I might only catch glimpses.

A door had been opened for me. I now knew profoundly that everyone around me also contained universes of unrealized possibilities. Hamlet was right about what he said to Horatio. Everything we say or think is only a glance at the infinite.

Zen.

I never saw Jenny again. She'd definitely turned me on to something new. I never got the chance to thank her. Perhaps, because she was left in peace for the night, she thought about options other than exchanging sex for safety. Perhaps that was my gift to her.

CHAPTER 27: SOME OTHER ENCOUNTERS

The Woman Who Interviewed Cops

In the summer of 1970, *El Teatro* went to Los Angeles to perform as part of the Chicano Moratorium against the war. This was a series of demonstrations, boycotts, press conferences, and teach-ins that focused attention on the grossly disproportionate number of Latinos killed in Vietnam as well as on the streets of Los Angeles.[51] Police brutality, especially in Los Angeles, was reaching epidemic proportions. There was no redress of any kind. The Brown Berets' community protection program of observing arrests was not stopping the police violence.[52] It was said that the L. A. County Sheriff's Department had distributed recruiting fliers in the Southern states with a "no high school education required" description, essentially actively recruiting white racist applicants. This revelation added fuel to the charges of inherent racism in the LAPD.

El Teatro's performance was at the amphitheater in Olympia Park. It held more than nine thousand people. We shared a bill with Pete Seeger. (DOCUMENT #54: Pete Seeger and *El Teatro* in L. A.) The place was packed. This was the largest house we'd ever played. I shared a microphone with Pete on a duet of "This Land is Your Land." Pete sings better.

---

[51] In this period, my Draft Resistance work and my work as a member of Teatro coincided. Don Teeter and Doug Rippey, both Draft Resistance organizers, had also been members of Teatro, binding these two movements together.

[52] The Brown Berets, originally a nonviolent community action group, were beginning to take up an armed posture, much like the Black Panthers.

After the show, we went to a party in a large, Spanish-style house owned by a Los Angeles restaurateur who was supportive of the Grape Strike and critical of the Vietnam War. There was food and good liquor. The party was crawling with attractive, expensively dressed women sporting cashmere brown berets, Che Guevara buttons, spiked heels, and miniskirts. People were openly smoking weed in the house and the yard. This was the surreal world of "fashionable radicalism" for which Los Angeles was famous. It was Orwellian. It was Oz.

I watched a Brown Beret brother wander off to a back room with what appeared to be a tall, thin, provocatively dressed woman. The guy standing next to me laughed and said to me, "When he gets where he's goin', he ain't gonna find what he's lookin' for."

"What do you mean?"

"That guy's a famous drag queen. He likes to surprise straight guys."

"The surprise might be mutual. I happen to know the other guy's wearing a gun."

I rapped with a woman (a real woman with no Adam's apple) about the police treatment of Chicanos that was in the news. She worked as an interviewer for the Los Angeles County Personnel Department. I shared with her the report about the fliers found in Southern cities. I'd actually seen one myself. She was incredulous and more than a little indignant. She said, "I test and interview the new recruits. Things are getting better."

I had my doubts.

Before I left, she said, "I've never been to Fresno. Maybe I'll come and see you."

I gave her my address and phone number.

A week after this performance, the L. A. Chicano Riots happened. The cops showed what they could really do to wage war on a community. The newsreels made the police in Alabama look like Boy Scouts. The *placa* (street Spanish for PIGs/police) filled the hospitals with beaten and bloodied people. Field hospitals had to be set up combat zone-style in schools and churches.[53]

About two weeks after this event, my phone rang. Luisa, the interviewer for L. A. County, was calling from the Fresno bus station. I picked her up. She was a mess.

She started to cry in the car. When we got to my pad, she sat cowered in a corner of my bed.

"What happened?"

"I interviewed more candidates for sheriff. When I found tendencies for violence or racism, I noted it. I thought I was weeding them out of the hiring pool."

"Yeah?"

"Those were the guys they hired."

---

[53] "The biggest, bloodiest disturbance in Los Angeles since the Watts Riots five years earlier lasted several hours." What began as a fiesta day in the park after a nonviolent march turned ugly when the cops overreacted to a liquor store pilfering a few block away. In less than an hour, "A three-square-mile area was the scene of people running for cover and riot-equipped police advancing in military formations, trampling spectators and clubbing those who did not move fast enough. ... When it was over, Los Angeles Times columnist Ruben Salazar was dead and two others mortally wounded, about 200 people were under arrest, 75 law enforcement officers and untold numbers of demonstrators were injured, 95 county vehicles were destroyed or damaged, 44 buildings were pillaged and eight major fires had been set." For many in the community, it confirmed their complaints of abusive and indifferent law enforcement. (information and quotes from an article by Luis Sahagun, *L A. Times*, August 23, 2020)

CHAPTER 28: MORE FRONT-LINE TALES AND "YOUR FRIENDLY MOVERS"

During this period, I attended a political talk in the student lounge at Fresno State. The discussion focused on government efforts to foil the Movement with a counterrevolution. This topic was always fueled by wild paranoid assertions of nefarious plots involving everything from putting LSD in the drinking water—which the FBI in Berkeley had actually done as a test—to intentionally circulating drugs in the Black and Latinx communities. (What an outlandish idea!)

Rarely was there anything like hard material evidence to support these theories. However, on this evening, something unique occurred. A very serious, intelligent couple took the floor. The husband was a dedicated conspiracy researcher looking into the wiretap and COINTELPRO evidence just beginning to surface.[54] By pure chance, his wife had been hired at Bekins Van and Storage (yes, "Your Friendly Movers™") as an office temp worker. They liked her. So, without any kind of security check, she was hired to work in their Corporate Archives Division. She took from her purse and passed around brochures describing what the "Friendly Movers" in this office did for their clients.[55] I held this brochure in my hands and read it.

---

[54] Only a few years later, the Freedom of Information Act (one of the Movement's accomplishments) exposed the full range of surveillance and sabotage activities.

[55] My subsequent attempts to confirm this division of Bekins elicited different responses. Finally, in one call, someone picked up the line, confirming that this

For a reasonably exorbitant fee, Bekins provided top-level executives and their families a reserved berth at a secure bombproof bunker in a sprawling underground campus. A few of these facilities were already completed in defensible locations near military installations. The couple making the presentation believed that one of these facilities was being built west of Fresno near the Naval Air Station in Lemoore, camouflaged by construction vehicles on a nearby highway project.

"All fine," you might say. "If there's a nuclear attack or a flood, it's important that the executives of Soaky-Toy Corporation[56] can get back to the business of making sponge bathtub toys for the milk poster children of the Free World."

But wait! There's more! According to the colorful, fully illustrated brochure, in the event of an imminent nuclear attack, the promotion laid out the details of the perks. It promised to scoop up the executive at his office (or the golf course) and gather his wife from home and his kids from school before Armageddon rained down. While all hell broke loose topside, the wealthy clan would be chauffeured out to one of these self-contained, underground bomb shelters complete with food, water, living space, a gym, a bar, schoolrooms, movies, etc., for a period of up to two months.

"Wow, what a perk!" you might say. "We sure as hell want all the assholes who got us into a war to survive it so they can take over again!"

However, consider further. If these shelters were to protect these worthy leaders and their families from nuclear attack, *why were they being built near military bases that would be prime missile targets?* An ICBM missile from Russia takes forty minutes to reach either coast from a submarine or a launch site. How could Bekins Van and Storage guarantee that they can scoop up your

---

division existed. However, my request for the brochure was rebuffed because I was not with a bona fide company.

[56] Soaky-toys were kids' plastic tub sponges in the shape of cartoon characters like Bullwinkle and Mickey Mouse. Soaky-Toy Corporation executives made Vietnam War speeches supporting the war because "communism threatens our way of life." We needed those toys to maintain our freedom, yeah.

records, your family, and your poodle in time to dodge the blast? There is only one way: *They would have to know in advance that the need for the shelter is coming.* Only with days or weeks of prior knowledge could they make this guarantee. And how would they know? They would know because the real reason for these facilities is to protect the Corporate Elite while the government arms and moves out to put down the insurrection they'd heard about on their wiretaps. The only reason that these locations make sense is that military sites could protect the executive folks against a domestic insurrection. I'd bet my best gas mask these underground castles are still around.

Getting My Picture Taken and a Whole Lot More

In late 1969, a lot was happening around the world and at Fresno State. The heat was rising, and not just from the desert. There were rising body counts, troop increases, city riots, CIA coups engineered in democratic countries, and government corruption. Every Friday afternoon, the Draft Resistance group took over the Free Speech Area in the middle of the Fresno State campus. We had guest speakers and our own commentators presenting feedback about the war, civil rights, the Grape Workers Strike, government corruption, and university politics. The crowd usually totaled a few hundred. Sometimes there was guerilla theatre. Once, we dressed in Nazi-style uniforms and praised the university for some ridiculously backward decision.

I was a consistent speaker at these occasions. I had a dedicated following—the plainclothes FBI and police. The same overweight guy with greasy black hair and big sideburns was always posted on the balcony of the Student Union, holding a camera with a lens like a cannon. There was another guy down in the crowd, not even trying to hide the tape recorder. I used to address part of my speech to them directly and even pointed them out to the rest of the gathering. When we passed the hat for donations, a pretty girl usually went over to them to get contributions. They were too embarrassed to turn her away, so we usually got something from them. We thanked the government for contributing to the Revolution.

One day, out by the Student Union, a friend called me over for a private chat. Dennis was a student in the Law Enforcement Training Program. He told me that his police training class had taken a field trip to the Fresno Police Department headquarters. The trip included a visit to a special room where the local cops liaisoned with the FBI.

He said, "Hey man, there's pictures of you guys all over the walls in the basement of the Fresno Cop Shop. They have shots of you all over campus and out in front of your house. Hell, they've got a camera with a giant lens mounted on the college water tower, taking long-range photos of y'all out on your front lawn."

I thought of the times I'd smoked weed out there and made love under the fig trees. I remembered the morning my roomies were passed out naked on the lawn. "You're not for real."

"Saw the pictures myself. Big red circles around you, Paul, Patrick, Don, and a few other folks. Watch your back," he said, and we parted.

I borrowed a pair of field binoculars and took a gander up at the water tower on campus, just over a mile from my front door. Sure enough, up there on the twelve-story-high water tower, a camera with a giant telephoto lens—and an office chair for the comfort of the snoop—were permanently installed. I now flew the finger at them or urinated on the lawn. My housemates mooned them often.

About that time, things got more interesting. Occasionally, we'd see dust kick up at the borders of the orchard and occasionally a glint of light. We suspected it could be from binoculars or a camera lens. It might have been happening before, but it was definitely happening now. Just before dusk one evening, I heard a "thip-thip-thip" around me. It was bullets whizzing past my head, cutting through the big fig leaves. Some buried themselves in the fig tree trunks. One slug buried itself in the wall of my house. I made a phone call to some ex-Vietnam vets in the Brown Berets and explained the situation.

A few days later at dusk, a Brown Beret name Ramón came to my front door. Ramón was a big guy, well over two-hundred pounds, fair-skinned with a black handlebar mustache. He was an even-tempered guy with a very droll sense of humor.

He smiled and said, "You were right. We found a couple-a cowboys out by the road. Their weapons were relieved of ammunition. One of them fell down a couple a times and hurt his face." Ramón shook my hand with the Brown Beret handshake and drove away.

At the same time that this occurred, Dale and Gail, the married couple in the house across the little dirt road, began getting death threats on their phone. They'd had a baby boy a few months before. Dale sent Gail and the baby away. He and I loaded the printing press into the back of his VW van. I think we took it over to Dr. Ed Dutton's garage.[57] We now kept the sprinklers running on the lawn every night and the outside lights on. They don't make flak jackets in purple paisley.

More than Rhetoric

As the conflict in Asia escalated, the rhetoric escalated as well. We would often harangue the ROTC frat boys, warning them about fragging.[58] We used to say, "Watch your back, fellas! The Black and Latino guys you call 'nigger' and 'spic' now will be in your squads over there, and they'll be heavily armed."

We also challenged teachers to devote class sessions to the truth about Amerikan history, especially current events that affected the students who were right in front of them. The worst

---

[57] In June 2019, Fresno leftist organizer Mike Rhodes informed me that after this old Multilith 1250 printing press left the Draft Resistance, it became the tool of the *Fresno Free Press*. Eventually, it was crated up by Mike and Lang Russell and shipped to El Salvador to serve the people in the hands of the FMLN, the liberation front in El Salvador.

[58] Fragging was when soldiers had had enough of an incompetent officer who was leading them to die without cause. They would shoot him or roll a grenade into his tent.

insult to an academic is not being relevant. The most vocal and active antiwar and anti-racism teachers were the philosophy teachers, history teachers, and a few of the outstanding poetry teachers, notably Wren Mabey, Bob Mezey, Phillip Levine, Bob Johnson, Pete Everwine, Alex Vavoulis, Ed Dutton, and Everett Frost, all nationally recognized in their fields. These men were real heroes. Their jobs and family livelihoods were threatened by the college administration for criticizing the war, racism, and repressive university policies. (There were no Blacks, Latinos, or women hired in these departments.)

Phillip Levine, a published poet and professor of writing, lived on a working ranch in the foothills. He wore shit-kicker boots, Levi's, a work shirt, and a rolled and crushed straw cowboy hat. A deeply concerned student raised his hand and asked Phillip, "What can we do to stop this? What can we do to be heard?"

Phil walked over to the fire alarm on the wall, raised his booted foot, and kicked the alarm off the wall. Over the din of the wailing horns in the halls, he said, "You can start with that! Now get out of here and save your ass from Nixon's war!"

The university was soon to exercise a full-scale purge against all of these brave, outspoken professors.

CHAPTER 29: 1969—WOODSTOCK AND THE POLITICS OF LOVE

"By the time we got to Woodstock, we were half a million strong,
And everywhere was a song and a celebration.
And I dreamed I saw the bomber jet planes riding shotgun in the sky,
Turning into butterflies above our nation.
We are stardust, we are golden, we are caught in the devil's bargain,
And we've got to get ourselves back to the garden."
("Woodstock," Joni Mitchell, 1970)

The Woodstock weekend concert held August 15–18, 1969, was the ultimate spontaneous, revolutionary gathering. I didn't go myself, but one did not have to be at Woodstock to be part of it. It reached out to all of us. It was political because it changed the colors of the background behind everything we did or said. Other than the 1963 Washington Civil Rights March and the Vietnam Moratoriums, the Woodstock weekend was the most important American meta-theatrical demonstration of the decade. It was our anti-conventional convention. Our amplified Bill of Rights was declared electric by our leaders in leather fringe and tie-dye.

The counterculture was an undeclared revolution. It was a far deeper and wider insurrection than the organized movements for social justice. We were in same war occupying different trenches. It had its own manifestos in songs, poetry, and artwork in free "street rags" like the *L. A. Oracle*, the *Haight-Ashbury Free Press*, and the *Berkeley Barb*.

The Woodstock weekend was held at Max Yasgur's 600-acre dairy farm near White Lake in Bethel, New York. With its dozens of rock and folk-rock artists, it attracted an audience of more than 400,000. It was the counterculture's national unconvention. Woodstock was a declaration of freedom of self-expression in just being who you were in any damned way you pleased. Woodstock was not organized to be about civil rights or the war. It was fundamentally about *the whole goddamned thing*. Freedom was declared in our appearance, (tie-dyed) clothing, freewheeling taste in music and food, and above all ... hair. There even was a Broadway musical, *Hair: The American Tribal Love-Rock Musical*,[59] originally produced with a garage band, that declared its importance as our symbol of freedom.

At Woodstock, our inalienable manifesto of political and cultural expression was declared in the simple *fact* of this event. Our generation ratified our rights by smoking a joint and dancing naked under the open sky. They were, as the sacred words declare, *inalienable*. For the Establishment, that was the craw-sticker. Radical action took many forms. Sometimes it was getting arrested for sitting in front of the tanks. Sometimes it was dancing naked under the moon.

However, despite the good vibes and painted naked bodies, more than thirty-thousand soldiers and nearly a million Vietnamese had died by the end of the Woodstock summer. Dancing to groovy music ripped out of your head wasn't going to convince the State of Alabama to let Black people vote or bring the kid you used to party with home from Vietnam. Flower Power wasn't enough. It was still necessary to translate this yearning into forms of expression that the "square," "straight" world could understand. That was the function of the political manifestations of our Revolution. This was rock 'n' roll against the atom bomb, and we couldn't afford to fail.

---

[59] *Hair: The American Tribal Love-Rock Musical* by Gerome Ragni and James Rado, music by Galt McDermott, originally produced by Joseph Papp at the Public Theatre, off-Broadway, on October 17, 1967.

CHAPTER 30: BECOMING THE PEOPLE WE WERE WARNED AGAINST

If the disjointed, unpredictable, surreal quality of these times is becoming clear, then you're getting into the groove. By early 1970, it was clear from the headlines that we were living in a crumbling, broken society. Fact-based stories and editorials about the war as a colossal mistake now flooded the news.

There were minor skirmishes or major street battles someplace in Amerika almost every day. The rioting increased. Black neighborhoods burned. Cops were getting off scot-free for brutality while the whole world looked on. Preemptive "thought crime" detention bills were introduced in Congress. This was heavy shit.

Mainstream Amerika was more interested in saving face than in making the changes that were needed. Painful rifts were tearing at the fabric of our families. As I have already recounted, this included mine. The level of denial was insane. Families sat and watched their own kids being gassed and beaten on TV all for wanting to bring our soldiers home. They cheered as the Army fixed bayonets on us at Berkeley. They dug into their TV dinners as the National Guard shot down and killed four students in cold blood at Kent State in Ohio[60] and two at Jackson State in Mississippi. They resented us exposing the lie behind their lives, even at the expense of their own children, not to mention the lives of the people of Vietnam. This was a cultural civil war, not only

---

[60]Despite the government's insistent claims that the shots were fired by random soldiers with nervous trigger fingers, modern computer-filtered sound equipment has clearly isolated the voice of the commanding officer giving the order to fire at unarmed students.

city by city and campus by campus, but family by family. We had become the people our parents had warned us against.

Trouble on Campus

More and more white students, even in conservative Fresno, were becoming disaffected with Amerika's direction. Many were now desperately hopeful that they wouldn't be called up for military service. As the struggle intensified, however, they were truly torn. They might attend a rally if it was peaceful but never tell their families. Many wanted an end to the war but didn't want the kind of trouble we were attracting. Just to make it harder, a law was passed in California that anyone *arrested* in a demonstration could not become a schoolteacher or a nurse, and their student draft deferment was automatically removed. *Actual conviction of any crime* was not required for this penalty to be invoked.

While leftists were subjected to derision from jocks, frat boys, and aggies, as well as explicit surveillance by the authorities, this was nothing compared to the ordeal that even the most well-dressed, innocuous Black and Latinx students experienced every day. Minority students were openly harassed, demeaned, and insulted in broad daylight just walking to class. Black and Latinx students carrying books on campus were routinely stopped by campus police and required to show library checkout slips for the books.

Fresno's tiny Black community was so demoralized by intimidation that when Angela Davis's sister, Fania Jordan, visited there in 1972, she would say, "Jesus Christ! This place looks like Alabama in the 1950s!"

Minority students returned to their cars to find tires slashed, headlights broken, the bodies "key-gouged," and occasionally, "KKK" spray-painted on them. Small groups or individuals—especially Black women and Latinas—were cornered, verbally abused, or physically roughed up in some isolated corner of the campus, even in broad daylight. If these encounters erupted into out-and-out physical defense against this violence, the students who were defending themselves were suspended or put on probation. The white student perpetrators were merely reprimanded if that. Documented cases, even with film and photographic evidence and witness testimony, were ignored. White professors who stood up for them were demoted, lost advancement to tenure, or removed outright.

Invariably, Karl Falk, the college president, and Don Fikes, the vice-president, would show up at the Ag buildings, the P. E. Department, or fraternity gatherings and socialize openly with the students who'd participated in these incidents. Falk was using the white students as his own personal Klan mob to keep uppity Black folks in their place. The comparison to a Southern plantation owner whipping up his white sharecroppers against "niggers who think they are better" was too obvious to ignore.

Under these conditions, it was no surprise that when we held large political demonstrations, blocked traffic, or occupied buildings—all behavior guaranteed to attract police interaction and reprisals—minority students stayed away. They had enough trouble without kicking the angry dogs ready to tear them apart. They lived in a different world that was painful to see.

Other Issues, Other Battles

On February 26, 1970, students from UCSB, my alma mater, burned the nearby Bank of America building (and the Wells Fargo a block away) in Isla Vista to the ground. Media sources were totally unreliable regarding the cause of this incident, so I went to Isla Vista to find out what really happened. I stayed with some Movement people there. When I arrived, there was a strictly enforced curfew. The crime-scene tape still enclosed the charred ruins. Riot cops were still patrolling the streets. The FBI was still going door to door. I had no reason to doubt my host's story. They may have been closer to the action than they were willing to admit.

This is the full story.

Isla Vista is the student enclave next to the University of California campus. It consists of block after block of student apartment buildings spreading north and east from The Loop, a circular boulevard of cafes, grocery stores, pizza and burrito joints, liquor stores, and bike shops. Around The Loop were six property management offices that rented apartments to students and saw to the complaints concerning living conditions. Centered on The Loop, like medieval castles lording over their fiefdom, was a Bank of America and a Wells Fargo Bank.

Isla Vista belonged to the university. It was sold off parcel by parcel to developers who built apartment buildings or retail stores with loans made by these two bank branches, primarily with money deposited by the students for living expenses. The university was doing very well with this arrangement—too well.

For reasons never explained to the students, leases on Isla Vista apartments were never allowed to last a full twelve months. Students had to leave their apartments in June. Even if they wanted to stay in their own apartments through the summer, they had to sign a separate lease. This meant that the property management companies collected a full month's rent for June and September *twice*, even it if was the same occupant. Thousands upon thousands of students were victimized by this scam for more than a decade. Student groups petitioned the university and the banks to do something about the situation. Nothing was done.

Justification for the restriction on year-round occupancy was that the apartments were zoned as "temporary housing." This put them in the same category as labor shacks. The Isla Vista apartment buildings were therefore built with inferior materials by non-union workers. These buildings were death traps. When I attended UCSB and lived in Isla Vista (1966-1968), a recently built, three-story-high, city-block-square housing complex was built so poorly that you could watch tiles pop off the bathroom windowsills as it sank. It was condemned after less than one year of occupancy.

I personally experienced two frightening incidents in one of these stucco slums. In 1966-1967, I lived in an apartment that was in a block of eighty units, each occupied by four students. One afternoon, I was ironing a shirt on the kitchen table (college boys don't own ironing boards). Without warning, the light fixture over my head exploded. The repairman said that he replaced several of these substandard fixtures every week all over Isla Vista, installed by non-union labor working for unlicensed contractors.

    A few months later, I was studying in the living room of this same apartment. My roommate Darryl was taking a shower upstairs. Suddenly I heard a crash and a scream. I ran upstairs to see the entire glass shower door shattered into penny-sized shards on the floor of the bathroom and shower stall. Darryl was standing wet and naked in the shower. There were small cuts on his body where shards of glass had hit him like shrapnel before they fell to the floor. I made him slowly shower his whole body without moving his feet. I put my arms around him and lifted him, naked, out of the shower stall. I slowly looked him over for tiny glass splinters.

    The repairman showed me why this happened. The substandard shower door was made without a rubber rim between the glass and the metal frame. It was manufactured with glass that was too thin, a strictly forbidden product under union building codes. A quick temperature difference or a slam of the door would shatter it. That was what had happened to Darryl. The repairman said he had steady work replacing these all around Isla Vista. The building owners gave him the identical door to replace the old one. Despite the tropical landscaping, these student rabbit warrens were no better than slums in Harlem or ranch labor shacks.

    The plot thickens. The Bank of America and the Wells Fargo Bank in Isla Vista used student money to finance this lucrative real estate. In this Orwellian scenario, the students were literally financing their own ghetto-like living conditions. The bank boasted huge profits from these holdings as well as investments in war industries, all financed by student dollars. Student money was used to fuel a war in which, if a student lost his deferment, he was expected to fight and die to defend this cozy arrangement.

Then the last act in this grim guignol was enacted. Almost five years of negotiations with the university and the banks yielded nothing. Finally, demonstrations erupted over the complicity of the university, the banks, and the six property management companies with offices around The Loop. The war-profits-for-death issue, wherein these banks took student money and invested it in war industries, was almost a footnote in the list of grievances.

On the day the bank was burned, the large, determined demonstration first went to each of the real estate company offices around The Loop and torched them. All of the county's fire trucks were occupied with these fires. The Bank of America was then torched. The bank burned to the ground because there were no fire trucks left to extinguish the blaze. (DOCUMENT #55: Bank of America fire, Isla Vista, CA)

This was a popular uprising of the most fundamental grassroots order, like the Harlem Riots or the American Revolution. White students had never before taken up real combat against the police, but this time they were not in a mellow mood. When the cops showed up, they were chased to side streets with hails of rocks and bottles. None of this was reported truthfully in the news. The university and local law enforcement agencies claimed that it was the work of "outside agitators." This was easier than admitting their shameful complicity in the real cause.

This is a small example of how Amerika was exploiting us against our own interests. Just as the revolutionaries in the Black communities were doing, there was only one possible response to this level of in-your-face oppression. It's in the first line of the Declaration of Independence: "When in the course of human events..."

Steve Salino and the Blasting Caps

By 1970, the disproportionate numbers of Black and Latino soldiers dying in the war made it clear that the poor were being used—once again—as cannon fodder to protect the holdings of the rich. As Malcolm X put it, "No Viet Cong ever called me 'nigger.'" To prove his point, a white racist politician said, "Dead niggers can't vote me out of office."

The situation for Chicanos in the San Joaquin Valley was especially bad. With no way out of the cycle of poverty, many joined up to affirm their manhood and to gamble their lives against cashing in on the G. I. Bill. Only six percent of the infantry were Chicanos, but they accounted for more than twenty percent of the casualties. It was as if the Angel of Death shaved the dice every time a Chicano rolled. The small farming town of Porterville, California, a few miles south of Fresno, lost more men in Vietnam, proportionately, than any other city or town in the United States. They were almost all Latino.

The Chicano vets had had enough. One night, I got a phone call from a friend in the Brown Berets, the Chicano community support group similar to the Black Panthers.[61] Steve was an ex-infantryman back from the war. I recognized the voice.

"Hey man, do you know where I can get like...blasting caps?"

The Feds were on the line. I said, "I don't know who the hell this is!" I hung up. I didn't answer when it rang again. Steve showed up at my place the next day. I was performing the revolutionary function of mowing the lawn. I turned off the rusty mower and laid into him. "What the fuck, man! You can't even joke about that kind of shit on my phone!"

This was his *palabra* (story). "It's like ... my *carnal* (brother) has some stumps on his land out in Parlier. He needs to get them out."

It sounded pretty lame, but I played along. "Okay. This conversation never happened. There's a feed and grain store on Tollhouse Road up in the hills. I remember seeing a sign on the counter about blasting caps; maybe they even sell small 'stump charges.' I don't know. People up there often use them like that, to

---

[61] *Los Berets* began as a police observation group watching arrests to protect against harassment and brutality against Latino youth. They worked to politicize youth and pull them away from the gangs. After the Chicano Moratorium in Los Angeles, they became more militant, modeling closer to the Black Panthers.

clear boulders and tree stumps off their land." I doubted his story, but I had no proof. "Just be sure that no one gets hurt," I said. Steve got on his motorcycle and rode off.

About a month later, I got a call from someone with a heavy Chicano accent. The man said, "Don't leaflet down by the draft board for about a week." Then he hung up.

On November 2, 1970, the *Fresno Bee* and *The New York Times* carried front-page stories on the predawn explosion and destruction of the Fresno Army Induction Center and the offices of the *Fresno Guide*, a racist right-wing weekly paper continually filled with salacious, fabricated stories that supported growers against farmworkers. (DOCUMENTS: #58, 58A: Induction Center Bombings in Fresno) Paul and Patrick risked getting busted and went down there for a look-see. The building fronts were blown away. There had been big fires, but nobody was hurt. For weeks afterward, we were all on edge. They never caught anybody.

I connected the dots. This story never happened.

CHAPTER 31: 1970—A PURGE AT THE UNIVERSITY, A LITTLE EXTRA ATTENTION

There can be no doubt that the administration at Fresno State was handpicked by the State Trustees to deal with the campus Anti-war movement, minority teachers, and teachers' union issues. Karl Falk, president of the college, owned a bank notorious for hard-hearted evictions in minority neighborhoods. His doctoral thesis had been on the ball-bearing factories in Germany in 1934. According to the treaty after World War I, Germany was not supposed to have ball-bearing factories. Karl Falk was allowed to visit these *verboten* factories as a guest of the Hitler regime. (DOCUMENT #56: Spontaneous anti-Falk rally, Fresno State) President Falk went nowhere on campus without an armed bodyguard.

His second-in-command, Vice-President Donald Fikes, was so paranoid of Black people that he wore a gun in a shoulder holster under his suit coat. When his coat flew open sometimes, anyone could see the weapon. I saw it myself.

These hatchet men engaged in what amounted to a racist *pogrom,* firing every Black and brown instructor on virtually no grounds whatsoever. Also axed were twenty-two white progressive professors, in some cases effective immediately in mid-semester. All were fired with no explanation, no hearing, and no mediation. Adjuncts favorable to the administration took over their classes. Not a single conservative "chair warmer" lost his or her job.

The firing of Dr. Eugene Zumwalt in particular was an act of political theatrics meant to threaten and dispossess. If it didn't really happen, it'd be funny. It wasn't funny.

December 4, 1970, was an unseasonably warm late autumn day for Fresno. At about 3:30, I had just come out of the Drama Department building and was sitting on a bench outside. I noticed some unusual activity around the English Department offices. There were cops with shotguns on each side of the door and several more with M-16 automatic rifles on the roof. Was there a bomb threat or a hostage scene unfolding?

Suddenly, two police officers escorted Dr. Zumwalt out of the building as if they were throwing a drunk out of a bar. He saw me and came over to sit down. Gene and I had become somewhat close. We often discussed Shakespeare and political theatre.

Gene recounted a tale right out of a low-budget Nazi movie. "One of the president's toadies walked into my office, handed me an envelope, and demanded I open it. I was fired forthwith. Two cops literally picked up my secretary and carried her out of the office. They then locked my file cabinets. Two cops escorted me out of the building. They said that since I no longer had business on the campus. I had thirty minutes to leave or be arrested for loitering on state property. When I asked if I could go back and retrieve my suit coat, two guys came in with welding gear *and welded my door shut.*" (DOCUMENT #59: Fired professors with gags, welded door, FSC) He began to cry. After twenty terrible, bottomless, rage-filled minutes, he left.

Dr. Dutton, Chair of the Department of Social Welfare, and Dr. Mabey from the Philosophy Department were similarly treated. (DOCUMENT #59) Falk had said that his administration "would be founded on clear communication." It was pretty clear what he wanted to get across.

SECTION VII

BREAKDOWNS

"Oh, what did you meet, my blue-eyed son?
And who did you meet, my darling young one?

I met a young girl, she gave me a rainbow
I met one man who was wounded in love
I met another man who was wounded in hatred

[Chorus]
And it's a hard, it's a hard, it's a hard, it's a hard
It's a hard rain's a-going to fall"

"A Hard Rain's A-Gonna Fall"
(Verse 4, Bob Dylan, 1962)

CHAPTER 32: CAUGHT IN THE CROSSFIRE

The war dragged on despite all our efforts. There was a change in the tide, but it was nerve-grindingly slow. More men came home in shambles or in body bags. There was more and more violence in the ghettos. Movement frustration increased with the intensity of the long, drawn-out struggle. Just when the Establishment's excuses for the war had become paper-thin and the message of the Left was more credible, factions arose like mushrooms in a cow pasture. Among them were more militant splinter groups.

On the national scene were the Students for a Democratic Society (SDS), the Peace and Freedom Party, the Ralph Nader folks, and the Eugene McCarthy Democrats. There were also the Communist Party, the Socialist Party, the New Left, the Young Communists, the Young Socialists, the Youth International Party (Yippies), the Maoists, and the Weather Underground. Even the Civil Rights Movement was bitterly divided over strategies; the Black Panthers had split into camps. The rows of recruiting tables at Movement events looked like a farmers' market.

Among these splinter groups, there arose a truly militant faction of the antiwar/anti-Imperialism movement: the Weather Underground. Because of their very provocative militant stand, the "Weathermen" became the target of the mainstream media, who routinely described them as "ruthless terrorists." Compared to what a plane full of napalm could do, who was a "ruthless terrorist?" This group's ability to carry out effective guerilla warfare scared the government because of its ability to succeed.⁶² The government's reaction was to intensify their program of sabotage against the entire progressive movement.

The years of sacrifice and the stress of the struggle were wearing our patience thin due to the slow methods of radicalizing the people and the uneven results. Factionalism was developing over rhetoric more than over solid strategies to achieve our goals. In the military, this is called battle fatigue.

Che Guevara once quipped, "When American liberals form a firing squad, they make a circle." Sadly, he was on the money. To the delight of the Ruling Elite, the Movement was degenerating into a cancerous cacophony of territorial intellectual bickering over theoretical phraseology instead of strategies for real action. People began leaving meetings over the wording of an idea instead of getting something concrete decided. Having one's watchword slogan be politically correct became more important than what was to be done.⁶³ Everybody was choosing up teams in the heat of History.

Just at the moment when we needed to pull together for victory, we were losing it.

Such groups as the Weather Underground were making it clear to the Power Elite that our patience with being shucked and jived was wearing thin. Though the Panthers' posture of declaring their right to defend themselves against police brutality was an entirely different posture, it sent a similar message of rising frustration to the power brokers. However, at that time, ordinary antiwar and civil rights activists were not ready to start digging trenches in an armed struggle. A leadership vacuum was developing between our slogans and the needs of the country. For years as activists, we had set ourselves apart from ordinary life. We had stood as lightning rods, calling attention to our generation's deep dissatisfaction with the bankruptcy of our culture

---

⁶² Ho Chi Minh, quoting George Washington, said, "The purpose of the struggle is not to amuse or frighten the enemy. The purpose of the struggle is to win."
⁶³ Future activists take heed. Some of this is a legitimate sign of burnout. Some of it is fomented by government plants and disinformation projects.

and our anger over current injustices. We were the self-appointed public witness against callous brutality perpetrated with arrogance and greed.

Millions with more ordinary lives marched behind us against the war or with our Black and brown brothers and sisters in their fight for dignity, hope, and peace. Ordinary peace-loving folks joined us to sit in and occupy buildings and block streets, stopping "business as usual." They were also beaten and went to jail. They burned their draft cards or waited for loved ones who went to prison. Some moved to other countries for their own safety or in disgust. These people *were* the Movement. However, it seemed they were not ready for a true insurrection that involved extreme tactics. *The Movement leadership's greatest failing at this moment in History was in spinning our rhetoric beyond what our rank and file would support. We did not frame a clear, unified message of how the changes we envisioned could be achieved with further political action involving them.*

As organizers who identified ourselves as the engines of this struggle, we held a position of both courage and vulnerability. We put ourselves in harm's way, and come to our lives it did. We took the forward brunt of repression, surveillance, harassment, jail, and intimidation. However, things within us and around us changed. We were, in the end, only human. This history we were making took a toll on us. After setting ourselves apart from ordinary life for so long, our factionalization was the first sign of our own personal breakdowns. The mental and spiritual fatigue that led to militancy ahead of the rest of our Movement indicated a level of frustration. We had lost our spiritual moorings just when redefining that anchor was crucial. We were acting out the breakdown in energy and focus from the stressful danger in our lives.

Our rank and file were experiencing this battle fatigue as well. Ordinary followers of the Movement were getting burned out on just being *against* something. They were looking to do something positive with their lives. They needed a philosophy they could hold onto that spoke to a daily practice. In this instinct, they were expressing a collective wisdom that we did not understand. The great Paisley Unwashed needed an ideology with principles of practice, a dogma with rituals, and clear codes of behavior in which they could engage right away.

Millions of spiritually shipwrecked young folks without deep political awareness began to search in desperation for a slogan to live for. Hungrily, they signed on to one of a plethora of patched-together Born Again (or born-just-last-week), Flavor-of-the-Month guru cults with a catchy slogan, a secret handshake, and a colored robe. By the early 1970s, this "anti-Movement movement" led to interest in Eastern-like guru cults such as those led by Rajneesh and Sun Myung Moon, as well as the Hare Krishna cult (whose followers were, if nothing else, colorful and noisome). Others found Sufism or one of the varieties of Buddhism.[64]

For those with a very shallow political commitment and a case of political burnout, any cult that smacked of being Asian now held cachet. All of them had rituals of simple daily practice that seemed exotic, mysterious, and new. Most of us already had Ravi Shankar records, incense, and a bag of brown rice around the house anyway. There was even a desperate cosmology known as Jews for Jesus. Even Saint Dylan took up with Jesus and wrote the signature excuse piece, "You Gotta Serve Somebody."[65] One of the things the great mass of our disaffected generation soon came to believe was that they could do without politics. They decided to leave the powers that be…well…to just be. It was the ultimate political capitulation.

****

This fracturing began to affect our local community. By late 1969, some of my friends were morphing into Maoists,

---

[64] The Zen practice of Karma Yoga—right action—was a cornerstone of my own politics from my earliest awareness. It was the framework around a socialist worker democracy.

[65] No, Bob, you don't gotta serve nobody.

quoting slogans from Mao's *Little Red Book*. "Serve the people" was the easiest to understand. (DOCUMENT #60: *My Little Red Book*) This was pretty much what we'd been doing anyway, but the slogan became important. The Maoists in our midst were alienating people just when we needed to pull together. One wonders what percentage of them were government plants.

In the flood of slogans and pamphlets, things became more serious under my own roof. My roommate Paul and our friend Don Teeter blossomed into Maoist neophytes. Maoism also fell under the rubric of Asian cults. Paul began to collect guns. He acquired an M1 carbine and a 9mm Parabellum pistol. He kept his little arsenal hidden under his bed, a hippie mattress on plywood and cinderblocks. So clever. Nobody would think to look there. Sure as hell he didn't have permits for them. Paul now kept the thin wooden door to his upstairs loft room locked. Maximum-security cracker box.

My comrade's new gun-toting posture was dangerous and unnecessary.[66] What was particularly bad form was that Paul brought his little arsenal into our house without asking me or our other roommate, Patrick. After all, I was a duly registered, nonviolent Conscientious Objector. If we were busted for the weapons, his little stunt would have scuttled the entire peace movement in Fresno. It would have undermined everyone from the older matrons in the Women's International League for Peace and Freedom down to the junior high school girl who faithfully and courageously leafleted in front of her school, risking expulsion, arrest, and juvenile hall. It was an arrogant and unforgivable stunt with no political mileage to be gained.

We were now more careful of who we draft counseled in the house, more circumspect on the phone, and removed every stem, leaf, and seed of marijuana out of the house. Just as a larger audience was beginning to understand the profound wrongheadedness of our foreign policy, this overt insurrectional

---

[66] It might be theorized that this increased militancy made it clear to the government that the Movement was becoming increasingly frustrated and angry.

braggadocio isolated us from the general Movement population. This was definitely not being "one with the people."

Nevertheless, this personal and collective transition was not fully understood at the time. We were struggling as a movement and as individuals to keep our values and the vector to our lives. At the same time, we continued to deal with the unexpected day-to-day activities of ending the war. The escalation of violent posturing soon became a two-way street.

Karla

One day, Karla Wilkins hitchhiked to our front door, knocked, and walked in. Karla was very blonde and blue-eyed, with a husky voice and a healthy farm-girl figure. She had a warm laugh that could melt a statue. Karla was a very grounded young woman. She confessed that she was a CYA (California Youth Authority) escapee, turned in to them for being a habitual runaway. Her drunken stepfather had been sexually stalking her. Running away was her only protection. The streets of San Francisco, Los Angeles, and other cities were crawling with girls living out this same scenario.

I hung out with her for a day or so. Then Paul showed up. After they laid eyes on each other, that was the last I saw of them for two days. Karla moved in with Paul and began baking bread for the house when she wasn't upstairs with him. They were genuinely smitten with each other. I never saw Paul so happy.

Paul knew that his only chance with Karla was to get her to negotiate something with the CYA. Karla's uncle Marty was a rookie Fresno police officer. Marty and I had known each other in high school. He liked Paul, and he respected that we made contact with him about her situation. He came out and talked to her. She agreed to return to court in Marty's custody, hoping for a haven under his roof. In the meantime, Marty felt she was in good hands. Before Marty left, he smoked a joint with us (in uniform).

The next day was Saturday. Paul had left early on an errand. Karla was sleeping upstairs. At nine a.m., she and I (in separate rooms) were awakened by the pulsing, punishing *WUMP! WUMP WUMP!* sound of a U. S. Army "Huey" helicopter hovering less than three-hundred feet directly over our house in the middle of the fig orchard. The din was so loud that we had to yell at each other, head to head, in order to hear and be heard. There was no one in the adjoining houses, not uncommon with our busy schedules. I could not imagine what the residents of the suburban houses a hundred yards away across the main road might have thought.

 The chopper was leaned over. A soldier was strapped in the open side gun hatch snapping pictures of our house. As far as they were concerned, we were The Enemy and therefore a legitimate target. Aside from flying the finger at them, I didn't know what to do.

 Karla said, "I know how to get them to come closer."

 She went upstairs and climbed out of Paul's bedroom window onto the roof of the first story of the house. (DOCUMENT #26, My house at the Resistance Community) She languidly stripped off her blouse and showed the Army boys what they were fighting to protect. The excited photographer signaled to the pilot to drop down closer. The chopper was soon another fifty feet lower. I could almost read the soldier's nametag over his pocket as he slammed away, taking pictures of Karla.

 Karla slowly reached into the bedroom window and deftly pulled out Paul's M1-carbine automatic rifle. She calmly opened fire on the chopper. Shells flew away from her bare arms, torso, and shoulders as fast as she could pull the trigger. She got off eight or ten rounds before the Army retreated.

 I yelled, "What the hell did you do that for? Now they're gonna be out here to bust us!"

 While putting her shirt back on, Karla yelled down, "Doubt it. They'd have to explain what the fucking Army was doing takin' pictures of us from a chopper in the first place."

 The Army must have figured it the way Karla did. The cops never showed up.

CHAPTER 33: 1970—PROGRESSIVE THEATRES REFLECT THE TIMES

By late 1969, more than half a million soldiers had been called up for the War. One in seven was dead or wounded, and we were no closer to winning. The protests were growing in size, frequency, and unexpected locations. The government had a popular revolution on its hands. They had to do something. That year, the draft was turned into a lottery wherein birthdates were chosen in random order. Each potential draftee's chances were based on the position of his birth date.

At first, this scheme seemed to diffuse the fear that fueled the "End the Draft" Movement. If you had a high number, you were safe for a year. However, the men with low numbers *knew* they were at risk. And any sense of security was a moving target. If the troop call-ups escalated without warning, your date could be called up anyway. Each year, the numbers were drawn again, repeating the gamble with the Grim Reaper. A birthday became a death sentence. At the same time, it was dawning on Milk Poster Amerika that serving in the war was a needless sacrifice. The number of young men willing to resist the draft was growing birthday by birthday.

Shifting Ground under the Counterculture

Meanwhile, the ground was shifting under the radical theatre movement. If there were several people living in a shared house or "squat" (unauthorized living space in a warehouse), you could make your rent. If your personal partner had a straight gig, you could do unpaid Movement or theatre work; otherwise, you needed a paying gig. Some of the actors now had families. The theatre groups were getting reviewed in both the "straight" and alternative press. As alternative theatre gained in popularity (as I'd predicted), some of the more dedicated and talented practitioners considered careers in theatre or teaching. Within the groups themselves, the sense of membership was shifting to a stake in leadership.

Founder R. G. "Ronnie" Davis Leaves the San Francisco Mime Troupe

In January of 1970, I went up to the Mime Troupe to borrow drawings for their outdoor stage. I arrived at their studio on Florida Street to discover that the flagship radical theatre was going through serious changes. When I arrived, I was informed that R. G. "Ronnie" Davis, the company's founder, was no longer with the company. He had taken a "leave of absence," but not of his own choosing. To say I was shocked is an understatement. This was a serious state of affairs.

The Mime Troupe was rehearsing *The Congress of Whitewashers,* originally written by Brecht and translated for them by Juris Svendsen. The show was directed by Davis. The critics panned the performance for being too talky with not enough action. The audience and the critics expected their signature style of slick one-liners and physical comedy. R. G. countered that the ideas *were* the action. I'd seen the show. The critics were right. It needed radical revision. Ronnie fought it tooth and nail. This was the crisis that had brought about an internal revolution.

The company members recounted their plight to me. The feeling in the room was glum. Many were fearful for the survival of the company. Morale was slipping badly. Ronnie had a reputation for being maligning and passive-aggressive with his actors in his modus for getting them to work harder. While his heart was in the right place—and he genuinely thought he was helping them to deliver a stronger performance—on a scale of one to ten among the methods available to a director, this one is at the bottom. An added layer of friction was that the women in the company, always forthright and outspoken, felt the brunt of his backhanded approach particularly hard. It seemed he belittled them more than he belittled the men. It was an unnecessary, counterproductive way of working. (To be fair, I've seen Black, and Latinx women, directors work the same way, and he didn't just dump on the women.)

One night, Ronnie fell asleep during a rehearsal. Everybody stopped. Somebody said, "If the director nods off, how do you think the audience feels?" While R. G. slept, the company held a meeting. When R. G. awoke, they informed him that he could stay as a company member but was no longer automatically the director of the shows.

Dan Chumley recalls, "This was a very sad and scary moment. Ronnie was our indefatigable energy source. If he was adrift then so were we."

R. G. had founded the company. He didn't want to accept the democratic/socialist reality that things had evolved. Brecht said, "You cannot run a communist theatre company in a capitalist manner." The company was now the collective property of its members. In the negotiations, Ronnie exposed a general contempt for actors-as-co-creators. However, they *were* the company. Attempts at a middle ground failed. Ronnie finally left the SFMT. His longtime girlfriend, Sandra Archer, left as well. I have no idea of Sandra's politics. Clearly, her relationship with Ronnie was important. Perhaps her politics coincided with his.[67]

R. G.'s exit from the Mime Troupe threatened the survival of this flagship ideological engine. The Mime Troupe was our Juggernaut. We had few tools in our arsenal that could raise our spirits and goad our enemies more cleverly than the SFMT. Fortunately, the company had the talent and the will to weather the transition. The SFMT became a collective and an Equity Union company that continues to perform more than sixty years later.

---

[67]Some years later, she took a teaching/directing job at Lassen College in Susanville, California.

This situation represented a symptom of concurrent cultural upheaval reflected throughout the Movement.

Bread and Puppet Move to the Country

Movement burnout and spiritual fatigue were also affecting the Bread and Puppet Theatre of New York. Peter Schumann, founder and director of the company, understood that urban activists were beginning to seek more spiritually supportive ways to express their politics. Peter and his troupe picked up stakes and moved to a farm in Vermont. This drastically improved their working conditions. It was an adjustment to the collective needs of the company, the makers of the work. The outdoor space and barns were perfect for large puppets, processionals, and circus-like shows. This was a constructive response to the changing times. It has allowed them to continue to thrive to this day.

Other radical theatres were going through reconfigurations as well. The Living Theatre went to Brazil. Earthlight left New York for Los Angeles. The Floating Lotus Magic Opera Company dissolved. These groups gave form to ideas that reached a far larger audience than they ever imagined.

El Teatro's Growing Pains

During the development of the *Bernabé* production and the TENAZ Festival, transitions were brewing, and I had to leave *El Teatro*. This is the moment where I had left off about working with the company to focus on my parallel life in the Draft Resistance Movement. It was an evolution similar to that of Bread and Puppet and the SFMT.

Soon after the TENAZ Festival, as I mentioned, *El Teatro* moved to San Juan Bautista, a sleepy little farming village in the heart of the fruit and vegetable growing region near Salinas, California. This appeared to be a rural exodus similar to that of the Bread and Puppet. In reality, it was a move deeper into the community they needed to serve. In this renaissance of the company, Luis left *rasquachismo* behind. He hired a mix of local people along with professional actors, designers, and technicians. Since the 1970s, the company has continued to thrive.

Broadway's production of *Hair*, an Unexpected Personal Connection

Even Broadway got into the act of counterculture Transformation Theatre, and I discovered an unexpected personal connection. Joseph Papp produced a radically different Broadway musical about the Amerika that was right outside the theatre. In this high-energy show, a white kid gets his draft notice. He and his Black girlfriend deal with his angst about the war and racism. This was the aforementioned *Hair: The American Tribal Love-Rock Musical.*

Papp opened a second company doing *Hair* in Los Angeles. The drummer on the Los Angeles production was Cubby O'Brien, the former big-eared little kid with a flattop haircut who played drums as one of the original Mouseketeers on the popular Disney show, *The Mickey Mouse Club.* On grownup Cubby's nights off, the other drummer on the L. A. production *of Hair* was my old high school beach buddy, Bob "B." (Robert Keith) Hobbs!

Because of the nude scene, The Los Angeles Vice Squad cops stopped the show every night and warned the audience that they'd be busted if the show continued. By declaring the act of witnessing the show an act of participation, the cops turned the play into a political event, thus radicalizing the entire audience. Movie stars and liberal politicians lined up to be arrested in front of news cameras. Attendance at the performances skyrocketed.

Bob told me that he and Cubby kept a pair of gym shorts under the drummer's seat so that during the bust, while waiting to get into the bus, their "talent" was protected.

The show ran for 1,750 performances. It presented alternative ideas to an audience that radical theatres could never reach. In 1969, Cubby O'Brien, the cute little Mouseketeer, became a Draft Resister and burned his draft card.

CHAPTER 34: DAYS OF RAGE: THE CAMBODIAN INVASION AND AFTER

At an antiwar sit-in at Fresno State, a reporter said that we were exaggerating claims about police intervention. About five minutes later, the cops took his camera, removed his film, and made him leave. *Then* they strong-armed us out of the building.

By the spring of 1970, the political scene was turning even more surreal. In late April, the fact that Amerika had been secretly carpet-bombing Cambodia hit the press, and the shit hit the fan everyplace. The U. S. Government claimed that the Viet Cong were using a corner of this neutral country as a supply shortcut. Rage and disbelief filled the newspapers. Even if it was true, we could have increased attacks at either end of the route while the supplies were still in Vietnamese territory.

The depth of the reaction to this arrogant, underhanded strategy was unfathomable. This campaign, based on paper-thin excuses, angered even our staunchest allies. It created waves of huge anti-American demonstrations worldwide. Most serious of all, it threatened to turn Laos and Cambodia—nations that were supposed to defend against the expansion of communism—into potential belligerents against us. This tactic would require expanding troop involvement into two other nations.

This unconscionable underhanded action was taken without the approval of Congress, causing even Republican "Hawks" to blink. The territory of who was opposing or supporting the war was rocked by an earthquake of shifting alliances. The government was ignoring the wisdom of its own military experts, a growing majority of the American population, world opinion, and the lessons of history. It was almost as if they were beginning an entirely new war.

The Anti-war movement discovered its full strength behind the outcry against the invasion of Cambodia. Opposition to the war exploded. Until then, the media always pointed the camera at the prettiest flower child and put the microphone into the face of the most wildly dressed hippie, feeding the impression that our ideas were fuzzy-minded and probably drug-induced. After the bombing of Cambodia, this manipulated perception of who was against the war was no longer even remotely possible. People from all social strata wanted to bring our soldiers home. Now even the jocks and frat boys, worried about getting called up, were stopping by our tables and picking up leaflets about draft counseling.

On May 4, 1970, the National Guard gunned down four students at Kent State University in Ohio. Two more were killed at Jackson State in Mississippi eleven days later. They resented the students rubbing their government's mistake in their faces. Amerika was still in full denial about the fact that they'd been lied to and that their sons were dying in an unnecessary war.

The guardsmen at Kent State were issued lethal ammunition. Sixty-seven shots were fired in thirteen seconds. Jeffrey Glenn Miller, 20, was shot through the face. He was killed instantly. Sandra Lee Scheuer, 20, received a fatal neck wound and died minutes later in front of all her friends. William Knox Schroeder, 19, received a fatal chest wound and died an hour later in a local hospital. Allison B. Krause, 19, received a fatal chest wound. She died later that day.

The story was much the same at Jackson State in Mississippi. A group of about one hundred African American students had gathered on the evening of May 14 as part of the national protest against the bombing of Cambodia. By 9:30 p.m., the students were starting fires, throwing rocks at motorists, and overturning vehicles. Their rage over what had been done in their name overcame their Movement fear of enraging the local racist police. The result was predictable.

The police in Mississippi responded in force. The Mississippi cops were going to get their chance to kill some "uppity niggers." Jackson State became a free-fire zone. The fire-at-will fusillade lasted for thirty seconds. The cops shot at the student dormitory as if it was an enemy installation. At least one-hundred-and-forty shots were fired from shotguns from thirty to fifty feet away. Every window on the Lynch Street side of the building was shattered.

Just being there and Black was enough. Phillip Lafayette Gibbs, 21, a Jackson State junior, and James Earl Green, 17, a senior at nearby Jim Hill High School, were killed. Both young men were ripped apart by the shotgun blasts fired at close range.[68] Twelve others were wounded.

This was the last straw. These incidents were our massacres at Lexington and Concord. Everywhere across the country, everyone from office secretaries to Boy Scouts was out in the streets. Students at more than eight hundred colleges went out on strike. This spontaneous insurrection involved more than four million students. Ordinary rank-and-file antiwar people were pushed to do things they could not have imagined doing only days before. The "People's Army" had come out in the streets.

On May 23, the antiwar groups on the Fresno State campus announced a walkout and march beginning at the Free Speech Area. There were easily more than a thousand people marching in this demonstration. (DOCUMENT #42 Free Speech Area, Fresno State College) We ended up out on Shaw Avenue, the major east-west boulevard in North Fresno, stopping traffic to end "business as usual."

Knowing that there was a possibility of violence, we'd contacted the cops and told them that some of us were clearly identified as medics carrying first-aid kits. When the group made its way around the corner by the Ag Sciences Building, however, we were greeted with a posse of about twenty cowboys carry

---

[68] The President's Commission on Campus Unrest investigated this event. It concluded that "the twenty-eight-second fusillade from police officers was an unreasonable, unjustified overreaction."

baseball bats and ax handles, yelling, "Go back where you came from!" "Commie lovers!" "Nigger lovers!" And more. It looked like newsreels of Alabama or the Memphis bus station. There were no cops to be seen.

    The valley's right-wing rag, the *Fresno Guide*, reported the day's events accompanied by a picture of the mob of yokels with the caption, "Fresno Ag Students Protect their Building." *But the ax handles and baseball bats were crudely airbrushed out.* Even for the *Guide*, this was too obvious a lynch mob to publish. (DOCUMENT #61: Aggies airbrushed)

    At four p.m., nearly a thousand people invaded Shaw Avenue and stopped traffic. Several busloads of riot cops swarmed out of the campus. As soon as the bus doors opened, the first cop saw me and yelled, "There he is! Get him!" Obviously, they'd been looking at their rogues' gallery in the Cop Shop basement. Forty-seven people were arrested, including several young women. (DOCUMENT #62: Newspaper article from our arrest) They busted only the leaders, then chased off the rest of the crowd. There were more demonstrations across Amerika on this day than any other in American history. The wrongness of the Vietnam War was getting through the haze of bullshit.

    I was cuffed and taken to the police van. (DOCUMENT #63: My arrest record) A police photographer was there. It was the same fat, sideburned guy I'd seen at the Free Speech Area for months. They searched my shoulder pack, clearly marked with a red cross, and took the carabineer I was using to hold my helmet on my belt. They opened the commercially purchased first-aid kit in my pack and found a pair of round-nosed bandage scissors. The Camera Cop starting making smartass remarks.

I never heard an order to disburse. I was standing right in front. I was put in the van with Ron Thiesen and a few other people. Although Paul Dunham was not with us at the front of the demonstration, somehow he also ended up in the police van.[69] Most of us were charged with obstructing traffic and failure to disburse. We were released at the jailhouse after processing.

My charges included obstructing traffic and failing to disperse as well as felony possession of a weapon for both the carabineer (called "brass knuckles!") and the round-nosed bandage scissors inside a commercially purchased first-aid kit. (DOCUMENT #64: My arrest photo)

Inside the police van, Paul said, "You know, if you get out of here before me, it would be nice if you *cleaned the house* in case we have company." Somebody needed to get rid of the guns. Though they weren't my property, they had become my problem. It was going to be me.

****

It was your typical Friday night in the Fresno County Jail. In the tank were the usual vagrant Mexicans, knife-fight victims, barfing heroin addicts, and drunken barflies. The usual cast was provided with some variety by our political contingent. I was held on nine-thousand dollars bail. This was a lot in those days. I figured I'd be in jail until I could get a lawyer on Monday.

Somebody had called my folks and a lawyer. Four hours later, Counselor J. V. Henry showed up with my bail, put up by my parents. Mr. Henry wanted to chat. I told him I had an important errand to run. He didn't ask questions. I planned to see him the following Monday.

I went to my place in the fig orchard. I sat outside for fifteen minutes to be sure I hadn't been followed. I scanned the

---

[69] Paul later informed me that he was grabbed out of the middle of the crowd with hundreds of people around him. He was charged with possession of a deadly weapon for a small hammer handle the police claimed was found in his bag. Paul does not remember putting it into the bag.

property for anything moving. With all the lights off, I went to Paul's room and broke off the lock. I grabbed the duffle bag containing his weapons from under his bed. I waited again, then put the bag in my car trunk and drove away.

The only guy I knew who might be up at midnight was my occasional grass connection, Benny Delario. Giving a bag full of weapons to a drug dealer wasn't much brighter than hiding them in a Movement house, but Benny was my only shot. He took the weapons and hid them under *his* bed, next to a huge suitcase full of upscale weed.[70]

Understandably, my dad was mortified. My arrest would drag his name through the papers. Somewhat arrogantly, I said, "Listen, in five years, millions will be busted for draft evasion, drugs, or demonstrations. It's our 'Movement Merit Badge.' Even members of Congress and big movie stars have been arrested." My mom reminded him, "We had a lot of union friends who got arrested back in the Thirties, and in the Fifties, we had friends blacklisted. It all blows over." He didn't like this, but eventually, it turned out to be true.

Paul got out a few days later and thanked me profusely. I was pissed all the same. He got the message and didn't bring back the guns. Eventually, Paul was convicted of destroying his draft card. He served ten months in Lompoc Federal Penitentiary. He was never nailed for the weapons. We never spoke of it again.

Back to the Struggle

Our arrest and that of millions of others in angry marches and walkouts across Amerika that day had several effects. One of these was to add exponentially to the FBI's 'enemies' lists. This was job security for the guys on headphones in basements and phony utility trucks. Because probation was required for those convicted, the arrests had a chilling effect on student activists. A

---

[70] Evidently, Benny had found his life's calling. In the late 1980s, Benny Delario was busted in New Jersey for major cocaine trafficking and Mob connections. He went to federal prison.

subsequent arrest for anything, real or trumped-up, would put you in jail for the probation violation. You'd be kicked out of school, drafted, and given an all-expenses-paid trip to Da Nang Airport in camo clothing.

Another ripple effect of the Cambodian bombing was that we were cursed with our own success. Just when burnout was hitting us from leafleting, demonstrations, marches, weekly potlucks, phone taps, and being followed, the number of calls for draft counseling went through the roof.

When we gave a talk or counseled a young man, someone in the room—including the guy getting counseled—might always be an informer. With the increased interest in counseling after the Cambodian invasion, this tactic escalated. The snitch could be the wild-haired new guy in tie-dye overalls who says he "hates the war." (He was FBI.) It could be your smokin' buddy who's defaulted on his student loan and the government offered to cancel it in exchange for information. It could be that longhaired, doe-eyed chick from "the valley," who just wants to "help out" (a police science student planning a CIA career). We encountered all of these and more.[71] This resulted in a general erosion of trust.

Like foot soldiers in combat, years of this were taking a toll on us. Factionalism was becoming rampant. It was getting hard to get three people in the room to stop shouting slogans at each other and come up with a unified action on anything. I'm sure the headphone guys caught all of the harangues on tape.

At the same time, the war effort was truly falling apart. The Canadians (representing the U. S.) were engaged in informal discussions with the Russians (representing the North Vietnamese), hosted by the Parliamentary Union in Geneva. The dance of disengagement was beginning. It was clear that at some point in the hoped-for, not-too-distant future, the war could be over. Ordinary concerns returned to the front page of our lives.

---

[71] In one case, I drew the short straw to deal with a planted snoop. I gave him ten minutes to clean his shit out of my place. I gave him a ride to the bus station. I made him sit in the back seat.

But we soon discovered that we had been forever changed by our immersion into this struggle. Once we had been at the edge of events, that "plugged in" feeling stayed with us. An electric sense of *being there on the front lines of history* became who we were. I discovered that I could never just step back into an ordinary life. In this changing landscape, the idea of finishing my degree began to take form. Beyond that, a plan to direct a theatre company or teach theatre was lapping against the shore of my personal future. However, before I got hired or famous, I had to go to trial.

CHAPTER 35: 1971—GOING TO COURT, FRESNO COUNTY JAIL

I sat down in J. V. Henry's small, cluttered law office. He pointed to a manila file folder on his desk. It was almost two inches thick. He said, "That's your FBI file."

"Holy shit."

"You've been a busy boy."

"What does that have to do with my case?"

"It shows that with the ridiculous felony charges, they were trying to railroad you."

I then told him what the cops who jumped out of the bus said when they saw me and about the photos in the police department and the camera on the water tower.

Smiling, he wrote all of this down. He was not surprised.

"Also, the time noted for your arrest was before an order to disburse was given. Also, the indictment is confused. First, they say that you were found with a pair of brass knuckles…"

"That was a carabineer I used to hold my helmet to my belt. You can't use it as brass knuckles; it's too wide and springs open if you push on it."

He noted this. "Then they say something about scissors."

"They're small, round-nosed bandage scissors in a drugstore first-aid kit, the kind you give school kids to cut up craft paper."

"Well then, it's really bogus. Besides, they mention *both* in the arrest but only one count in the charge of a weapon. They can't have it both ways. I think they're going to drop the charge."

"Does that get me off?"

"No. They're going to insist on the charge of blocking traffic. They have video footage. I recommend you plead *nolo contendere*—no contest—to the misdemeanor. It's your first offense. You'll probably get probation."

"Okay."

"I'll tell them I have your FBI file and that I'm looking into civil rights violations. This will convince them to accept the '*nolo*' plea. In the interest of justice—which means kissing the judge's ass—they'll drop the felony thing."

Can I look at the FBI folder?"

"No, I have it, but I don't have it if you know what I mean."

"No, but yes."

"Okay. See you in court."

My Little Trial

Before my court date, J. V. Henry submitted a laundry list of procedural violations to the District Attorney and the judge. He noted the glaring contradictions in the police work, the surveillance of my activities before the event (as shown in my FBI file and police records), and the comments the cops made when they sought me out even before they'd declared an illegal assembly.

He noted the sloppy indictment for possession of one weapon while mentioning two weapons. He then showed the judge and the D. A. that neither could serve as a weapon under any circumstances. The cops had fucked up big-time, and it smacked of conspiracy.

The D. A. ran for the hills like a rabbit.[72]

When the trial began, the D. A. offered to drop the trumped-up felony charges in exchange for our dropping the civil-

---

[72] In 2020, while working on this book, I discovered a letter from the Fresno District Attorney admitting to the procedural error in the felony arrest for a weapons charge. What is also extremely telling is his reference to my FBI file, thus thoroughly giving the lie to the FBI claim in the early 1990s that such a file did not exist. (Document #65)

rights countersuit. I was charged only with "failure to disburse" and "blocking traffic." Counselor Henry entered the plea of *nolo contendere* to these charges "in the interests of justice" so they could sentence me for something.

I wasn't totally happy with this. The fact was that without a "failure to disburse" order being issued, everything after it was entrapment. J. V. said that given the mood of the times, this was the best he could do. It all took about thirty minutes. J. V. was right on all but one point. I was sentenced to six days in jail for a first offense, a nonviolent misdemeanor. This was significant. I was the only demonstrator from that day to do any county jail time. On the way out of the courtroom, J. V. said, "Wooo-wooo" like a *railroad* train whistle.

After my trial was over, everyone else left the courtroom. As I walked past the District Attorney's desk, I reached into his file and liberated one of my arrest photos. (DOCUMENT# 64) It's on the cover of this book.

Time in Jail

Before I did my time, J. V. Henry gave me some survival advice. "Check yourself into the jail near five p.m. This means the first day of your sentence will be counted as an overnight. You'll be released on the morning of your sixth day. At breakfast on your first morning, sit in a corner. Check out the troublemakers before they try to rattle your cage."

"Makes sense to me."

"Don't be too talkative. They can tell if you're nervous. It's not likely that anyone will fuck with you. Most of them are working off light sentences. They won't want another charge on their jacket and a heavier sentence. Besides, the cops would punish them for making extra paperwork."

The jailer who booked me wore a smirk on his face. He definitely had an attitude about hippies. They let me take in a paperback and a pad for writing, but I had to ask for a pencil every day from the guard.

The inside of the jail smelled like bleach and bologna. In addition to two-man cells, there was a large day room with welded steel tables and bolted-down benches. The day room had a TV way up on the wall. It looked like a student sports bar except there were steel bars all around and no beer.

The inmates were mostly middle-aged Chicanos. They were not an especially rough-looking bunch, but they were not currently on drugs, alcohol, or adrenalin. They were shaved and wore jail-issued blue jeans and denim shirts. It was just like in the movies, but nobody walked off the set at the end of the day.

Most of the men in the jail treated incarceration as something that just happened to them from time to time. In their world, this recycling was a "given." In jail, they learn skills to survive in the 'hood. Like an undergraduate degree, the average first stay in a state or federal penitentiary is just over four-and-a-half years. Prisons are the universities of the poor. Doing time gains them macho credibility. The younger they started to get a "jacket" (prison record), the more respect they got. It's their Ghetto Merit Badge. Truly, theirs is a different country. Each stretch in the Joint is marked with a teardrop tattoo under one eye or on one knuckle. Prison makes them into the men they think they are supposed to be.

Before breakfast, some of the men lined up at a small table outside the day room. A guard gave each of them a small Dixie cup with a pink liquid in it, then a cup of juice. This was their methadone ration, like Soma in *Brave New World*. They then went in to breakfast as another guard checked them off his list. Then the rest of us filed in and were checked off.

Breakfast was cold cereal, skim milk, coffee, unseasoned scrambled eggs, and warm, dry, white toast with a pat of butter and prepackaged jam, like a really bad Denny's. There was coffee, but it was mixed by the gallon and decaf to boot. I would have ironed somebody's shirts for some salsa or an espresso. Silverware was counted in and out. There were no knives. Food in jail was soft and bland, nothing requiring the use of a knife. You spread your butter and jam with the spoon handle.

TV was the main attraction in the day room. There were two main types of shows: stupid family shows and cop shows. In jail, the macro message of TV programming becomes very clear. *Here's a family that makes no trouble. Daddy is a well-meaning buffoon. See how happy they are!* Then, over on the other channel are the cop shows. *Here are some people who break the rules.* (Mostly Black, Latinx, crazy, or rich, white, and corrupt.) *Look what happens to them.* I never really got it before. It was a simple formula for subliminal mass communication. The exception was *Lost in Space*. The *vatos* loved to watch the flaming-gay bad guy camping it up.

Watching the news in jail was surreal. I thought, *these guys may have seen the footage of my arrest. They all know who I am.* Watching the news was painful because it showed you that real life was still happening outside.

Each of the cells had four narrow bunks, but they now allowed only two men to a cell when they could. Four men to a cell allows gang-ups. The bunk was a solid steel sheet welded to a frame. It hinged up so the guards could lift it to see if a weapon or drugs were hidden under it. Each bunk had a thin, cotton, ticking mattress in a striped fabric, like lawn furniture. Mattress pads were taken out and exchanged weekly to ensure that no razor blades or silverware were hidden in the pads. Disinfectant in the laundry kept the lice down and removed bodily fluids dispelled into them.

The steel toilet bowl had no lid. A guy coming down off heroin could get "the cranks" and slam the lid against his head. Your head could be forced under the lid with your neck on the toilet rim. You could be gang murdered in jail. No more lid. There were no magazines. A magazine could be rolled up and rammed into soft body parts. You would bleed to death. Magazines could be used as clubs. The only magazines were Jehovah's Witness rags. Too small for a weapon, thank God.

The lights were controlled remotely. The lighting was all fluorescent. There were no regular incandescent bulbs. The glass of an incandescent bulb could be broken open, the filament wrapped in toilet paper, and the glass bulb put back with soap. This would almost be invisible. When this jerry-rigged incendiary device was turned on automatically, you'd get a big explosion and fire. The chaos that ensues is an opportunity for all kinds of things to happen. No more incandescent bulbs.

My cellmate was a Chicano named Jésus, about five-foot-four, thin, and angular. Jésus was a quiet man. Before mandatory quiet/lights dimmed (the lights were never turned off completely), he stood on the toilet rim to be closer to the light to read his Bible. The light shined like a halo over his head. His blanket was wrapped around his wiry shoulders. This was a great image. I did a sketch of him like this on the inside cover of a paperback book, now long gone.

I couldn't figure out what such a quiet man did to get himself ten months in County Jail. But then again, he was not strung out on anything at the time. With his *carnales* (tight buddies) on the outside, he might be an entirely different beast.

When Jésus talked about his girlfriends, the descriptions were always the same. "Ah...man, Lupe! She was really pretty, nice ass, not dark, *really light*..." For some reason, the more his girlfriend looked like a *gringa* (white girl), the more desirable she was.

I asked him, "Hey, man, why do all your girlfriends have to be light? What's wrong with dark brown girls?" He stopped dead. He'd never thought about it. He was quiet for a whole day. I hoped he wasn't mad.

There was a TV camera over the day room. Nobody was going to fuck with you there. The men didn't seek out conversation. "Hi there, what are you in here for?" was not the right icebreaker from me. However, since I was the new guy, they could ask me this question. This began some interesting discussions. "I got busted in a demonstration because America bombed another country." This registered with them. Most of them probably knew someone in the service. They knew the unfair ratio of Latinos killed in the battle zones. They were not particularly motivated to fight and die for the country that ran on skin privilege and skin punishment. Nevertheless, going to jail for that kind of *pedo* (trouble) was totally out of their universe. Doing time happened to them often enough just for being who they were. I also mentioned the Grape Boycott and the strike. They all knew about that. This got me major points.

Just after lunch on my second full day, one of the guys came up and asked, "You good at readin' and writin'?"

"Yeah, I think so."

"I'm writin' a letter to my lawyer. Can you look it over?"

"Not sure I can help, but okay." He was trying to get a hearing on something like a reduced sentence. I told him, "Makes sense to me. It's simple, direct. No bullshit."

"It don't sound like I'm begging?"

This was a big deal to these men. They didn't want to sound dependant on the system even though they knew it was going to jack them around. "Naw, I think you're asking for something reasonable. If they're gonna fuck with you, they're gonna fuck with you."

By the middle of the next day, I had guys in the cell waiting to talk about legal stuff, letters to girlfriends, etc. This passed the time and got me respect. They were just trying to improve their situation and stay connected with the outside world.[73] It felt good to help them in a small way.

When you're in jail, your rhythm slows waaaaay down. Your thinking slows down. Even simple thoughts expand to fill the vacuum. Thoughts introduce themselves to you, and you can examine them slowly. It's like an idea sits down and visits you. If you see an unexpected implication, you're free to follow it where it leads. Jail is like a Zen meditation center with no scenery and lousy food. I have no doubt that many of the spiritual transformations that men report from long-term incarceration, like finding Jesus, Buddha, or Muhammad, are real and profound. You also have the time to rehearse a line of bullshit about being

---

[73] The longest sentence in the Joint was ten months for non-support or drugs. Guys who didn't support their families didn't get much respect.

reformed. Jail inmates are consummate actors. Theirs is a performance of survival.

I slept a lot. I got into TV program details I'd never noticed. My director's eye went to work like an uncontrollable addiction. Costume continuity mistakes like loose necktie knots in a cutaway or tie clips moved or forgotten in subsequent shots were all over the place. Drapes were closed then opened. Coffee cups moved in the next shot. A cigarette would be burning in an ashtray then gone when they cut back to a wide-angle. The continuity crews on *The Partridge Family* and *Kojak* should have been fired.

As I lay in my bunk, counting cracks in the concrete ceiling, I contemplated how I'd gotten there in the first place. Somehow, I'd avoided jail up to that time. I attended uncountable demonstrations, sit-ins, and marches. How I'd missed getting busted at the strike at S. F. State was something of a miracle. I came to the Zen/fatalist conclusion that for some reason, this was the right time.

I checked out of jail early in the morning on my last day. It was still cool. I needed to walk. It felt good to be able just to walk anyplace I wanted. I walked about two miles from downtown to Olive Avenue. Soon the heat began to rise, so I took a bus home.

Getting Arrested and Not Going/Going to Jail

In your organizing, always play hardball with The System. If you make it clear you're willing to go to jail, the more likely the authorities will be to want to resolve your issue some other way, but don't count on it. They get off on fucking with you. The whole situation is based on having the power to determine your life.

Nevertheless, avoid arrest if you can. It involves more hassle than glory. The cost should be weighed carefully against what you hope to achieve, such as getting rid of an oppressive law itself.

You pay a price in terms of your freedom even if you don't go to jail. After you're arrested, you're on their radar *forever*. Any political activities while on probation constitute probable cause for search and re-incarceration. Nevertheless, if you intend a life of political involvement, it comes with the territory. Many people around you will have been through it.

If you have to do time, make it on your own terms. In planning an action that might involve an arrest, don't forget the value of theatricality for the media. It's not a "demonstration" unless someone sees it. If a hundred women, aged seventy or older, demanded "illegal" abortion information from a clinic or a public library (for their granddaughters), imagine the power of showing the cops cuffing and stuffing a hundred old ladies into jail buses.

Did the thousands and thousands who went to jail during the Civil Rights and Anti-war movements change things? Damn right. It made everyone—our friends, neighbors, acquaintances, and even our enemies —think about the price we would pay to end the carnage of the war and the wrongness of racism. It made more people get active. That was the victory.

Would I go to jail again? It depends on the situation. Would I do time for something like torching a police car? A burning police car at the right moment of anger is a sign of the level of rage. However, getting caught in a guerilla action proves that you didn't plan well. Before such actions, know your way out of the scene of the action. You can assume somebody is going to catch the action on camera, so wear a good disguise. As in all kinds of theatre, planning is everything.

****

Soon, everything changed.

Years of making others think, of working to clarify the contradictions, had finally crystallized in my own life as well. Everything had come to a crossroads. I'd stood in that crossroads. I'd paid the price for my ideals. I had some "cred" in my own 'hood. I'd come out clearer in my vision of a future path. That clarity of self was the outcome of a week in jail.

A few months after my jail time, out of the blue, I received a new draft card and reclassification (1-Y) "to be taken for active service [still as a Conscientious Objector], but only in extreme national emergency." (DOCUMENT #66: My draft card) I asked J. V. about this spontaneous reclassification. He said, "Evidently, the government looked at your continually fattening file and figured that if you went in, you'd be organizing in the military." This kind of *tsuris* they didn't need. They didn't want me in the Army unless we were invaded by Martians.

New draft card.

A short time after my time in jail, the terrible visions of war and death in my head stopped as mysteriously as they had arrived.

Daring Them To Tell The Truth

As the embattled soldiers captured and recaptured the same hills and villages over and over with high casualties, morale eroded. The grunts began to smoke weed or shoot heroin to deal with it all. Hunkered down in a rice paddy as VC machine-gun fire ripped into their buddies around them, some of the GIs remembered that before they got on the Army bus, a longhaired hippie had handed them a leaflet warning them about all this…

This kind of painful personal tragedy reached into my own family. My sister Sandy and her husband David got married just before David was sent to 'Nam. David was from an Oklahoma family who migrated to California during the Dust Bowl. He had sandy red hair, freckles, big ears, and a toothy smile. David was the boy on the milk poster.

Before being drafted, the most danger David ever encountered was crossing a big street on his bicycle on his paper route. David was off to boot camp. Ten short weeks later, he was in his camo work clothes, hunkered down in the jungle. For reasons David never determined, his C. O. had a hair up his ass about him. The jerk continued to rotate David's duty as a radio operator with point patrol. A point patrol is a small unit who sets up on a hill in order to direct fire. They're the guys the enemy tries to locate and kill first. His C. O. sent him into dangerous action with each rotation. David somehow survived ten months of this duty. He was a mess.

My sister went to visit him on leave in Hawaii. When she came home to Fresno, she intimated that his situation was serious. He had the shakes and repeated himself all the time. A real conversation was impossible. By the time he finished his hitch and came home, David-the-paperboy with big ears and freckles was a heroin addict. He and my sister divorced. Ten years of his life were lost to drugs and mental torture before he returned to something like wholeness. David was lucky. His family stuck by him. Other men with stories like this were destined to end up on the streets sleeping in cardboard boxes until they died of hypothermia or an overdose.

By the late 1970, the guys in the mud and in the hospitals had figured out what we'd been trying to tell them. Returning vets began to tell the truth about the war. The antiwar sentiment among returning Vietnam vets boiled into rage. These men felt abandoned and exploited by the lies behind what they'd been asked to do. In a televised demonstration on April 24, 1971, hundreds of decorated veterans in wheelchairs and on crutches, who'd left pieces of their bodies and souls in the jungle, threw their war medals onto the steps of the Capitol. My dad, who'd earned a Purple Heart in World War II, watched this on TV. Tears began to roll down his cheeks, his fists clenched at his sides.

The Big Light Bulb went off in our house. Dad was a changed man.

It went on all over the country. I now met many vets who apologized for being pumped up with macho and patriotic claptrap instead of paying attention to the message of the Resistance. The returning vets and the Resistance joined forces.

The war had truly come home.

The Pentagon Papers

The revelation of the Cambodian bombing resulted in a national change of heart. However, it was not the only political bombshell that was dropped on Amerika. In the summer of 1971, *The New York Times* published the entire text of the Pentagon Papers. This document, purloined by Daniel Ellsberg, a defector from the Hawks' camp, contained the transcripts and clandestine letters of all the presidents from Truman to Nixon on our involvement in Asia. Much of it had been hidden from Congress and even members of the cabinet *for decades*. The Hawks not only hid the truth from the public; they also lied to each other. This dossier made it clear that the Hawks had always known that the Vietnam War was unwinnable and therefore a waste of money and lives. Five presidents had continued to send young men to be butchers and to be butchered. The depth of the anger was unfathomable.

Would you die and kill for a government like that?

America had invaded a foreign country with a mission that was a hallucination conjured up in the boardrooms of Wall Street and the war rooms of Washington. We'd been hoodwinked into sending our sons into this hell. We'd killed innocents by the millions, ruined their land, and turned their nation into our enemy. Men like my brother-in-law David were part of it. The percentage of men who came home with Post-Traumatic Combat Stress Disorder stood at forty-five percent. Others didn't come home at all. None of this had to happen. This was the message that a powerful faction within the government wanted to silence at any price.

The media had willingly colluded in this criminal deception. Reporters were always handed leaflets from our organizers. *To my knowledge, this material was never quoted in any news report— ever.* On the occasion of a sit-in at Fresno State, I challenged a young reporter to quote from our leaflet and to air an interview with me. He did the interview and promised to quote the handout. The interview was never aired. The quotes never appeared in his article.

More men died.

DOCUMENT #42: Fresno State College free speech area. This image is the Fresno State College Anti-Cambodian Bombing rally. May 21, 1970, just before the crowd headed out to block traffic on Shaw Avenue. Note two people on the speaker's podium at left. I will be the last speaker before the crowd begins the march. (Photo: University Archives, Henry Madden Library, Cal State Univ., Fresno)

DOCUMENT #43 Agitprop theatre at Rally, Spring 1970. Note: Author in pom-pom ski cap. F S C Yearbook, 1970, p. 89. Univ. Archives, Henry Madden Library, Photog. unknown)

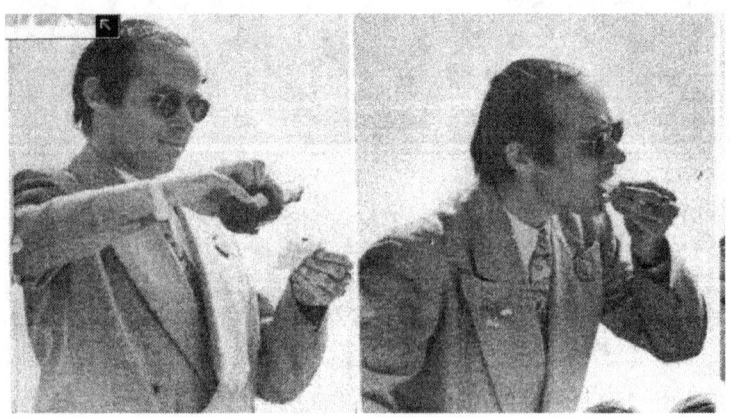

Professor Byron Black eats his draft card, Spring, 1970 (F S C Yearbook, 1970, p. 89. Univ. Archives, Henry Madden Library, Photographer unknown)

DOCUMENT #44:

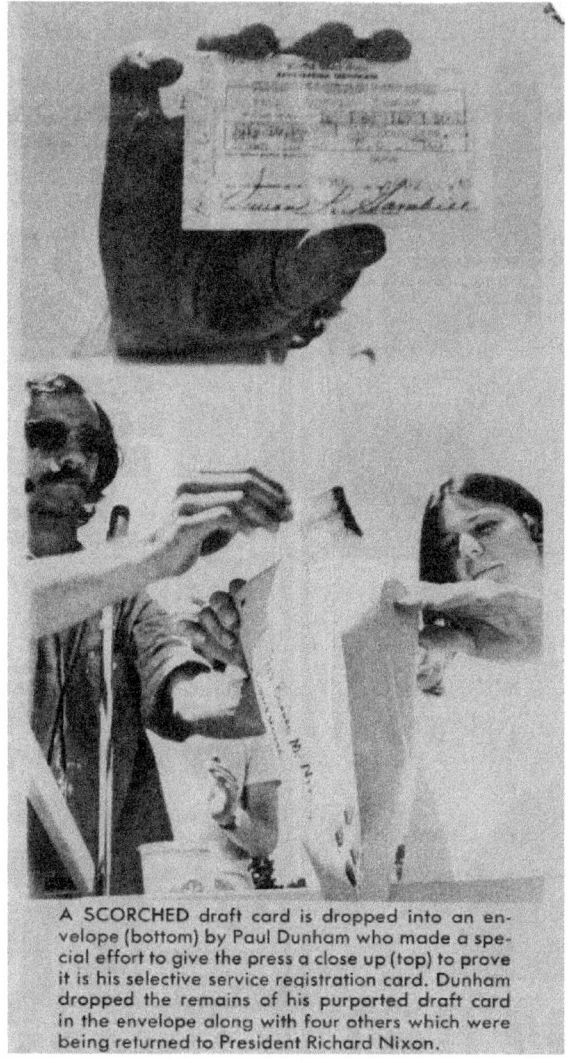

A SCORCHED draft card is dropped into an envelope (bottom) by Paul Dunham who made a special effort to give the press a close up (top) to prove it is his selective service registration card. Dunham dropped the remains of his purported draft card in the envelope along with four others which were being returned to President Richard Nixon.

Paul Dunham burns his draft card, Spring 1969. They didn't believe him so he did it again. (Photo, Fresno State Collegian)

Summons

Cr. Form No. 19 (Rev. July 1953)

United States District Court
FOR THE
<u>EASTERN DISTRICT OF CALIFORNIA</u>
at Fresno

UNITED STATES OF AMERICA

v.

PAUL ANDREW DUNHAM

No. F-421-crim

To Paul Andrew Dunham

You are hereby summoned to appear before the United States District Court for the Eastern District of California Courtroom #1, U.S. Courthouse Bldg., at the 5th Floor, 1130 "O" St. in the city of Fresno, Calif. on the 18th day of August 1969 at 10:00 o'clock A.M. to answer to an indictment charging you with Destroying & Mutilating Selective Service Certificate in violation of 18 USC App. 462

Dated: July 24, 1969.

WILLIAM C. ROBB, Clerk

By D. D. BUTLER, Deputy Clerk

RETURN

This summons was received by me at _____ on _____

_____ Defendant

Paul Dunham's Indictment for destroying his draft card, 1969. (Courtesy, Paul Dunham)

High school students receive indoctrination from Resistance leaders. Don LeBaron

DOCUMENT #45: Draft Resistance Organizers Dale Klemm and Ron Thiesen council young men interested in all of their options. Note bias in the original caption (Photo Fresno State Collegian, 1969)

DOCUMENT #46: David Harris, my roommate Paul Dunham, and Joan Baez speaking at Fresno State, 1969 (University Archives, Henry Madden Library, California State University, Fresno. Photog. Unknown.)

DOCUMENT 48: People's Park in the 21st century, cared for and cultivated by volunteers. (Photo, Michael Delacour?)

DOCUMENT# 49: May 15, 1969. James Rector, shot on the third floor roof of his apartment over Telegraph Avenue. The police excuse was that he had thrown a chair down at the cops. No chair was ever found. The video footage showed no chair in his possession. (Original image says "Daily Cal, P.7 May 23, 1969." photo: Kathryn Bigelow)

Document #50: Two men in dark glasses in the foreground are clearly Patrick Conroy (left) and Paul Dunham (right) in a 2-second shot from People's Park news footage (authorship unknown). I am probably just out of frame.

DOCUMENT #51 Stake side truck with a load of rolled sod. At some point, I am directly behind this truck handing rolls of sod to people laying them over the pavement. (Photo W. Haigwood)

DOCUMENT #52: People's Park demonstration, Berkeley. May 17, 1969. Fixed bayonets. It is clear from this shot what the government was willing to do. (Photo: Dick Corten)

DOCUMENT #53: The iconic poster, from 1968, "GIRLS SAY YES to boys who say NO" features Joan Baez, and her sisters Pauline and Mimi Farina. (Photographer unknown).

DOCUMENT #54: Notice of show with Pete and El Teatro, in the L. A. Free Press, April 25, 1969, Just after our return from France. (Permission, L.A. Free Press Archives.)

DOCUMENT 55: Activists turned the image of the burning bank in Isla Vista, February 25, 1970, into a mock image of a decorative check. Note spelling of "Amerika." There were posters and "T" shirts of this image all over hell. (Original photographer unknown)

DOCUMENT #56: The general opinion of the president at Fresno State just before the Cambodian invasion and the firing, without cause or due process, of two dozen popular, progressive professors, was not good. (Photo, Fresno State School Yearbook, 1970. University Archives, Henry Madden Library, California State University, Fresno)

Document #57: Image of the bombed out Fresno Induction Center, Nov 2, 1970. (Image appears Permission, Fresno Bee)

2 Bombings in Fresno Damage Draft Center and a Newspaper

FRESNO, Calif., Nov. 1 (UPI) —Two predawn dynamite explosions ripped a military induction center and the office of a conservative newspaper today.

Agents of the Federal Bureau of Investigation and city policemen, who were investigating the blasts, said they had no suspects, although the authorities were looking for a Volkswagen bus seen in the area before the bombings.

The explosions ripped off doors, shattered windows and heavily damaged the lobbies of both buildings.

Dynamite bombs were apparently placed against the doors of the Fresno Induction Center and the office of The Fresno Guide, a triweekly with a strongly conservative editorial stance. The blasts occurred less than a minute apart. The two buildings are about a block apart in downtown Fresno.

The police said that numerous bomb threats have been received in recent months by newspapers, radio stations and police stations, but that no specific threats had been made against the two targets.

Lieut. Jim Packard of the Fresno Police Department said that the odor of dynamite lingered in the area after the blasts. Witnesses said that the first explosion occurred at the newspaper office and was followed seconds later by the induction center blast. The blasts were heard as far as three miles away.

Fresno, a city of 200,000 population, is about midway between San Francisco and Los Angeles in an agriculture center.

RIPPED APART—

Police, FBI Net Few Clues In Blasts At 2 Fresno Buildings

Document #58A/B (left) Article on the bombing of the Fresno Induction center appeared in the N.Y. Times (Nov. 2 1970 (Image appears Permission NY Times) (Right) Image and article Fresno Bee, Nov 2nd, 1970.

DOCUMENT #59: Office door welded shut, tenured and respected professors Ed Dutton (left) and Wren Mabey (right) fired without due process, take to the streets with grass roots theatre. (Fresno State Yearbook, 1970) (Image courtesy, Fresno State Yearbook, 1970. University Archives, Henry Madden Library, California State University, Fresno.)

DOCUMENT #60: My Little Red Book. I've still got mine. How about you? (Photo, Toni Labori-Eis, 2017)

AGGIE STUDENTS PROTECT THEIR BUILDING FROM MARCHERS

DOCUMENT #61: Image of "Aggie" students from the ultra-right wing paper, *Fresno Guide*, 5-25-70. Note the hands that appear to be holding nothing at all. These students were holding axe handles, baseball bats, etc., as we marched by. Evidently, this obvious, illegal vigilante activity was too much even for the Guide, so they crudely airbrushed out the weapons and blurred the faces before printing the picture. (Photographer unknown)

FSC Protest March Down Shaw Brings 47 Arrests

Students Are Released On $1,100 Bail

By George L. Baker

Forty-one of 47 persons, most of them Fresno State College students, who were arrested yesterday afternoon by law officers sweeping down Shaw Avenue, have been released on bail.

The arrests climaxed the third day of demonstrations at FSC.

Also released on $11,250 bail was Virgil Lewis, 18, a student suspected of setting the fire in the college's $1 million computer center Tuesday night. Most of the other students, arrested for blocking Shaw traffic, were released on $1,100 bail each.

The normal bail for misdemeanor unlawful assembly is $250, but Municipal Judge George Hopper set it at $1,100 apiece.

Sympathizers of those arrested canvassed the town to raise the bail money, with some parents posting bond for their children.

Four deputy public defenders handling the youths' cases met with Hopper to ask him to reduce bail, but he refused.

One girl, Sharon Org, charged with assault on a peace officer and unlawful assembly, has to post bail of $7,350 when in normal situations the combined bail for the two offenses would be $2,350.

SHAW AVENUE ARRESTS—Two girls in police van yell to companions, one of them asking for a babysitter, as police arrested 47 persons, most of them Fresno State College students along Shaw Avenue.

DOCUMENT #62: After the original 6 of us were busted, the demonstration continued until 41 more people were arrested. (Photo Dick Daring, Image : Permission, Fresno Bee, Sat. May 23, 1970)

In the Municipal Court of the Fresno Judicial District of the County of Fresno, State of California

THE PEOPLE OF THE STATE OF CALIFORNIA,
  Plaintiff,
vs.

DOUGLAS M. GUSTAFSON, PHILLIP D. ESPARZA, PAUL A. DUNHAM, JOEL D. EIS, CALVIN PRESTON NORRIS, DAVID LEON WARD and KENNETH STUART PARSLEY,
  Defendants.

Complaint—Criminal

No. 44627

Docket........... Page.........

File No. 70-1532

STATE OF CALIFORNIA, } ss.
COUNTY OF FRESNO,

Personally appeared before me, this 23rd day of May 19 70 C. HESS of FRESNO POLICE DEPARTMENT in the County of Fresno, who first being duly sworn, complains and accuses DOUGLAS M. GUSTAFSON, PHILLIP D. ESPARZA, PAUL A. DUNHAM, JOEL D. EIS, CALVIN PRESTON NORRIS, DAVID LEON WARD and KENNETH STUART PARSLEY of the crime of a misdemeanor, to wit: VIOLATION OF SECTION 407 OF THE PENAL CODE Committed as follows:

The said defendants, on or about the 22nd day of May 19 70 at and in the said County of Fresno, State of California, did wilfully and unlawfully assemble together with two or more persons to do an unlawful act, or do a lawful act in a violent, boisterous and tumultuous manner.

DOCUMENT #63 Our arrest record at Fresno State, 1970, (Courtesy, Paul Dunham.)

DOCUMENT #64: My arrest picture for May 23, 1970, stolen from the prosecutor's file after my trial. Property of the Fresno City Police (Photographer unknown).

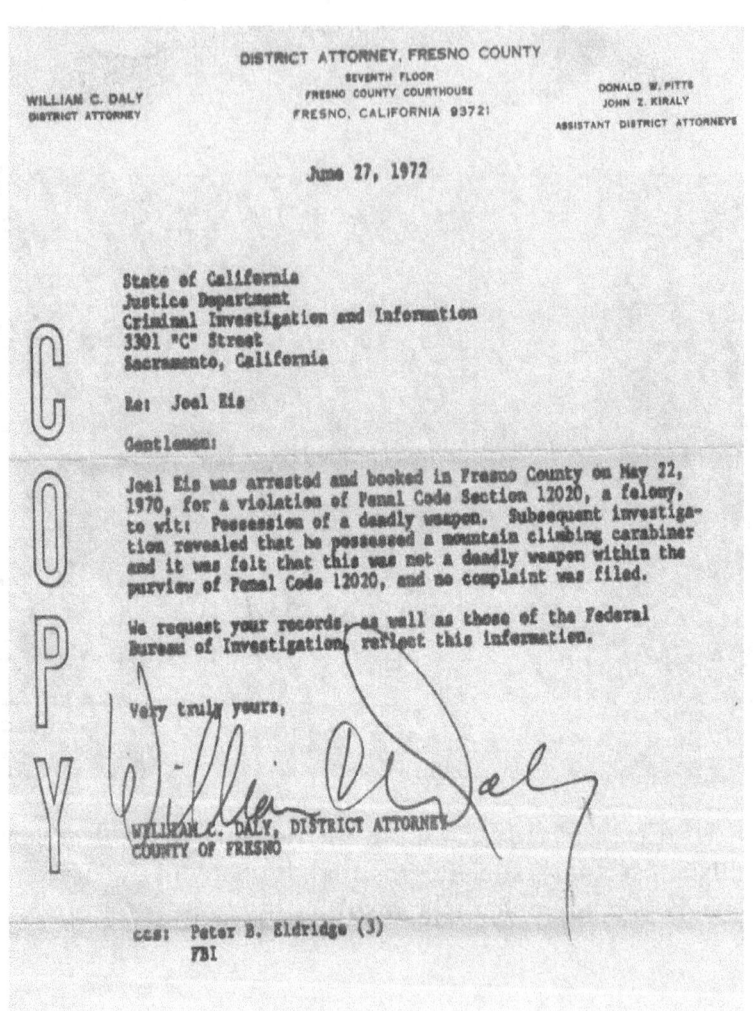

DOCUMENT #65: Fresno County DA accidently exposes the existence of my FBI file seventeen years before the Freedom of Information Act of 188 (Archives, Joel D. Eis)

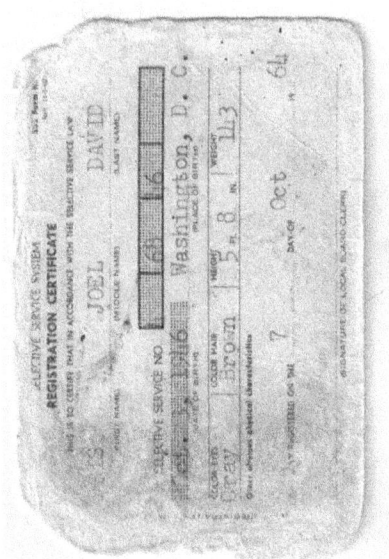 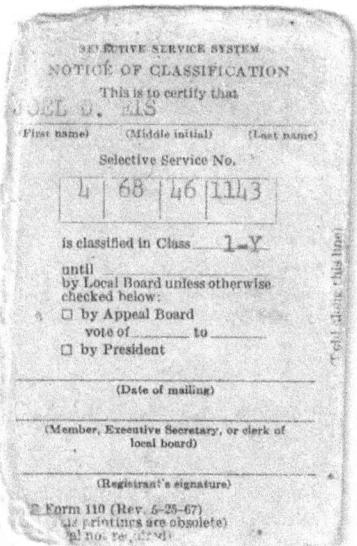

DOCUMENT #66: The condition of my draft card in 2017. Note Classification 1-Y ("To be taken only in extreme national emergencies, sent to me unrequested after my time in jail.") (Photo J. Eis)

SECTION VIII

TIMES CHANGIN'

"And what will you do now, my blue-eyed son?
And what will you do now, my darling young one?
I'm a-going back out 'fore the rain starts a-falling
I'll walk to the depths of the deepest dark forest

Where the people are many and their hands are all empty
Where the pellets of poison are flooding their waters
Where the home in the valley meets the damp dirty prison
And the executioner's face is always well hidden
Where hunger is ugly, where the souls are forgotten
Where black is the color, where none is the number

[Chorus]
And it's a hard, it's a hard, it's a hard, and it's a hard
It's a hard rain's a-going to fall"

"A Hard Rain's A-Gonna Fall"
(Verse 5, Bob Dylan, 1962)

CHAPTER 36: 1971—*SAY 'UNCLE' SAM!* AND THE UNRAVELING TIMES

> "They killed us for wanting to live in peace."
> (Chief Joseph, leader of the Nez Pierce Nation)

This is where I left off in the two threads of my story—my work with *El Teatro* and my life with the Resistance. Both had now changed drastically. After my jail time and leaving *El Teatro*, I was at a personal crossroads.

Things were unraveling in Fresno. Soon after I got out of jail, the fig orchard was sold to housing developers to be bulldozed and turned into tract homes. After the Cambodian invasion, the growing factionalism in our ranks, and the wholesale firing of all the progressive Fresno State professors, it felt as if the Movement in Fresno had been run over by a squadron of tanks. After my bitter end with *El Teatro*, I felt as if one of these heavy machines had personally rolled over me.

Danny Valdez had said that the Bobby Seale and Soledad Brothers Defense Committees[74] in San Jose needed a committed, politically savvy director for a play to be produced as an organizing tool and fundraiser. It was only to be a four-month gig, but because I was at "sixes and sevens," I needed to do something constructive. It would give me time to think.

---

[74] Three politically active Black prisoners in Soledad Prison near Salinas, California, had been publishing accounts of racism in the California prison system. Attempts had been made on their lives by white prisoners who were offered time off their sentences in exchange for acting as hit men for the system. The defense committee was working to protect them and seek parole for their railroaded sentences.

This was an important project. The Soledad Brothers and Bobby Seale defense efforts were two pivotal events unifying Black, brown, and white justice reform groups. Our prison system was warehousing and degrading young men by the millions. It costs twice as much to keep a man in prison for a year than to pay for a year of college. As these men and women rotted in prison, Amerika turned their future into a toxic half-life. This struggle was a logical move in my calling.

The Bobby Seale Defense Committee

The Bobby Seale Defense Committee was working for a fair trial in the case of the Black civil rights leader who was being railroaded into prison. Seale was accused of planning demonstrations at the Chicago Convention that had intentionally turned violent. This was a blatant fabrication. Police provocateurs had been identified in the crowd egging on the peaceful marchers into committing violence. Then the cops beat up and arrested the demonstrators. The cameras caught it all, including the famous film clip showing thousands of demonstrators chanting, "The whole world is watching."

Instead of being allowed to conduct his own defense, a basic right granted by the Constitution, Bobby Seale—the only Black man in the Chicago Seven—*was literally gagged and tied to his witness chair* during the proceedings in full view of the jury and the press. (DOCUMENT #12) Nothing more outrageous could be imagined for a Black man in the middle of the civil rights struggle. Millions shared the rage over this legal lynching. The project in San Jose was to educate and facilitate his struggle.

The Soledad Brothers

The Soledad Brothers Defense Committee was part of a larger movement concerned with the cruel, racist prison system in Amerika. The Prison reform movement had been escalating for years. Riots and strikes in prisons across the country, including

Rikers Island, Attica and the Tombs in New York, and prisons in Illinois, Washington state and Texas had been n the news. My Department Chair at San Francisco State had done a play about the exploitation and corruption in the prisons in Kentucky. For his truth telling, he was forced to resign.

This struggle put the California prison system under intense scrutiny for a long history of blatant abuses in which incarcerated men and women serve as forced labor for private industries using prisoners for profit. The prison system divides and brutalizes white, Black, and Latino inmates against each other as a premeditated strategy to undermine the unity inherently shared by everyone incarcerated.

The Soledad brothers—George Jackson especially—had arisen as leaders in the movement that identified Black inmates as political prisoners because they had been targeted in American society as an exploited population in active revolt in open society. The prison system therefore served as a form of intimidation to keep Black people "in their place."

The stories of the Soledad Brothers (John Clutchette, Fleeta Drumgo, and George Jackson) somehow touched people. More than merely read and understood, theirs was an all-too-familiar tale that we somehow truly felt. It let white people peek into a tiny window of what it was to be Black in Amerika. Their constricted lives touched us with the chill of cruelty and inhumanity that was Amerika for people of color.

These three had followed the tragic path of young Black men into the prison system. (DOCUMENT #67: Soledad Brothers leaflet cover) While in prison, they'd educated themselves about the history of the system that kept Blacks as second-class citizens while siphoning off intelligent, deeply angered men into incarceration. Black men in prison were essentially political prisoners in a racist system. The Soledad brothers—and George Jackson-especially—had arisen as leaders in the movement that identified Black inmates as political prisoners because they had bee targeted in Amerikan society as an exploited population in active revolt in open society. The prison system therefore served as a form of intimidation to keep Black people "in their place."

George Jackson began to educate fellow Black prisoners as well as Latino *and white* prisoners, about how the system pitted them against each other with a "divide and conquer" strategy instead of improving their lot as a social class. He published a prison newsletter and wrote articles for major newspapers as well as the left-wing press. He gave radio interviews about a system that used the men as slave labor.

George was agitating for reforms such as real education, better medical care, and a fair review of prisoner treatment. When he began openly meeting and befriending white and Latino prisoners, he became a marked man.

A state of war existed inside the walls of Soledad Prison. The situation for the Soledad Three had become dangerous. The guards at Soledad had engineered an altercation among the inmates then fired into the melee, killing three men. The guards were exonerated. In an understandable reaction to officially condoned murder, a riot broke out. A prison guard was thrown from the upper tier of the cells and died. Despite no tangible proof, Drumgo, Clutchette, and Jackson were charged with the crime. They faced the death penalty. It is common for "troublemakers" (read: politically educated activist-inmates) to be framed with "witness statements" from other prisoners in exchange for favorable treatment and early release.

The Soledad Brothers' lawyers found solid evidence that these men were repeatedly denied parole *because* they'd become political leaders among the prison population. Additionally, they'd discovered that white prisoners had been offered reduced sentences for acts of violence against them. The Soledad Brothers case focused a searing light on the California Gulag system's strategy for keeping them in their place. The power structure, used to operating with a free hand, didn't know how to handle facing up to public scrutiny. This was when the defense committee had contacted me to direct the play to gain support for their cause.

Their cases drew media attention and important political figures all the way up to presidential candidates. The powerful Black theorist and activist, Dr. Angela Davis, was drawn into this struggle. I had first heard Dr. Davis speak as I stood among a crowd of thousands of striking students at San Francisco State in late 1968. Dr. Davis was J. Edgar Hoover's worst nightmare, a brilliant, charismatic, female African American civil rights activist. She was an outspoken member of the Communist Party and allied with the Black Panthers. She knew who the enemy was, straight up. She is one of the most dynamic speakers I have ever heard.

Dr. Davis took up the cause of the Soledad Brothers. This incensed the Federal Government and the California Correctional System. Angela Davis began to write to George Jackson and visited him. This liaison grew into a deep, genuine, shared affection. Her connection with the case was soon to draw Dr. Davis into a nefarious whirlpool of dangerous manipulation.

The Bobby Seale and Soledad Brothers cases were taken up by a broad coalition of progressive and labor groups spearheaded by the San Jose Peace Center. This coalition struck upon the idea of a play as an ideological weapon and fundraising tool. The project brought together the Peace and Freedom Party, the Brown Berets, the Panthers, the liberal wing of the local Democratic Party, and the Communist Party, among others. In contrast to the factionalism plaguing the Movement in Fresno, this project had a united front. The situation felt very positive.

I went up and met the producer of the project, Emma Gelders Sterne. Emma was a seventy-six-year-old author and activist. We hit it off famously. (DOCUMENT #68: Emma Gelders Sterne, 76 years old) I packed my stuff and headed to San Jose. This gig was exactly what I'd been looking for.

Emma was the daughter of a well-to-do Jewish family in Birmingham, Alabama. At the age of eighteen, she attended a speech by W. E. B. Du Bois and was converted to social activism. She married Roy M. Sterne, one of the lawyers for the Scottsboro Boys, nine Black men accused of the rape of two white girls on a train that never happened. Emma joined the Communist Party in

1950 in the midst of the McCarthy era *pogrom* against progressives. Talk about *chutzpah!*

Emma was a straight-talking, no-nonsense, energetic young spirit. She was the author or coauthor with her daughter of thirty-four published books for children. She read a book a day and was working on two novels at the same time. She was at her rose garden at dawn every morning. She was a chain smoker. I once said to Emma, "You know, every cigarette takes eight-and-a-half seconds off your life."

Without batting an eye, she riposted, "The end they're takin' it off of, I'm not gonna use," and lit up another.

During the project, I lived in Emma's little house in the Willow Glen area of San Jose. I cooked for us often, but when it was Emma's turn, I enjoyed her simple Southern cooking. She'd been to Russia and now drank her vodka ice-cold. Her daughter had married an organizer in the Printer's Union, and her granddaughter was also an organizer. Hers was a family of leftists. Being under her roof felt like home.

The play to be produced, *Say 'Uncle' Sam!*, was donated to us without royalties by its author, Lester Cole, one of the infamous "Hollywood Ten." The "Ten" were screenwriters who'd been active in the Screenwriters Guild in the 1940s, working against the big studios for fair writers' contracts. After the Second World War, the big studios were looking to gut the power of the Guild. At the same time, the House Un-American Activities Committee was looking for a big news splash to justify its appropriation, so the HUAC used the power of the government to go after activist writers and break the union.

Lester's play, *Say 'Uncle' Sam!*, takes place in the waiting room of an Army Induction Center. Among the inductees are a biker and his sidekick, a Draft Resister, a kid who is a closeted gay, a militant Black kid, and an unassuming Black kid who just wants to make his family proud of him. Every one of them knows they could be sent to die. The military characters are a gung-ho sergeant and a doctor who hates the war. Tension exists between them as well. The play was real, accurate, and timely as hell.

Lester and I got along well as a creative team. We made a few adjustments to the staging and were ready for auditions. The man who had volunteered to do the set for the show turned out to be my old college friend, James Bertholf! It was terrific to reconnect and work with Jim again. His ideas were on the money, he was easy to work with, and he always had good weed.

Emma's house teemed with multiracial, left-wing writers, poets, and professors. The circle included the famous Italian sculptor, Benny Bufano, and members of the Black Panther Party. George Jackson's mother, Georgia Jackson, and his seventeen-year-old brother, Jonathan, came by often. I was hanging out in the stratosphere of left-wing movers and shakers. This was a breath of fresh air compared to the scene I'd left in Fresno.

The show was cast from notices published in the papers, leaflets at various cafes, the Peace Center, and college theatre departments in the San Jose area. Our cast was a wonderful ragtag bunch. Among them was a real-life biker (played by Eddie Church), his sidekick (Geoff Pond), a real hippie (Russell Bedillion), the "momma's boy" (Michael Connolly), a closeted gay man (Eddie Green), a real-life smart-mouthed Black guy (Jose Reed), and shy Jesse Richards, who played the timid Black kid openly scared about going to war. Nobody, especially Lester, could believe we got such a great group together. All they had to do was play themselves. We rehearsed the show in an auditorium at San Jose State that was almost identical to the performance space. Rehearsals began on an enthusiastic note.

Around the project was a middle-aged couple named Fred and Ginny Hirsch, friends of Jim Bertholf. They were old-line labor organizers. Fred and Jim believed in direct action that didn't hurt people. During the Grape Boycott, Fred and Jim went out on Saturday nights to the San Jose railroad yard. With high-powered rifles, they shot out the compressor tanks on the refrigerator trucks full of grapes destined for strike-breaking grocery stores. When the trucks were opened, the grapes were all rotten.

Organizing meetings and parties were held at the Hirsches. There I met Bettina Aptheker, a major force in the Free Speech

Movement at Berkeley. During our meetings at the Hirsches', I was entrusted with the heavy front-line revolutionary duty of feeding and diapering Bettina's young son Joshua while the meeting was going on in the next room.

****

One day, while working on, *Say 'Uncle,'* I was standing in a grocery store line picking up some snacks and beer. To my amazement, in the line right in front of me was Bryce "Pig-Pen" Barrett, my old roommate from my freshman year at San Jose State in 1964. This was now six years later. I surprised him with a "hello," and we spoke. He said that he hadn't been in San Jose in the intervening years and was only there for a short stay. What were the odds!

Bryce confessed, " Ah… We picked on you pretty bad."

I told him what I was doing in San Jose.

He said, "Of all the guys at Miss V's (our boardinghouse), you made the biggest impression on me."

"Oh yeah?"

"Yeah. I remembered everything you said about the war. I burned my draft card."

The Politics, the Struggle

I was at a planning meeting for the Soledad Brothers Defense Committee. On a table in the vestibule were some of the handwritten letters between George Jackson and Angela Davis, gathered for publication. Filled with real friendship and love as well as a sense of hope, they were profound and beautiful. In only a few months, my serendipitous connection with Dr. Davis would become more important.

Without warning, in the middle of the *Say 'Uncle'!* rehearsals, George Jackson and the other two men had been transferred from Soledad Prison to San Quentin because their lawyers felt that a change of trial venue out of the Soledad area because the chances of more aware white and Black people on the jury in the San Francisco Bay Area was significantly greater.

Soon thereafter, a fundraising party was held at Lester Cole's rooftop patio on Potrero Hill in San Francisco. The cast of the play—Emma, her family, and Georgia Jackson and her younger son, Jonathan—were there. I sat with Jonathan on the back steps of Lester's flat and tried to make conversation. He sat across from me on a warm afternoon, completely inside himself. I did not know what I could say to this seventeen-year-old who had been described by his brother George as a "man-child." It was an apt description. I could feel his pain and his rage. His was a boy's spirit already made joyless and weary with just living and living with the fear and worry for his brother, not to mention what he himself dealt with every day that threatened to herd him down the same slaughterhouse path that was the fate his brother and millions of others were living. I had to get up and walk away. I went and had a nice conversation with his mother, Georgia. She thanked us for our work on behalf of her son. She was looking forward to the play. We all did pitches for contributions. The party was a success.

George was transferred to San Quentin. This would get him the chance of a better jury but removed him from the protection of whatever allies he had developed in the Soledad population. As our efforts drew more and more scrutiny of the prison system, intimidation of the Soledad Brothers increased. Jonathan was frightened and desperate for his older brother's safety.

On August 7, there was at a hearing in the Marin County Courthouse, not far from San Quentin Prison, for Ruchell McGee, a Black prisoner. Seventeen-year-old Jonathan Jackson brought weapons into the courtroom. He kidnapped the judge and several jury members. (DOCUMENT #69A: Hostages outside Marin County Courthouse, bullet-riddled van) As I read the story and heard the details from others on the defense committee in San Jose, it occurred to me that when I had sat with him on the steps of Lester Cole's porch some two weeks before, this wild suicidal scheme was already simmering inside him.

This frantic, regrettable plot was totally uncharacteristic of Jonathan. No one could believe it was really happening. The press accounts glibly declared that the motive for Jonathan's desperate plan was to use his hostages to bargain for his brother's release, typically casting the victim as the perpetrator. This could not be the thinking of a streetwise, recently radicalized young man who'd been reading his brother's publications, the Panther paper, and the ideas of everyone from Malcolm X to Martin Luther King. Jonathan was wise enough to tell no one of his plans, and so even those closest to the tragic situation were only left with conjecture. One of the people close to the event, Bettina Aptheker, a major participant in the Free Speech Movement labor and feminist organizer, summarized, "Jonathan was not intending to hold hostages to free the Soledad Brothers. He never stated that at any time during the courtroom drama. We think that he intended his act to be a dramatic revolutionary one, to expose the prison system, and to broadcast an appeal on behalf of the Soledad Brothers."[75]

For Jonathan Jackson, History was personal. Whatever his motive might have been, this desperate act of revolutionary street theatre was doomed, ending in a tragic finale. The San Quentin prison guards closest to the van, ordered not to allow an escape of a prisoner even in a hostage situation, opened fire from outside the van and slaughtered everyone inside without any attempt at negotiation. Neither Jonathan nor the men inside the van ever fired a single shot.

The press presented this gruesome event as an insane, thug-generated massacre. However, all of the deaths were perpetrated by a storm of police bullets fired *into* the van from the outside. I am in possession of a photograph published in the *Marin Independent Journal* on August 8, 1970. It shows bodies of innocent jurors inside, slain by the blizzard of law enforcement gunfire inside the open rear door of the *Hertz* rented van that Jonathan Jackson used in the hostage plot. So shocking and brutal

---

[75] Email to the author, 7/26/22.

is this image, that the legal department of the "*IJ*" will not allow it to be published.

Jonathan's mother and his brother George, incarcerated and unable to comfort her, were devastated by this tragedy. When the funeral for Jonathan Jackson was held, there was a place reserved for me in the limousine with Georgia Jackson, Emma Sterne, and her family. Unfortunately, I had business that weekend in Fresno. Those who did attend with the family have related that a crowd of thousands of young Black people mobbed the streets around the church. The throng was so large that they could not get near. Clearly, this was the audience for which Jonathan's demonstration was intended. They had gotten the point. They were moved and further radicalized by his revolutionary sacrifice.

I still deeply regret that I didn't attend.

However, the penury for Georgia Jackson's family and supporters was not over. The Soledad Brothers case was drawing attention to the obscene collusion between the prison system and private industry. One of these uppity Black men had to serve as a lesson, and it had to happen soon.

A year after the bloodbath at the Marin County Courthouse, George Jackson was gunned down by a prison sniper in a tower at San Quentin. The State claimed George was given a nine-millimeter automatic pistol, smuggled in by his lawyer, and that he had hidden this large three-pound pistol in his short Afro! The guard in the tower that day was not the usual guard in rotation but a trained sniper. George Jackson's death proved his point: Outspoken Black inmates were political prisoners.

As a result of these events, the attention around the play exploded. It also increased the surveillance, both official and vigilante, focused on us. We were offered Black Panther escorts but declined these offers. The project was already enough of a target without a cordon of leather-coated, black-bereted, African American armed men around us.

Tom and Carol Valentine and the Secret Tunnel

While working on *Say 'Uncle!,'* I met Tom and Carol Valentine, a mixed-race couple living near San Jose State University. Carol was a white social worker and organizer of the Municipal Employees Union. She was a clever woman and a strong supporter of civil rights. Tom was African American. He was a small, ebullient man with a wicked sense of humor. At a demonstration in Mississippi in 1961, Tom had been beaten nearly to death by a crowd and left to die. (DOCUMENT #70: Newspaper article: Tom Valentine's beating and rescue)

Due to lifelong dyslexia, Tom couldn't read. Ever resilient, he earned his living as a photographer. The camera was his weapon. Due to his dyslexia, whenever Tom laid out his darkroom chemicals or cooked food, someone had to read the labels and directions to him. I did this on several occasions.

Tom was the photographer for the San Jose Community Alert Patrol (CAP). This group, organized in the Chicano community, was led by Tony Estramera. Fred Hirsch and Jim Bertholf were very active in it, and the cops took a polite step back when the two white men, each over two hundred and fifty pounds and six feet tall, stepped out of a car to watch the cop's shenanigans. In order to curtail police brutality, the volunteers in this group watched arrests of Black and Latinx youth from a respectful distance. Tom was a constant police target. When Tom shot photos of demonstrations and speeches, he needed someone to watch for the cops coming after him to "teach him a lesson." He kept two cameras in his car. When the cops stopped him and demanded his camera, he'd give them the camera with pictures of the food-smeared face of his baby daughter or the neighbor's dog. Many times, it was only the fact that his wife and baby were in the car that kept him safe.

Tom called me over to his place one evening. He was laughing on the phone. "You gotta come over! I got a story you're not gonna believe, and I'm cookin' up some catfish."

After that opener, I couldn't wait. Tom made the best damned blackened catfish I have ever eaten. When I arrived, he was in great spirits. "You're not gonna believe this! I got a call to do a freelance shoot for IBM."[76] They had a campus several miles south of downtown San Jose.

"Somehow, they hadn't checked my security clearance. I've got an FBI and local cop file as thick as a phone book. They took me to the Federal Building in downtown San Jose. This was weird, but I kept my mouth shut. We stepped into the elevator, but instead of going up, the guy in dark glasses opened a box under the elevator buttons, put in a key, and the elevator went down! There's a secret tunnel under the Federal Building in downtown San Jose. *I think it goes all the way to the IBM compound, several miles south of town!* This is what they wanted me to shoot. I don't need to make this stuff up. It's there, big as life."

"You got any pictures?"

"You've *got* to be kidding. They took all my film. It's just my say-so. Now I'm scared they're gonna discover who I am and come for me, so I'm tellin' somebody about it. I don't need this James Bond stuff!"[77]

****

Say 'Uncle' Sam! was booked at the old San Jose Civic Auditorium for September 11 and 12, 1970. The posters were out. (DOCUMENT #71: *Say 'Uncle' Sam!* production poster, San Jose, 1970) There were write-ups in the left-wing papers and even some notice in the regular press. There was enough mention of the radical sponsors of the production to make us a few enemies as well. On the days before the show, there were death threats and calls about bombing the theatre. This was not new, but somebody decided these were serious. About forty-five minutes before

---

[76] International Business Machine Corporation, makers of cash registers, Univac computers, and assorted defense systems.

[77] Bizarre and unbelievable as this story is, Tom's wife Carol confirmed this as fact for the writing of this book in 2019.

opening, some local Brown Berets showed up and introduced themselves. Each was carrying a hefty shoulder bag.

One guy came up to me and said calmly, "Don't worry, *ese* ("man"). You-all just do your thing. We got your back." He opened his shoulder bag and showed me a very large pistol. Our innocent stage manager, a high school girl, asked, "Who are those guys in berets and dark glasses hanging around the auditorium?"

I improvised. "Ah…volunteer ushers."

The show went off without a hitch. It was well received with full houses. It met its goals as a fundraising project and was great publicity for the defense committees. The project is noted in Lester Cole's autobiography, *Hollywood Red.* The script we developed was used in Los Angeles for a production supported by Donald Sutherland and Jane Fonda. My dream of using my theatre skills for the Movement was working out. The theatre company wanted to stay together, so I decided to stick around and see what other trouble I could get into.

It came along soon enough.

CHAPTER 37: SMOKIN' WITH "A FEW GOOD MEN"

I couldn't have been any deeper into left-wing politics. By now, I'd organized for the strike at San Francisco State in '68. I'd been with the Farmworkers Theatre. I'd been a draft counselor and public orator with the National Draft Resisters. I'd been busted and done jail time for leading a thousand people into the street. I'd just finished directing a play sponsored by the Communist Party, the Black Panthers, the Brown Berets, the Young Socialists, the Soledad Brothers and Bobby Seale Defense Committees, and a host of left-wing radical lawyers. Sure as hell, I was on somebody's radar.

I'd lived through enough scenarios that I started to jot down story ideas that grew out of my experiences. After *Say 'Uncle' Sam!* closed, the actors said they wanted to stay together. I was offered free rent for house-sitting on San Jose's East Side in a house where a Mexican *folklorico* kids' dance troupe rehearsed. It was in a rough area. They needed the place watched to prevent vandalism and discourage squatters. When the moms came for rehearsals, they always brought home-cooked Mexican food for the kids and left some for me. (DOCUMENT #72: *Folklorico* house, East Side, San Jose, kids in the backyard)

Shortly after I moved in, I pulled together most of the *Say 'Uncle' Sam!* company and put together some skits I'd written. We called ourselves "The Underdog Theatre." We used the *Folklorico* house to rehearse and store props. Our most successful show was a gig at U. C. Santa Cruz. A reviewer called our show something like "a vulgar, flagrant diatribe of left-wing propaganda." Great publicity for the audience we wanted. We used this quote on our posters and press releases. Poor bastard called up and begged us to remove it. I made sure he got press releases for all our shows. In the next six months, we did four or five gigs. We even opened for a San Francisco Mime Troupe show in Berkeley.

On evening walks from the *Folklorico* house to the Baskin-Robbins or the San Jose Cheese Company on King Road (a distance of about a hundred yards), the cops regularly threw me over the hood of a squad car. This answered my questions about being on the cops' radar. One time the cop asked, "You got any weapons?"

"Just my mind, man. But that seems to be enough."

It took a few days for the bruises to heal.

I continued to live at the *Folklorico* house and do political work. Amazingly, despite my significant radical record in a glitch in the Security State the size of the Grand Canyon, I was hired as a stock clerk in the grocery PX on the Moffett Field naval base. In my long hair and Mexican serape coat, I drove my trusty Dodge Dart past the Marines at the gate every day without an ID check or an inspection. There was enough pot in the floor rugs that you could probably smoke them and get high. They never searched the car. I could have smuggled in a carload of drugs, weapons, or horse manure. So much for security.

Once inside the gates, I had free run of the entire base. No one ever stopped me or asked for a pass or an ID. I could have planted explosives in the hangars full of new jets or near the fueling depot. A soldier could have gone AWOL in my trunk or under a blanket in my back seat. I'd encountered tighter security trying to get into a drive-in movie, where they check your trunk to see if you're sneaking anybody in or out. I currently have serious doubts about Homeland Security.

One evening, at the end of my shift, the guard flagged me down at the gate. *Shit,* I thought, *just my luck. There's a shakedown when I'm carrying a joint.*

I rolled down the car window and turned off the radio. "What up?"

"Good evening, sir. We see you coming and going out often."

"I work as a stocker over at the grocery PX."

"Thought so. Which way are you heading when you leave the post?"

"South, down 101 into San Jose."

"Would you mind giving a couple of Marines a ride to the bus station?"

"No problem."

I wasn't going to be searched, but I was going to have two spit-and-polished jarheads in my car for an hour. Two big, squeaky-clean, cologne-washed "Good Men" got into my car.

We pulled out of the base and said our hellos. Both of these guys had thick Southern accents. These were real deep-country boys. I'm your Haight-Ashbury poster child in boots, bellbottoms, Indian print shirt, hair hanging out of my wool watch cap. Peace button. We were from different planets. Hell, we were from different universes.

One of these guys said, "What do y'all think about that there bombin' o' Cam-bodia?"

I wanted to get home in one piece, so I waxed philosophical. "Well, it sure as hell was unexpected."

The other giant-with-a-flattop drawled, "Shit yeah! Them faychist bastards will try any-thaing!"

Color me surprised. "Would you guys like to smoke a joint?"

"Is a wet hound heavy?" one said.

The Marines and I roasted one up. By this point in time, antiwar sentiment was so pervasive that even Marine plowboys from deep in Dixie were reading leftist news. Goes to show that you can't tell a man by his cover.

Shortly thereafter, I was laid off from the PX gig. I started collecting a nice unemployment check. After some of my suggestions had been accepted by Lester Cole, an Academy Award-winning writer, I thought about writing a play myself. Writing short *actos* for the Underdog Theatre boosted my confidence. I didn't have to worry about government scrutiny. After the *Say 'Uncle!'* project, my FBI file was probably the size of the large-print version of *War and Peace*.

****

Just after the odometer on the lucky "EIS" Dodge Dart rolled over to three-hundred-twenty-thousand miles, the transmission gave up the ghost. I was collecting unemployment insurance and had a little bread saved. I wouldn't need to look for a regular gig for a while, so I decided to move back to Fresno. I had no clear plan. This was the first time in my life I'd made a move without a clear idea of what I was going to do. The writing bug was taking over my mind. I needed to find some seclusion to sort things out. I was hearing my dad's admonition in my head again.

CHAPTER 38: ANGELA DAVIS AND A FEW OTHER THINGS

During the *Say 'Uncle'* project, I sat with Dr. Angela Davis at Soledad Brothers and Bobby Seale Defense Committee meetings. I'd first heard her speak at the student strike at San Francisco State in '68. Everything she said was serious. Even when she asked for a cup of coffee, it sounded important. I was in the presence of a true revolutionary. J. Edgar Hoover probably lost considerable sleep knowing she was alive and well.

To Dr. Davis, it was self-evident that nonviolence was not going to stop the ruling class from extracting wealth from the sweat and blood of Black people. While she respected Dr. King, she embraced nonviolence as a single tactic to achieve fundamental change. What had been stolen from working people—and Black people especially—would have to be taken back through whatever means were necessary. Fredrick Douglass, the nineteenth-century Black freedom fighter, said, "A slave is a person who waits for someone else to free them." We didn't need permission to act for our own survival.

We were soon to discover that there was a plot in motion to silence her. Some months later, I would be pulled into this scenario.

<u>Return to Fresno</u>

After *Say 'Uncle!'* and my own small theatrical endeavors, I returned to Fresno a more mature artist and organizer. It seemed anticlimactic, but it felt right. However, I had no clear plan. One cold, fog-soaked night soon after I got back to town, a good friend drove me out to the old Resistance settlement. The property had been sold to build tract homes. The beautiful, gnarled, half-century-old fig trees had been bulldozed over. They were lying on their sides. Their ghostly, ragged roots and naked branches awaited the chainsaw. Our little farmhouses were abandoned. The doors were ajar. The windows were broken out. My old horsehair easy chair was rotting out on the lawn, soaking up the misted air.

    As she waited outside, I climbed the stairs and ducked out of Paul's old bedroom window to the roof. I looked down. At my feet were still shell casings from the day that Karla held off the helicopter. I looked up around my old home. The surreal rows of supine trees disappeared eerily off into the quiet mist like gravestones. Soon the entire area was to become a neighborhood of mundane tract homes, lulled into secure conformity by the mantra of lawnmowers and ballgames wafting from open garage doors. I thought, *the children who grow up in these new houses may have to deal with their own corrupt wars.* Sadly overwhelmed, I got into her car and we drove away.

    For a few weeks after my arrival, I was crashing at my old roommate Patrick's new place. I told the Movement folks up in San Jose how to contact me. I started doing political work again. It had all moved to the newly relocated Movement Center called "The Building." I knew the place well. The Building had previously been my own rehearsal hall and shop, the home of *El Teatro Campesino*.

    A collective of Movement groups had taken over the lease. It housed a small food co-op and health food market, a hotline office, a women's political center, and the Draft Resistance/Antiwar office. Larry Sheehy, the ex-Green Beret, opened an office for Vocations for Social Change. David Harris, just out of federal prison, had a desk for the Vietnam Veterans Against the War just behind mine. I was crashing with the same roommates, working in the same building. Everything was the same but different.

    Weird.

What was even more bizarre was that we began to hang out at an after-hours dance club in an abandoned storefront on a side street in downtown Fresno that I believe was owned and operated by an ex-cop, my former friend and nemesis, Chuck Hess, who danced with everyone. Goes to show you never know the paths that any of us will take.

Then, unexpectedly, events up in San Jose took an ominous turn. On October 13, 1970, Angela Davis was arrested for murder and conspiracy in the Marin County Courthouse shootings that resulted from Jonathan Jackson's failed attempt to break the Soledad Brothers out of custody. The cops' story was that the guns found in Jonathan Jackson's possession were registered in Angela Davis's name and she therefore was part of the plot.

Yeah, right.

Due to the countless death threats made against her by mail and phone, Dr. Davis had purchased a gun. If some right-wing nut can have an entire basement arsenal ready to rekindle the Civil War, a Black activist with a price on her head can be packin'. However, if she'd planned to be part of this impossible plot, would she have used weapons bought over the counter from a reputable gun shop under her own name? I've seen better cartoon stories on Saturday morning TV.

Busting Angela Davis on this charge was almost as stupid as trying to kill Fidel Castro with an exploding cigar (which the CIA tried). If she knew anything about this idea, Angela would have tried to talk the boy out of it. Besides, it would have been easy for Jonathan to take the gun from her apartment without her knowledge, especially if he knew she would have disapproved of the idea. She didn't have jack shit to do with what went down. The cops knew this too. This was an opportunity to discredit, intimidate, and neutralize her. She was already followed, her mail was opened, and her phones at home and work were tapped. The government produced no other evidence. I was hearing my lawyer J. V. Henry's locomotive going "woo-woo" in the background. The truth wasn't going to get in their way. They were desperate.

Angela Davis languished in jail for months. Everyone around the Soledad Brothers case feared for her safety. Then, one night down in Fresno, I got one of those phone calls. It was the Angela Davis Defense Committee up in San Jose. "Hey, Joel, it's Fred Hirsch."

"What's up, Fred?"

"Some farmer down there named Roger McFee just put up his farm as bail for Angela Davis."

I was glad for Angela, but I rolled my eyes when I heard Roger's name. Roger may have presented himself well to the leadership in getting Angela's bail arranged, but our experience with him as a disciplined comrade was not good. If he was ever handed a mike, he rattled off scatological, disconnected polemics. He was always kept at arm's length by Movement groups in Fresno. Though he had come through at an unexpected moment for Angela, they didn't need to feed the media a clown.

Fred asked, "What do you know about this guy?"

I sighed and delivered the bad news about Roger. "The bail deal for Angela is great news, but don't let him get in front of a microphone."

"Too late. He's on a plane for New York. He's going on late-night TV with Dick Cavett. They spring Angela tomorrow."

I rolled my eyes again.

Fred continued. "He wants security for his place. He's worried about redneck backlash. Evidently, this is an important part of the deal."

"He's got a point there."

"The Grape Strike is still going on, and the County Sheriff says they can't spare the manpower to protect him."

"It's probably the sheriffs' deputies who would be his biggest threat. Good thing they're busy."

This was different from the Saul Alinsky/Dolores Huerta event at Fresno City College. I'd never run a field operation. I sighed. "I'll drive out there and handle it."

I had no combat experience, but they had no choice. The Brown Berets had their own troubles with supporting the Grape

Workers Strike, and they were a guaranteed cop magnet. Fred trusted me to get it done. This was not the first time someone had tossed me a dangerous job out of nowhere. Somehow, all my life, my phone has been hooked up to a Fate Network.

    The next morning, I talked to Roger's foreman at the farm. "Clear away anything between the house and the fences that someone can hide behind. Mow down any tall grass around the house and soak down the lawn. Put up hay bales six feet high, about twenty feet beyond the house windows, then soak 'em down too. No lights on in the windows after dark unless the drapes are drawn. Don't walk around unless the perimeter has been scanned with binoculars first. If anyone with a press pass shows up, call their paper to make sure they're legit. Prepared statements only, no interviews. See you tonight."

    I arrived at McAfee's farm just before dark. Everything was set up pretty well. The foreman had his property clean. It was a working dairy farm, so there were plenty of hay bales to protect the windows from Molotov cocktails or snipers. The cattle were all in the barns. We put a person in the barn and took turns walking the area beyond the house. No one could sneak in close. We had an occupied car a hundred yards down the main road from town.

    There were no incidents. I couldn't bring myself to watch Roger on TV, but I heard they had him under control.

CHAPTER 39: DAVID HARRIS, THE VETS AGAINST THE WAR, AND "THE BUILDING"

The year 1972 rolled in so fast, I don't even remember changing my wardrobe. In those short years, the air in Fresno had become laden with smog. Now, you could see the snowcapped Sierras only on the clearest days. My unemployment checks were running out. I was not sure I'd get an extension.

David Harris, The Building, and The Farm: A New Tactic

I returned to Movement activities with the War Resistance at The Building. By 1972, Vietnam vets, broken in body and spirit, were coming home in great numbers. The Vietnam Veterans Against the War had an office in The Building. They were a resourceful bunch. Faced with strict provisions against leafleting on military bases and denied the use of billboards for antiwar messages near military posts, they hit upon an ingenious solution: the dollar bill-as-leaflet. The vets converted their paychecks into one- and five-dollar bills. Using a rubber stamp, they marked the bills:

**"YOU'RE NOT ALONE!
TALK TO A VET!"**

The phone number to a local counseling center was also stamped on the bills. Thousands of these guerilla leaflets made it into the hands of soldiers.

The brutality and futility of the war had destroyed the minds and bodies of guys like my brother-in-law David. Someone had to notice these deeply troubled men and take them in. David Harris was that man. He leased a ranch south of Fresno as a haven for some of these wounded men. Harris had his office in The Building in Fresno, the town where an induction center was located. We were ground zero for federal surveillance again.

I'd known David since high school. We were on debate teams for rival schools. We ran into each other often at the Me-n-Ed's pizza parlor on Blackstone Avenue. David bought us beers at the pizza place; the counterperson sold him beer even though he wore his high school letter jacket,

While David may have been a Regular Guy, he was far from ordinary. Even in high school, he had an air of grounded, thoughtful maturity. When something was self-evident, David was compelled to act on it. The wrongness of the Vietnam War was one of those paradigms.

As Student Body President at Stanford University, David was probably headed for a law or congressional career. Instead, he refused induction into the Army. He said that if millions did the same, resistance to the draft would be an unenforceable crime. He proved to be correct. The courts were backlogged with cases, and the law became moot, but not before David went to federal prison. Between the time he'd returned his card and was locked up, he met Joan Baez on the antiwar lecture trail, and they were married.

David's desk/office space in The Building was right behind mine. We had many discussions about the direction (or lack of it) that the country was headed. For thousands of veterans coming home, there were profound problems with readjusting to family life, holding down a job, and keeping away from addictive drugs that dulled the pain, confusion, and nightmares in their heads. At David's farm, he and his small team helped these sad men readjust to life in a world that was now so alien and frightening that the chatter of an electric typewriter made them drop to the floor because it sounded to them like a Viet Cong machine gun.

In true guerilla warrior fashion, David had shifted his ground to the nature of the struggle, affirming the notion that doing socially responsible work was a continuation of our cause. Right at this moment, his example coincided with my own thoughts about what might be next for me. I recognized that continuing as an artist—and possibly a teacher—was now my strong suit.

Times Changin'...Again

By late 1972, our efforts were bringing results, but only after a terrible price in lives lost and lives destroyed. With mass support for an end to the draft and the war itself, Draft Resistance cases were now dismissed with fines and probation instead of incarceration.[78] We'd nearly won. However, living with this struggle for years on end was exacting a price from our souls. We'd been fighters on our own front line. Each of us was a point man the government had tried to pick off. Now, even as our message was getting through, we were not as we had been before.

The spokespeople for the "End the War" groups were now folks in clean, collared shirts and fashionable dresses. They had regular haircuts. The Draft Resistance Movement as a radical outlaw organization had succeeded in putting itself out of business. We reassessed our work and returned to professional studies. Our self-imposed tour of duty seemed nearly over. We began to think of having children in families that believed in peace and harmony as a revolutionary act.

My life was about to change again.

---

[78] By 1970, fifty percent of the men of draft age never even registered. Of those cases that were pursued, most received only bench probation.

CHAPTER 40: RIDING OFF INTO THE SUNSET

> "Sometimes the light's all shinin' on me,
> other times I can barely see.
> Lately it occurs to me, what a long, strange trip it's been."
> (Jerry Garcia and Robert Hunter, Grateful Dead, 1970)

A hero's exit down the main street of town, heading off into the sunset accompanied by swelling background music, has never been my favorite movie ending. It seems patently artificial. An unceremonious departing down a side street with no soundtrack at all seems more like real life. No one knows what happens to the hero thereafter. However, inevitably, something of the experience of saving the town has to stay with him into the future.

The student murders at Kent State and Jackson State in 1970 made it clear how far the government was willing to go to hold on to power. We were just collateral damage in this struggle. The revelations of the Pentagon Papers and the Watergate scandal in 1972 made it equally obvious how truly craven and self-serving the leaders were. Everything the Left had said for years about the war and violence against minorities began to appear in the mainstream media as if it was their discovery. This was a sign of some kind of a victory. Though it was without background music, it was a victory nonetheless.

The Woodstock generation had matured. We now sought ways to put our values into practice, focusing our energy on supporting veterans, championing women's rights, and operating free clinics. Others worked on "Back to the Land" organic food concerns, Feminism, or legal and civil rights. Still others focused on alternative schools. In this regard, the cultural revolution we envisioned was a success. As Boomers took over leadership roles, life in America became significantly humanized. Everything was washed over with a "soul" ethic. Even redneck truck buddies now greeted each other with a "soul hug," replacing the traditional handshake.[79] Times truly were a-changin'.

By the early 1970s, we were burned out from the organizing, phone taps, undercover agents, protests, and arrests. Nobody was shouting our slogans anymore.[80] We didn't have a name for it, but we were feeling displaced and anachronistic. We were experiencing our own kind of Post-Combat Stress Disorder. Just as the Continental Revolutionary Army had felt the need to go home to tend the farm, hippie families packed up their macramé plant holders, woks, and waterbeds, got into their VW vans, and moved to small, remote towns or farms. Rural neo-socialist communes started popping up all over America like mushrooms after a hard rain.

Those of us with professional aspirations set aside to end the war began to return to graduate school and pursue positive careers. The morphing of Movement activists into decent, law-abiding professionals and taxpayers was more like my preferred movie ending, at best accompanied by a solo strain in a minor key.

Along with simultaneous millions, my housemates from the Resistance Community moved on to regular lives, making their peace with the changes required. This action garnered no headlines. It caused no cops to put on guns and gear. Nevertheless, this quiet collective action of our generation changed the future. It became the revolution in which we would play a part for the rest of our lives. We had gone underground.

There was a book that came out with a bitten apple on the cover entitled, *Teaching as a Radical Activity*. It was my exit music. I was findin' "mah own guit-tar solo." However, sliding off

---

[79] The Black Panthers had a specific handshake. This unique greeting included a minor variation that informed the participants in the shake if one or the other was carrying a weapon.

[80] Folks made jokes about the crowd response, "Right on," accompanied by a raised "power salute" fist. Now people joked with, "Right arm" or "Hard on." There was nothing funny about our struggle.

the shore into the Main Stream proved to be more difficult than I imagined.

"The Label Don't Peel Off Easy"

The unemployment checks ended. I needed to find a straight gig. I relinquished my strident demeanor and my slogan-laden vocabulary. I got a haircut (a trim!) and ironed my hippie shirts. I applied for several jobs in Fresno, only to be refused an interview. A friend who was the personnel manager at one of these agencies met me away from his office. "You're qualified, but we can't hire you. A lot of people can't hire you."
"Why not?"
"Well…there's a list."
"A list?"
"Yeah, a list," he said, bitterly ashamed.
"Where did it come from?"
"I can't tell you, but they have a big office building downtown."
The FBI.
This amounted to punishment for "thought crime." We were still The Enemy. When I told my old poet friend, C. W. "Chuck" Moulton about the blacklisting, in his gruff, Okie twang, he said, "Guess th' label don't peel off so easy." Taking my mother's pronouncement on faith, I counted on the blacklist waning as the years of activism retreated into the past. I returned to graduate school to focus on classes at Fresno State.

In January 1973, I met Connie, a woman with two lovely precocious children. I soon moved in with Connie and her family. Connie had come by her feminist politics from necessity. She was confronting life as a single mother after her first husband left her for another woman. Fending for herself with two young children, she struggled with the public welfare system and the limited employment choices for single women without a college education, consistently offered work that paid less then single men without children. She had been radicalized by life, not leaflets.

Connie was intelligent and outspoken. Her life experience and discussions with other women in the same situation led her to more theoretical reading. When we met, she was in a nursing program to get off welfare and earn a decent wage.[81] Connie and I became the perfect New Progressive family. Along with working to end the war, we joined a food co-op and a childcare co-op, and we used a free clinic. Everybody did less LSD, but the pot was better.

The folks in our feminist babysitting co-op believed in direct action. When the local welfare office refused to set aside a playroom for mothers who had to bring their children to appointments, the mothers all got appointments at the same time, gave their kids sugary snacks, and let them loose around the welfare office. A few weeks later, an office cubicle was turned into a play area.

Connie and I married in Roeding Park in the fall of 1973. It was the perfect hippie wedding. She wore a peasant-style wedding dress. I wore a blue velvet shirt that made me look like a cross between an Indian Guru and a waiter in a Russian restaurant. We even let the homeless guys sleeping on the park benches have some wedding cake. I intended to finish my master's degree and seek teaching work. We were planning to be happy.

A Surprise at Fresno State

In the spring of 1974, my first directing project toward my master's was a production of *The Exception and the Rule* by the Communist playwright, Bertolt Brecht. Brecht was all the rage. This *Lehrstücke*[82] play had been produced all over the country, even off-Broadway.

---

[81] Connie was no slouch. When she took her nurses exam, she received the highest score of anyone in the history of the program. Ten years later, her score still stood as the highest on record. As Connie worked in hospitals in various cities and towns, she was encouraged by male doctors on many occasions to consider becoming an MD.

[82] Literally "teaching story" or "teaching piece."

The Exception and the Rule is about a cruel boss who is taking a small party across the desert. Due to his stupidity, they become lost and run out of water. Late one night, the boss's "coolie" comes to his tent holding an object out to him. The boss fears he's being attacked. The boss shoots the coolie. The coolie was holding a canteen of water. In his trial, the boss argues that considering how badly he'd treated the coolie, the coolie should have been trying to kill him. Therefore, the boss shot him in presumed self-defense. The coolie's kindness was "the exception." The assumption of retaliatory violence was "the rule." The boss is acquitted.

The show went extremely well. That was the problem. When I went to calendar my final directing project for my degree, the letter of agreement that guaranteed my final directing slot—required to complete my degree in the next season—had disappeared from my file. No one would talk to me about it. Finally, Phillip Walker, Chair of the Department, a virulent conservative, leaned out of his office door and said to me, "We're not giving you a date because all you did was bring a bunch of street theatre stuff in here."

This was a patently biased fabrication. Dr. Walker was well aware that all the staging techniques used were in Brecht's original stage directions. Ironically, my old friend Eddie Emanuel from San Jose State was now a professor at Fresno State. He was my advisor and defended the Brecht play. I have no doubt that Dr. Walker threatened him with dismissal if he was more strident in my defense. The politics was in the story, not in any arcane effects tacked on to my production. The real issue was that Dr. Walker knew my politics and my association with *El Teatro*. With his remark, he'd confessed that he'd personally lifted the agreement from my file. Due to his own politics, Dr. Walker had intervened, sabotaging my family's future. I felt like the coolie in my own play.[83]

---

[83] Dr. Walker made a personal crusade of slandering and railroading Robert Mezey, a nationally known poet and teacher, of writing, for his progressive

It was clear that I wouldn't be allowed to get a degree at Fresno State. With no chance of completing a degree, along with the revelation of the blacklist, Connie and I began to consider our next move. Other aspects of our lives helped make up our minds.

In the summer of 1974, as we considered our next move, our community imploded on itself as if the water had been laced with bad acid. The progressive community—including the feminists—engaged in an orgy of wife and husband swapping, extramarital affairs, and divorces all in the name of "liberation." There were cases of serious domestic violence. The counterculture had degenerated into a paisley *Peyton Place*.

This was part of a larger cultural upheaval. People now rejected earlier decisions made under the expectations of more buttoned-down self-images. The whole idea of commitment itself was under scrutiny. It was some kind of simmering disappointment bred from a kind of feminist consciousness because the women involved were certainly well aware and even active politically. They were dropping out of unfulfilling careers and poorly defined marriages with a kind of slash-and-burn vengeance. The men around them were also making major readjustments. High-powered executives walked away from corner offices to become fry cooks or farmers. Whatever it was, it hit the subculture in Fresno like a ton of bricks.

With the blacklist, my problems at the university, and our entire social network in freefall, our life in Fresno appeared bankrupt. Connie and I gave in to the cultural tsunami. We packed up and left for the small mountain town of Westwood in the lower Cascades, east of Chico, where Connie's mother and four of her sisters were living. The war was nearly over. I had a 1-Y deferment, and the Martians weren't even close.

---

views. The resulting legal case from this wrongful, vindictive firing lasted ten years and cost the college millions in restitution costs.

SECTION IX

THE RUSTIC INTERLUDE AND BEYOND

"And what will you do now, my blue-eyed son?
And what will you do now, my darling young one?

And I'll tell it, and speak it, and think it, and breathe it
And reflect from the mountain so all souls can see it
Then I'll stand on the ocean until I start sinking
But I'll know my song well before I start singing

[Chorus]
And it's a hard, it's a hard, it's a hard, and it's a hard
It's a hard rain's a-going to fall"

"A Hard Rain's A-Gonna Fall"
(Verse 5, Bob Dylan, 1962)

CHAPTER 41: POLITICAL THEATRE WHERE YOU CAN

"Seize the time."
(Bobby Seale, 1967)

  Westwood, California, is a town of about fifteen hundred people in the lower Cascade Mountains,. For us urban refugees, it appeared to be an idyllic place. The air was crisp. The nearby lakes and streams were pristine. The mountains were jaw-dropping gorgeous. Bears were sometimes seen in the backyards in town. There were no stoplights and no sidewalks. It could snow so deep that the first story of the houses would be buried entirely. (DOCUMENT #73: Westwood, CA, in the Cascade Mountains) However, for the locals as well as the newly arrived hippies, it was a town plagued with an Appalachian lifestyle.
  The official unemployment rate was about thirty percent. It was even more in the sub-zero winter. If you weren't on welfare, unemployment insurance, or disability checks as a wounded Vietnam vet, you had some kind of under the table job or your 'o lady had a straight gig. Usually your survival formula was some kind of equation involving several of these. Older folks were on union retirement pensions or Social Security. Almost everyone wore thrift store clothes and had hand-me-down furniture that had been traded around at least once already. We all received commodities[84] until that program ended. Then we were all on food stamps. During the long, jobless winter, many survived on unemployment insurance and odd jobs.

---

[84] Commodity food was a monthly food allotment for people on public assistance (welfare). If you were early in line, you might score a canned ham or a canned chicken. If you were lucky, there were a dozen eggs and a cake mix.

The urban refugees began attending the local college. We traded in our paisley shirts for lumberjack plaid. We started making families and plans to stay. If not, we could move away and go on to four-year schools. We were changing the politics and lifestyle in town. At first, we were resented except for the fact that we spent most of our money in town on rent, food, booze, and stuff from the hardware store. Then a few of us got jobs teaching at the high school or the college. Some took jobs in the local mills and stores. The resentment began to wear off.

Housing was cheap, and wood to keep the little homes warm in the winter was plentiful. Rumors of the closure of lumber mills in the area and changes in the price of heating oil were the major topics in the coffee shop, the bar, and the grocery store line. Everything else was out of their universe. The next nearest town was twenty miles away.

The local young men joined the Army as a way out of poverty. It was common for local girls to get pregnant before they got out of high school and get married instead of graduating. There were American flags on almost every house on the Fourth of July. There was one Black person in the entire town. She was my wife's six-year-old adopted sister, Lydia. Lydia was bullied often in school and stared at in the local stores. This put the whole family on civil rights watch duty 24/7.

We grew our own marijuana off in the woods with near impunity. I'd moved to a place where the blacklist seemed as far away as the moon. I'd definitely moved someplace totally different. I thought, *wherever there is a community, there's a need for culture. Perhaps there's a chance to do theatre here.*

Life in a small town in the Cascade Mountains seemed far away from my former life. However, when I wrote to Lester Cole about settling there, he told me that he'd discovered it when he was there for a big lumber mill strike in 1938 and that he was often up there trout fishing.

Soon after moving into a little house in town, I had a most unexpected encounter. I discovered that my across-the-street neighbors, Mr. and Mrs. Andriani,[85] were the parents of Sandra Archer, cofounder of the San Francisco Mime Troupe. What were the odds? Not only that but R. G. "Ronnie" Davis was due for a visit.

    It was snowing when R. G. arrived. I made a snowball and lobbed it at him from across the street. When he recognized me, he couldn't believe it. Away from the city and everyone we knew, he opened up about his disappointments and his dreams. For Ronnie, the loss of the Mime Troupe was like the death of the love of his life. To my knowledge, aside from a single project shortly after leaving the SFMT[86], he never directed a company of actors again.

    It seemed that my old life would not let go. I would do some theatre as soon as I got the chance. I soon got that chance.

Progressive Theatre in the Deep Woods

    Educated people were needed for the local school systems. I landed a part-time gig teaching theatre for Lassen Community College for their satellite program right in Westwood. I seized the opportunity to direct Kenneth Cameron's biting satire, *The Hundred and First,* a play about being poor in America. There couldn't be a better script for this community.

    The Hundred and First is a hilarious farce about a poor guy in the Bronx who tries to get on *The New York Times*' list of "The Hundred Neediest Families" in order to cash in on the money given to the unfortunates on the list. However, every year, this sorry-ass con artist just misses the cut. He's always "the hundred-and-first." He's such a loser that he even fails at being poor.

    There's not a lot to do in a town where it snows so heavily that sometimes the food has to be dropped in by helicopter, so the

---

[85] Descendants of the famous Andrianis, the seventeenth-century Italian Commedia family.

[86] A production of Dario Fo's, *No se Paga! No se Paga!* (*We Won't Pay! We Won't Pay!*), performed in a storefront theatre off-off-Broadway in NYC, produced simultaneously with the SFMT's production of the same show in San Francisco. I saw both shows. They were alarmingly similar.

play project was greeted with great anticipation. *The Hundred and First* was tailor-made for hippies, poor rednecks, and people on Social Security and welfare struggling to make ends meet—my family among them. Just as the work of *El Teatro* was for *la Raza*, *The Hundred and First* was a "theatre of survival" for this community.

The show took place in the elementary school auditorium with thrift-store costumes, dumpster-scavenged or borrowed furniture, and an entire cast who had never been in a play in their lives. This was hippie *rasquachismo*. It was a thoroughly enjoyable project. It was wonderful to see people blossom and do things they'd never done before. Unexpected raw talent came out of the woodwork. My sister-in-law Melinda and her younger sister Roberta, both in the show, were always in competition in real life. This rivalry spilled over into their acting and served their mother/daughter characters. They competed to be funnier within the play.

This was the kind of theatre that Brecht talked about. The cast and the audience all lived the experience in the play. For this community, political theory wasn't necessary. The ideas in the script were self-evident. With the production, something happened in the town. Seeing themselves on stage validated their struggles. Their lives were acknowledged, and their laughter at themselves lifted their horizons. They were *somebody*.

A Visit in a Blizzard

In the winter of '74, I'd landed a job as a print shop teacher at Susanville High School, twenty miles away. Along with the money from teaching theatre classes two nights a week, we were getting by.

One raw snowbound Saturday, there was already four feet of snow on the ground and the storm was coming in sideways. Connie was now pregnant with our daughter. Through the frosted windows, Connie saw the hazy outline of a car pull up in front of the house. No one in their right mind was out on the road in the middle of such a storm.

"Who do you know who drives a powder-blue Ford?" she asked.

I took one look out the window at the guy in a thin tie, Oxford shoes, and black socks coming up the unshoveled walkway. I knew who it was. "Hide the dope!"

"What?"

"Hide the dope, and get in the back room with the kids!"

"Why? Who is it?"

"It's the fucking FBI!"

"Why would they come up here?"

"Because all the stories I've told about what I did before I met you are true."

Her eyes were the size of half-dollars. I tossed her the weed, the papers, and the bong then shooed her and the kids into a back room.

Sure enough, it was a guy from the Feds.

I had no doubt how they'd found me. The few people I wrote to were on FBI lists, so their mail must have been opened and their phones tapped. As the guy dusted the snow off his pants and prepared to knock, I wondered, *How long have they been watching me here? How many of our friends and neighbors here have they questioned? What did the people around here suspect about me? How badly had they already fucked with my new life?*

The guy showed a badge and asked to come in. I thought, *If I refuse, he'll just come back with a warrant and half a dozen officers. They'll turn the place upside down just to fuck with me for making them come out twice. End of teaching career.*

I let him in.

He sat down at my coffee table and opened a manila folder that was almost two inches thick. It was my FBI dossier. I'd seen it before in J. V. Henry's office. It looked bigger now.

He began, "You made quite a lot of speeches when you were at college."

"The government was doing a lot of shit that pissed us off. It turns out we were right."

He was not amused.

I craned my neck and peeked across the table as he leafed through the file. I couldn't read the documents, but I could see some of the grainy black-and-white photos. Some were taken on the Fresno State campus. Some were images of my house taken from the water tower at Fresno State. I thought I'd glimpsed a shot from Roger Alvarado's house in San Francisco and maybe a shot from the strike at S. F. State. There were shots of me performing with *El Teatro* and a few taken in front of "The Building" in Fresno.

Not wanting to waste the taxpayers' time and money, he started right in.

"What do you know about Isaac Waller or his brother and the SDS?"

"I don't rat on my friends."

He then quoted something from one of my speeches, transcribed from a tape recording. He was trying to rattle me. "Isaac Waller is a foreign citizen. He can't join groups that advocate the overthrow of the American Government."[87]

What went on in our meetings was none of the government's business.

He closed the folder and seemed to be finished with his inquisition. Without any warning, he asked me, "What do you know about the bank burning in Santa Barbara?"

This was right out of nowhere to say the least. The bank burning happened two years after I left Santa Barbara. Clearly, the apartment I'd visited in Isla Vista two years later was under close watch. The folks I'd stayed with must have been in pretty deep. In truth, I didn't remember the people's names. I told him so. He knew their names already.

---

[87] One of our tactics was to meet and play soccer while we talked strategies. A lot of our soccer pals were from other countries. We always played a booming transistor radio next to the field to mangle any long-range microphones. I doubt the Feds ever got any texts from these meetings.

What was baffling is that he didn't ask anything about my work in San Jose with the Soledad Brothers Defense Committee, Lester Cole, Angela Davis, the Apthekers, the Hirsches, or Emma Sterne and her family, all of whom were known Communist Party members or affiliates. Go figure.

"Now I have to ask you, are you now or have you ever been a member of an organization whose avowed purpose is the overthrow of the government of the United States by force or violence?"

"Every American has the right to belong to any organization they want."

"Do you intend to answer the question?"

"No, I don't, and it's illegal for you to ask it in the first place."

"Well, do you know anyone who's against the government?"

I happened to have an Oakland phone book in my home office. I used it to get hard-to-find prop items for my theatre projects in this remote mountain area. Oakland was at least forty percent African American, ten percent Latinx, and another twenty percent white working-class labor union and leftist sympathizers, not to mention the progressives who lived in the Oakland hills. I said, "Wait a minute, I have something for you!"

I got the Oakland phone book from my office. I dropped it with an explosive *bang* on the coffee table. "You want to know if I know of anyone who is pissed at the current government? Start at the front page and just go door to door!"

He got up to leave. "Here's my card. In case you…"

"Keep it."

He left my home and skidded away on the icy roadway in his powder-blue Ford.

In a small town, your life is everybody's topic of conversation. Thirty seconds after the guy pulled away, my neighbors would be on the phone trying to find out what had happened. The talk in the grocery store line and coffee shop would begin within the hour. Whatever details Connie—an addictive gossipmonger—didn't foolishly share on the phone would be filled in by the rumor mill.

Connie came out of the back room, her eyes wide. She was shaking. "Is he gone?"

"Yeah. I'm going out to the shed to split some wood." I rolled a joint and went out to the woodshed for a little solitary time. I kicked open the door then slammed it closed behind me. A country philosopher once said, "He who heats by wood is warmed three times: once in the splitting, once in the stacking, once in the burning."

Backwoods Zen.

I went into my own personal woodshed for some quality time. It was quiet in the old shack. The snow was now falling gently, hushing even the small sounds of the town around me. It was clear from the FBI visit that I was still very much on their radar. I might have left the Movement, but the Movement hadn't left my life. Like Oedipus who had tried to avoid his fate, mine had found me. This Orwellian encounter taught me most clearly that you're never through with who you are.

By the end of my third year of teaching in the mountains, Connie and I had three kids: her two by her previous marriage and our daughter together. Our money needs were pressing. However, without a completed M. A. degree, full-time teaching was not possible. The nearest graduate school was at Humboldt State University, one-hundred-fifty miles due west on the Northern California coast. My family was off to live by the ocean.

An Unexpected Confession

Just before we moved due west over to the North Coast, I went down to Fresno to see my dad for Father's Day. In the middle of dinner, I asked him a question I'd never asked before.

"If it hadn't been for the Depression, what would you have been doing?" I'd caught him totally off guard.

He said, "I wanted a career in the theatre."

You could have knocked me over with the salad fork.

For the first time in my life, Dad had opened up with some details. "In 1933, I worked with the Labor Theatre."[88]

My dad had worked with this famous Communist-affiliated theatre; maybe he'd even been a young Communist himself!

"I couldn't make a living at it, so I hitchhiked to Chicago to work in the auto factories, and then out to San Francisco to work in the shipyards."

He'd been there in time to be part of the General Strike of 1934, maybe even on Bloody Thursday.[89] In an irony of ironies, his life journey at the same age was a mirror image of my own, complete with a self-searching, cross-country trek. He knew that there was more than just the view on the other side of the mountain. I felt as if his life and mine were two slow revolutions of the same Zen wheel. After my troubles at Fresno State and the blacklist, I felt my father's frustration with his life. I understood his fears for mine. I did not inform him about the FBI scrutiny. Years later, that dinner conversation would be the inspiration for a play about generations going their own way.

I went home and packed up my family for my next guitar solo…

Humboldt State, *Ubu,* and the Pacific People's Theatre Festival

My stepson and I drove toward the coast with our family possessions in a rented truck. A few miles before I got to Highway 1 near the ocean, we passed a large hillside meadow just east of the town of Blue Lake. The sun broke through gloriously as the fog lifted. Spiders had spun their webs in the tall, amber-colored grass. As the sun exploded through the rising mist, the dew was captured

---

[88] Late in life, my mother confessed that before she met my father, she dated the theatre reviewer for the Communist newspaper, *The Daily World*. From her association with this important Communist writer, she may have been subject to FBI scrutiny.

[89] The general strike peaked with the shooting deaths of two workers on July 5, 1934, "Bloody Thursday," when the police attacked the strikers and shot into the crowd, killing two men.

on these webs spanning three or four feet across. They're called "fairy quilts." Tiny rainbows scintillated in the captured droplets on the warp of a hundred webs sparkling like giant mandalas. In the redwood forests of the North Coast, the ferns grow six feet tall, and all the un-dammed rivers run wild. It is a wonderful place.

****

For some time before Connie and I moved to the North Coast, our marriage had been on shaky ground. Sadly, some months after we moved and settled and I was deep into my graduate studies, Connie and I divorced. Aside from missing my children deeply, this was a positive turn of events. She seemed happy in her new life with a third husband. I did what I could for my children. I devoted myself to succeeding so that I could have my two-year-old daughter live with me later on.

****

By 1976, psychedelic was out. Punk was coming in. Dylan and the Doors were out; the Clash and the Sex Pistols were in. Weed was now designer stuff and very expensive, but everybody in Humboldt knew somebody who was growin' their own. The idea of "I'll do my thing, you do yours" seemed like a sweeping victory for personal freedom. In reality, it was the beginning of "The Declaration of Me." The new generation was focused on careerism, not social change. I still hoped to find a work situation *because* of my specific slant, not in spite of it. I thought the callous attempt to sabotage my degree by Dr. Walker at Fresno State and the threatening of progressive teachers' careers, including Frank Verges—along with the firing of dozens of tenured progressive professors—was an isolated case of a craven abuse of power.

I had a lot to learn.

Sadly, as I pursued my degree, I discovered that the urban and suburban regional theatres were afraid to alienate their audiences or their funding sources with confrontational material.

Actors no longer came to auditions because of the politics of the play. In order to produce something progressive, the first people I'd need to educate politically was the cast itself.

Therefore, the emphasis of my thesis project at Humboldt State would be the development of an actor training methodology that included a focus on the ideas in the plays. This was something that is rarely discussed in traditional rehearsals. Built on the ideas of Augusto Böal[90] and Brecht, this methodology included educating the actor on the social background of the characters they played. If a director could ask actors to learn an accent, a period dance style, or how to fight with a sword, I could ask them to learn about the life of their characters within the time and place of the play.

For my thesis production, I chose Alfred Jarry's *Père Ubu* (alternately called *King Ubu, Ubu Roi, or Ubu Rex*). I would direct it using this method. This text, hailed as the first modern avant-garde play, debuted in Paris in 1884. *Ubu* was Jarry's savage, farcical rant against imperialism and rampant militarism in Europe. It was a rip-roaring prophecy of the twentieth century. The characters were all greedy, id-driven cartoon types, much like the S. F. Mime Troupe and the characters in *El Teatro*'s *actos*. It was modern political *commedia del Arte*.

Shocking symbolic costume choices were employed, such as "the People" costumed in black plastic garbage bags and the Army wearing disposable diapers as battle helmets. (DOCUMENT #74: *Ubu Roi* production, Humboldt State University, Arcata, CA, 1977) The young actors got into the political education part of the training. The project was well-received. I got my degree in 1978.

For audiences addicted to shopping-mall community theatre about love gone bad, I hoped that outrageous political theatre would be a breath of fresh air. This wasn't going to be easy.

---

[90] An important activist director who went to such places as villages in South America and used radical theatre techniques to teach poor villagers to read and to feel empowered by the ideas, much like *El Teatro* and the production of *The Hundred and First*.

CHAPTER 42: UNEXPECTED CHALLENGES

The miracle of my professional debut didn't happen as scheduled. Mere days after my graduation from Humboldt State in 1978, the infamous Proposition 13 property tax law passed, drying up the funds for arts and education programs all over California. Virtually every job for which I'd been invited to interview was taken off the table. The chances of my landing theatre teaching work in California dropped to near zero.

Then, out of nowhere, the phone rang…again.

It was from *El Teatro Campesino*. I hadn't had contact with them since 1971. They were co-producing the Pacific Peoples' Theatre Festival in San Jose, sponsored by the Rockefeller Foundation and the United Nations' UNESCO Fund. Twenty-five theatre and dance groups and two dozen solo performers from indigenous nations around the Pacific Rim and beyond were invited to perform.

As if that was not enough unexpected serendipity, the folks who'd come up with the idea for this event were none other than the mothers who'd run the children's *folklorico* dance company in San Jose back in 1970. I'd crashed in their *centro* after the *Say 'Uncle' Sam!* project. Small world. Their company had matured and prospered in the era of multicultural pride and awareness. They badly needed a technical director to organize the entire festival.

A general movement for multicultural awareness had grown out of the African American, Latinx, Native American, and Asian Power Movements. San Jose, with its many growing ethnic populations, was the perfect host city for this event. This was progressive politics married with cultural activism. Once again, I was in the right place at the right time, and the phone bell chimed for me.

Groups as diverse as the Japanese solo performer Kazuo Ohno, a Maori dance company of forty-five men and women, and a dance/storytelling company from Pago-Pago *with ninety dancers* were due to appear. Fifty performances were planned in indoor and outdoor venues during the monster ten-day festival. The event involved four-hundred-fifty artists. It was the biggest gathering of international performers in America up to that time.

Piece of cake.

The wonderful *madrecitas* (little mothers) who had given birth to this idea had no inkling of what went on around them when their children performed, and they had most assuredly had absolutely no idea what would be involved in a project this complex. When I got the fateful call, it was only three months before the festival's opening. Right out of graduate school, the ink still wet on my diploma, I headed down to San Jose.

When I arrived, I discovered that no information had been gathered about the technical needs from any of the fifty-plus foreign groups or individual artists. The performance spaces had not been surveyed to determine the equipment on hand. Rehearsal times had not been planned in those performance spaces. No one had done an assessment of dressing rooms, which was especially important for groups from traditional cultures and groups with children.

The TD/Production Coordinator they'd hired was going to be unavailable until just two weeks before the event. They were in deep trouble. That's when *El Teatro* called me. Truckloads of gear had to be ordered. Crews had to be hired for load-ins, to run shows, to transfer gear from space to space, and for load-outs. It was all about the details…and lists. Lots of lists. There are three kinds of electrical plugs used in theatres. Having the right adapters in each theatre had to be arranged. I would have to live with this project 24/7 until it was done. Having lived in San Jose twice before, I used previous contacts to gather information and crews. I slept in the festival's offices, a bank building in downtown San Jose. Calls came in at all hours from the likes of the Maori Dance Company in New Zealand, the South Korean National Dance Company, and a storyteller from Trinidad.

As information came in, the festival began to take shape. I generated a dozen light plots, plugging charts, and equipment manifests. We probably rented or borrowed every foot of spare theatrical lighting cable in a fifty-mile radius. A crew of nomad technicians was hired to move gear from theatre to theatre, match up the right adaptors to the theatre plugs, and set up and break down.

There were nights without sleep, countless miles of driving, and untold hours of lending a hand in theatres all over town. I didn't stop moving for four weeks before the festival, the ten days of the event, and the three days of load-out and final paperwork afterward. I don't remember where or when I ate. Nevertheless, the project was a fantastic experience in promoting cultural pride for the performers and the audiences. That is, until the bookkeeper cleared out the bank account and disappeared. I was never paid.

There was a real-life drama in the festival that I helped to resolve. A family dance group from Bolivia was being pursued by their repressive government. The father was active in labor struggles in his village. After I alerted the *folklorico* women to the situation, the family was granted political asylum. I was doing what I had hoped to do.

Back in the World

Exhausted after the festival, I seriously needed downtime. I was spiritually content but broke. I also had personal priorities. My very young daughter and stepchildren were still living in Westwood, so I moved up to Chico, a valley town eighty miles southeast of Westwood, to be near them. Chico had a state university and theatre groups. I hoped to find a gig while being close to my children. I was out of school, out of a job, and very much on my own in a different world. My long-range plan was eventually to settle in the Bay Area as a designer or teacher, but I had no idea what to do next. I got a straight gig working in a copy shop. I was not connected to the theatre or politics in any way. The *regularness* of this unaffiliated existence felt bizarre.

One afternoon in the early fall, I was sitting on a bench on the Chico State University campus, eating a salad. It was now almost ten years since my arrest in Fresno. I was just over thirty, older than Jerry Rubin's "trustable age."[91] I started a discussion with a young woman also sitting on the bench. She was majoring in International Business. She was much younger than I was.

She said bitterly, "Your generation sold out. Before the revolution was finished, you gave up and moved to the mountains or *wherever!*"

Her indictment wounded me. I riposted self-righteously with a litany of victories that had made her world a better place. "We ended the Vietnam War. There was the passage of environmental laws and advances in civil rights and rights for women."

"But when the war was almost over, you all just *stopped.*"

I tried to explain. "We were exhausted from persecution by our own government for speaking out."

It wasn't possible for her to understand. In a bitter poetic irony, we were acting out "Rubin's Axiom." We were looking at each other across a different History.

She picked up her bottled water and her textbook on International Business and walked away. Our discussion left me deeply disturbed. The Ruling Class had learned an important lesson from Vietnam—that overt wars were very costly—so Amerika now engaged in small, covert "boutique" wars financed by CIA slush fund money in remote places. They kept it off the front pages in a trade for easier victories. In exchange for a few bargain-price social concessions here at home, the same forces were still in charge.

---

[91] In 1968 Jerry Rubin, founder of the Yippie Movement and one of the Chicago Seven, had declared, "Never trust anyone over thirty."

The Woodstock Nation had showered up and finished graduate school. We were now teachers, lawyers, business people, and nonprofit managers. Right there on the sunny bench, my salad fork dripping Thousand Island dressing, I was having the confrontation with my life I'd avoided for too long. I was still hanging on to the slogans of the past. Nobody was in the street anymore.

This was the other movie ending.

Many of our role models didn't fare well in the transition to quietly productive lives. Some had morphed into unimaginable forms. Eldridge Cleaver had become a fashion designer, inventing "penis pants." Jerry Rubin, of the Chicago Seven, was so trapped inside his own neuroses, he couldn't get out the door except to consult a guru or buy another bottle of celery juice. Abby Hoffman, another of "The Seven," was busted for cocaine in 1973 then disappeared. Ralph Nader proved to be a whining, elitist wimp. Huey P. Newton was pretty much a rambling street person. Strident feminists were now getting interviewed in slick glamour magazines. The counterculture was becoming mainstream. The times were a-changin.'

Nevertheless, some of our role models turned to productive yet progressive pursuits. Angela Davis was now writing and teaching. Tom Hayden of the Chicago Seven became a progressive politician. David Harris wrote a powerful, insightful analysis of the Vietnam War called *Our War* and then became a very good journalist. Luis Valdez and Peter Shumann were still doing effective theatre. Jack Weinberg, famous for his involvement in the Berkeley Free Speech Movement, went to work for Greenpeace. The vets form the Movement became the troops that have made America a more human place to live.

The same transition happened for the more regular movement folks. Many became lawyers or powerhouses in NGO agencies. Some, like me, became teachers, professors, and artists in every medium. Several became important folk and rock singers. Many photographers for the free street papers continued in journalism to do important documentary work. One of the young "movement chicks" I'd known as a fifteen-year-old high school girl became a Public Defender.

At that moment, I didn't know how to rate my life against my dreams. Suddenly, I had a filmic image of myself. I was like one of those crazed Japanese soldiers who'd come out of the jungle and went running down to a beach—now festooned with tourist bungalows. In my own movie, I'd break through the foliage in the ragged tatters of a blue work shirt and bellbottoms, yelling "Power to the People," brandishing the remains of an antiwar placard and a wrinkled copy of the Port Huron Statement.[92]

My salad was wilting in the Chico noonday sun.

No revolution has ever ended as it was envisioned. The future we were living in wasn't exactly what we'd hoped for, but it was better than it would have been if we'd left things alone. Had we not gotten out into the streets, "International Business" would not even be a choice in this young woman's universe, nor would her interest in it be taken seriously. She was a victim of the ruling class's campaign to disassociate the younger generation from history, to eclipse our legacy from the narratives in the news and in her textbooks. To make history distant and *impersonal*.

"What are you doing after the revolution?" was a question we'd often asked. Sitting on that sunny bench after my exchange with the college girl, I remembered the voice my girlfriend Sharon and I had heard in 1968 when she had asked what I wanted most. The same answer came to me sitting with the half-finished greens in my bowl. The voice had clearly said, "Myself."

The cold wind of my future was blowing in my face. I was packed and gone from Chico to the San Francisco Bay Area before my next rent check was due.

---

[92] The Port Huron Statement was the first manifesto of the Students for a Democratic Society (SDS), a group at the top of the FBI list. I had a copy at home.

SECTION X

YOU'RE NEVER THROUGH WHEN YOU THINK YOU ARE

"Oh, where have you been, my blue-eyed son?
And where have you been, my darling young one?

I've stumbled on the side of twelve misty mountains
I've walked and I've crawled on six crooked highways
I've stepped in the middle of seven sad forests
I've been out in front of a dozen dead oceans
I've been ten thousand miles in the mouth of a graveyard

[Chorus]
And it's a hard, and it's a hard, it's a hard, it's a hard
It's a hard rain's a-going to fall"

"A Hard Rain's A-Gonna Fall"
(Verse 1, Bob Dylan, 1962)

CHAPTER 43: "SEIZE THE TIME"

"It's the end of the world as we know it, and I feel fine."
(REM, 1987)

Up Against the 1980s

The Power Elite in Amerika had most assuredly learned a lesson from the Vietnam War. The lesson they'd learned was that in order to avoid another mass Anti-war movement, they needed to hide their imperialist wars in covert actions with secret campaigns and mercenaries financed with CIA slush funds.

From 1978 to 1989, the Amerikan imperialist agenda went underground to avoid another uprising against its heavy-handed gangsterism. However, the power brokers really didn't have to worry. Everybody was busy getting interviews, jogging, or doing CIA-imported cocaine. Nevertheless, they weren't taking any chances. Clandestine commandos and mercenaries were sent to destabilize democratic regimes around the globe: Chile (1973), Argentina (1976), Cambodia (1977), Bolivia (1980), Grenada (1983), El Salvador (1980-89), Angola, Mozambique, and a host of others. Our government (under both Democratic and Republican regimes) decided it was safer for them to pay the salaries to mercenary armies or to finance local counter-democratic juntas from secret slush funds thus avoiding the political fallout from headlines about American soldiers dying to protect private interests in these remote corners of the globe. The excuse for destabilizing local democratic regimes all over the planet was "American lives saved and keeping our quality of life intact."

Only the San Francisco Mime Troupe said anything about any of this.

Finally, the small news stories from page eight started to creep toward the front page. Around 1985, the CIA finally admitted that they'd been training covert groups and right-wing death squads "since the late 1960s." When my dad read this, he laughed out loud. He said that in 1940, when he was stationed with the Air Force in Panama, planeloads of men were flown in and taken in unmarked trucks to barracks at the other end of the base. They wore unmarked fatigues and ate separately in the mess hall. They were being trained by the OSS (Office of Strategic Services), forerunner of the CIA, in how to torture people who objected to a government that tortured its own people.

So much for our government coming clean.

****

In late 1978, after my sojourn in Chico, I moved back to the Bay Area and crashed with my old partner in crime, Bob B. Hobbs. (DOCUMENT #75: Bob and I, very stoned) I knocked around doing whatever gigs I could find. I was hired as the Technical Director/Resident Designer at the Eureka Theatre in San Francisco.

The Tech Director gig is a serious time commitment, especially for a small theatre. The Eureka Theatre, housed in the basement of a church in the gay-dominated Castro District, was an important company. It had been the spawning ground for some of Sam Shepard's early work. (DOCUMENT #76: Eureka Theatre, 16th and Market Streets, San Francisco)

Labor Troubles Closer to Home

In the 1980's, compensation for actors, designers, and technicians in the small 99-seat art theatres[93] had degenerated below survival level. Public arts grants or shared box office "take" were not enough to live on.

---

[93] The number of seats allowed by fire law in theatres with a single exit door, for storefront or "found space" theatres.

I was called by one company and offered a design gig for $250. Though admittedly, their budgets were stretched, this was not even enough to cover the expenses of taking the job.

I countered, "Can you make it $400?"

The production manager crowed, "Hey, the show's going to be reviewed by the big papers and the Village Voice from New York!"

I parried, "that may be true, but *you* called *me*."

This situation was developing in other cities such as well. Small progressive theatres fueled by the dedication of their left-leaning companies were experiencing a "death by rent" and thus their progressive message was being censored by economics.

I was working for another theatre that did an extra Monday night show as a benefit night for the technicians. I volunteered to collect tickets. The reservation list looked like it would be a full house. When people showed up, I discovered that the producers had given out over half the tickets as free "comps.

This pretty much tore the rag. The actors and technicians in the 99-seat art theatres formed a wildcat union, the Bay Area Theatre Workers Association (BATWA). This was not a big headline but it was an important t memento for those of us who were inside it. The mounting tension in this situation put actors and their director/producers, who had been their friends for years, on opposite sides of the struggle. Directors were sometimes living with acting company members as housemates or even lovers. Breakfast chats were strained, to say the least.

This crisis put myself (and several others) in a unique, uncomfortable position. As the stage carpenter/painter/lighting technician for some of these outfits, we were the hired crew and definitely on the labor side of the table. As *also* designers and/or the Tech Directors, a few of us also sat on the management/leadership side. Those of us in this hot seat had to choose which side we were on.

I went with the rank and file. Right out of nowhere, I became an organizer for the union. My experience with the Farmworkers and the anti-war movement paid off. I was promptly blackballed by the producers at several theatres. I had to meet the crew to "talk union" at parties or scoot into the theatre by the shop load-in door. Nobody got physical, but I could feel the chill. My name disappeared from "comp" ticket lists and crew call rosters. It felt like the bible-reading incident in seventh grade homeroom all over again.

Things came to a head when the producer at a "progressive" company refused to disclose how much he was taking off the top for his own salary. A threatened walkout at several theatres at the same time forced the art theatre producers to the bargaining table. Actor's Equity stepped in to represent the actors. Equity forced the small theatres to adopt minimum L.O.R.T. (League of Regional Theatre) pay scales, rehearsal pay, and emergency medical insurance for actors and crew… and no comps on benefit nights. You cannot neglect the survival needs of your cadre, even if they wear funny hats at work. At least now, we could afford a beer with our burritos.

The Battle over Political Content: The Price of Principle

In an era of theatres rapidly morphing themselves into bland companies with predictable cookie-cutter seasons to compete for grant money, the Eureka produced relatively progressive, important material. The Eureka had the legally required ninety-nine seats.[94] If seventy-five percent of the seats were filled four nights a week for a six-week run, approximately thirteen-hundred people were exposed to the message of each play. That's the size of many demonstrations. The Eureka Theatre felt like the right place at the right time. My very first show at the Eureka, David Mamet's *The Woods,* won a Bay Area Critics Circle Award for the set design. I also hired my childhood friend and co-conspirator from Fresno, Mark Loring—now living in San Francisco—as the Master Carpenter and Charge (senior) Painter for the company. We

---

[94] Dictated by fire codes for theatres with only two accessible exits.

were a loud, rambunctious team. I was actually doing what I'd hoped to do.

The Eureka Theatre Company held regular Monday night meetings where everyone shaped the direction of the theatre. There was pressure to do more homogenized "popular" shows to curry favor with corporate and government granting groups. This line of discussion put me in something of a snit. I rose to speak. "They're going to burn us someday for something. It might as well be for shows we're proud of, shows that say something we really believe in." Unfortunately, this turned into something of a prophecy.

Perhaps partly because of my harangues, the Eureka moved leftward the following season. The company mounted a production of Sam Shepard's *The Unseen Hand*, a great play about self-censorship in a repressive society. Several Bay Area Critics Circle Awards were handed out for this production, and I received the California State Drama-Logue Award[95] for the set. *The Unseen Hand* was my last show with the Eureka before I moved to a gig in Santa Cruz with the Bear Republic Theatre, another company known for progressive work.

Santa Cruz was the only city in America with a socialist mayor. At the Bear Republic, I served as TD and Resident Designer. I also designed lighting for a touring production of John DiFusco's powerful, important play, *Tracers,* about soldiers in Vietnam. This show went directly to the Kennedy Center in Washington, D. C., right after our run. They used much of my design there.

When I left San Francisco for Santa Cruz, I handed the design chair at the Eureka to Mark Loring. The next show the Eureka was doing was their most important political production to date, *The Jail Diary of Albie Sachs,* about a white lawyer (another Jew Boy) in South Africa who was jailed, tortured, and murdered for his defense of Black political prisoners. The show was an

---

[95] Given by the Critics Circle of *Drama-Logue Magazine* for the best set design in California for that year.

American premiere. It was a highly controversial, powerful play. This project would become far more than just stimulating theatre.

Before the opening of *Jail Diary*, the director and the actors all received death threats. Some moved in with lovers or friends. Because nothing had actually happened, the police wouldn't provide surveillance or protection. On the Sunday night of preview week, Mark left the theatre at around midnight. He'd been to a party then drove past the theatre around two a.m. on his way home. Nothing appeared to be amiss.

Early Monday morning, my phone rang in Santa Cruz. It was Mark.

"What the fuck, Joel! Man, oh, man! The theatre's gone!"

"Gone?"

"Gone! Burned down! The whole goddamned building!"

"How the hell?"

"The fire department says we did it! Everybody's a mess."

"Okay, I'll be up tomorrow."

I hung up in a cold sweat. Sometimes you seize the time. Sometimes it seizes you.

When I got to San Francisco, I met Mark beside the burned-out hulk that had been the church building. The interior of the early-twentieth-century structure, made of heavy timber fitted with rich wood paneling and plush velvet drapery, must have been a total loss within an hour. I looked down into a puddle-pocked, smoldering pit where the brick walls had collapsed in on the blackened ash of timbers. There was less than nothing left. It smelled of charred wood, dank water, and sadness. The dreams and sweat and love were gone. Mark was shattered. Everybody in the entire theatre community was in shock. (DOCUMENTS #77, #78: Eureka Theatre, before and after the fire, 1981)

The fire inspector declared that the fire started with a cloth thrown over the tabletop light board. Mark was absolutely certain this was not the cause. Standard procedure is to turn off the light board and then the breaker to each individual dimmer, and then to throw the master switch to the dimmer packs. This is three levels of safety. Mark was certain he'd followed this triple-level procedure that night. In fifty years of theatre, I've never known a TD or board op to forget this task, *ever*.

A few days later, the fire officials changed their story. They now said that the fire started with a small hot plate found in the paint room. Another bogus tale. *We never plugged that hot plate in because it didn't work.* Either they had no clue or they were covering something up. Nevertheless, the guilt over the possibility was eating Mark alive.

I returned to Santa Cruz. A few days later, the Board President of the Eureka Theatre called. He unraveled an unbelievable story. "The police think that the cause of the fire was arson."

"Holy shit! Street people?"

"It's much bigger than that. The FBI is involved."

"Why?"

"A radio-controlled incendiary device was found upstairs in the sanctuary along with the remains of a can of gasoline. It was left so that it could be found. It was of North Korean manufacture. According to the FBI, this gizmo is the 'calling card' of the South African Secret Police."

"Holy shit."

"My sentiments exactly."

"So, Mark or the crew didn't start the fire?"

"No. That's a cover story."

"Well that's some comnsolation."

"Evidently, they'd contracted a local neo-Nazi group to do the deed. They must have snuck in and hid while the door was left open during the show that night. A stakeout someplace nearby must have set it off around four o'clock in the morning.

"Why don't the cops come clean?"

"They figure that Americans aren't ready for international espionage, so we're taking the rap."

I gave my set of keys to the Board President to auction off for a thousand dollars to raise money. The company rallied. A production of *Jail Diary* opened at the Magic Theatre across town.

Everybody did their best, but the heart had been burned out of the company.

Sadly, my quip about "burning us for what we did" proved to be more on the money than anyone imagined. When you take on the forces of evil, they will let you know they've gotten your message.

CHAPTER 44: GHETTO TIME AND MORE TROUBLE

Just over a year after I moved to Santa Cruz to work with the Bear Republic Theatre, money problems forced the BRT to close its doors. However, before I left, I was called to do a few weeks' build in San Juan Bautista for *El Teatro Campesino*, about forty minutes south of "Sa' Cruz." I was welcomed by Luis and Lupe. It felt good to complete another circle. I then returned to San Francisco.

By 1980, the white theatre community was moving to the 'burbs in droves to reinvent themselves. They dumped their hippie wardrobes and relocated to suburban regional theatres that did middle-of-the-road shows. They paid better and offered steady work. Everybody had bills to pay. Nobody talked about the spiritual and political karma that was going unpaid. The art/progressive theatre scene was being gutted by the AIDS epidemic. Those who remained alive only came back up to the City to attend funerals.

I stayed in San Francisco. Shopping mall carpet gives me a headache. I found work with African American and Latinx theatre companies doing inherently important work. Everything they produced had an energetic edge. Their dedication to community was invigorating. As far as it went, I was accepted and treated as a member who belonged. You belong where your heart goes. It felt like home.

There were few trained Latinx or African American designers, stage painters, or carpenters for these theatres. Working in struggling nonwhite theatres that truly needed artistic support was deeply rewarding. Sometimes I even got paid. While I wasn't always marching in the streets or raging against the machine, I was never far from the struggle. They needed me, and I needed the work.

One of my gigs was as sometime resident designer and tech director for the Mission Cultural Center on Mission Street, the throbbing, honking, roaring, double-parked, bus-choked main artery of the *barrio*. I actually lived about two blocks away. This was my 'hood. The *Centro Cultural* was directly connected to the fight against police brutality in the neighborhood, American imperialism in Latin America, the farmworkers' ongoing struggle against pesticides, and the push for dignity and inclusion. I dealt with poets, actors, transvestites, city officials, junkies, street kids, painters, musicians, and schizophrenics. There's nothing like doing the lights for a drag queen Flamenco dancer high on mescaline to test the limits of performer-designer diplomacy.

I was directly *engaged* through my art with a dozen of these very grassroots companies.

For the next ten years, while working with these companies, I was also Designer in Residence at San Francisco's School of the Arts (SOTA).

The Lorraine Hansberry Theatre, a Typically Unique Experience

Between 1982 and 1993, I worked off and on with every African American and Latinx theatre company in the San Francisco Bay Area. Though I was the "other" in the company, we were partners engaged in doing worthwhile theatre. In this age of rampant careerism, the chosen sojourn of a Jewish activist working across racial lines was unique enough to gain the attention of the Jewish press in the Bay Area. (DOCUMENT #79, *Jewish Bulletin of Northern California,* Dec. 3, 1993)

The African American theatre companies were all run by dynamic personalities who were strong-willed, visionary captains. They had to be in order to deal with the bullshit they got from racist funding groups, city governments, and bureaucrats. They spoke the truth about the underside of the American experience. They and their audience were one.

Stanley Williams and Quentin Easter ran the San Francisco Loraine Hansberry Theatre like an ambulance careening the wrong way up a crowded street. For decades, these sometimes charismatic, sometimes troubling artistic commandos gathered both loyal supporters and confirmed enemies. The LHT always got attention but not always for the right reasons.

There was no need for political education for actors in the African American (or Latinx) theatre companies. Their politics was in their faces. The Black community truly loved and needed this theatre. The Hansberry was the ultimate shoestring operation. It was conjured up from a rag and a bone. It lived by the seat-of-your-pants, make-do tradition of "soul *rasquachismo*" and an on-the-outs, avant-garde ethic. Dumpster diving and alley cruising for props were SOP. Bringing in furniture from home and friends' apartments was normal. I grokked it completely. I was home again.

I had no place to live when I joined LHT, so I crashed on Stanley and Quentin's couch in their second-story walkup Victorian in the Fillmore District. I threw my food stamps into the collective pot. Their place was a never-ending depot for actors and dancers, painters and poets. It was like living in a Harlem Renaissance sitcom on weed. I learned how to cook black-eyed peas and greens with bacon as well as gumbo with hot links—definitely not recipes I would have picked up from Mom.

The Hansberry was consistently harassed. While I was with them, the fire marshal showed up *every night of every performance* for some of their shows. In my entire theatre career, I've never heard of such scrutiny, even of strip clubs that were rife with fire violations. We all knew what was happening. When the fire marshal showed up, we kept Stanley outside. He liked to get in people's faces. We would have been shut down.

The fire marshal never found out that we'd broken into the vacant storefront next door through the side door and turned it into a dressing and storage space. As Brother Stokely Carmichael said, "By any means necessary."

The stage space in our storefront theatre was about the size of a big living room. We brought the universe into that chamber. The first show of the season, a dance/performance text called *Transitions for a Mime Poem* by Owa was an *homage* to the powerful, painful relationship between George Jackson and Angela Davis. We'd been given the keys to the space mere weeks before the opening of the show. We worked around the clock to get the space and the show ready. The dynamics between the lighting and the setting for this poetry/movement pierce was crucial to the performance.

The setting included a double row of large, abstracted heads carved from a pair of cheap, cardboard-filled veneer sliding closet doors found in the alley behind the building. These were covered with a roughly "crunkled" and textured newspaper and mounted eight feet above the performance space. When the lighting shifted angles, they appeared to turn their heads. They were mounted to show that George and Angela's entire relationship was carried out under the scrutiny of the public eye of juries, prison guards, and the press. Their lives were entirely politicized. They never had a private un-judged moment. Though this effect was constructed quickly, it had been carefully conceived. Everything appeared to move. (DOCUMENT #80: *Transitions for a Mime Poem,* LHT, 1982)

The schedule was so tight that there was wet paint still on the set as the audience was coming in, so I turned on all the stage lights before the show and ran a fan hidden in the set to get it dry. Due to the breakneck schedule, we'd never actually rehearsed the show with light cues. The light board was a big, bulky mechanical hand-operated monster from the 1950s. Half the lights were household clip-light floods; the rest were beat-up theatricals brought in from God-knows-where. We were running by the seat of our pants with an audience there. I had the cues in my script but had to get them right as the play was going on. I felt through the cues, playing the lights as I improvised on the action. The lighting was definitely a performer in the piece. The two actor/dancers were giving me small looks and freeze moves that were obvious cues. After pulling off that opening, we all got shitfaced back at Stanley and Quentin's place.

The Same ol' Same ol' in Other Theatres

Working conditions at the Lorraine Hansberry were typical of the half-dozen African American theatres in the Bay Area. The story of the Black Repertory Theatre on the Oakland/Berkeley border is a classic tale of institutional racism. I was hired to design the first show in their new theatre.

The theatre that was finally built for them—after a wait of twenty-five years—was an enraging disappointment. Though it wasn't in the contract, in order to do get the show up, I had to do a "shakedown" of the space itself to be sure things were working. Every tech director who has to a put up a show in a new space has to exercise this function. Cables need to be run for backstage lights, speakers, and clear-com, shelving for storage has to be quickly provided, and the light plot for general lighting needs to be hung, circuited, and focused. Hundreds of feet of cable need to be rigged and hung as well because finding out what doesn't work and getting it fixed before opening all come into the bargain for the "shakedown process."

However, as a guest designer in the Black Rep's new space, this turned out to be way beyond the contracted job description. When I went in and turned on the work lights, I couldn't believe what I saw. Over the stage, nine bell-shaped industrial air ducts were affixed. When the air conditioning went on automatically, it was so loud that you couldn't hear the performers on stage. The access to the "off" switch was in a closet to which the theatre company was not given the key. I finally popped the pins on the hinges and pulled off the door to get the thing to stop.

The stage rigging was so substandard that it was dangerous. The stage floor upon which actors, dancers, and *children* were supposed to rehearse and perform was made of cheap, splintered, and pitted marine plywood. There was no time or money to face it over with more serviceable material. Me and another guy spent two all-nighters spreading ten gallons of paint to seal it and hold down the splinters before anyone could be allowed to walk on it.

Instead of the standard, true velour stage drapery, they had been handed cheap, hotel-style window "shears" in a hideous orange-brown. These were so thin that they fluttered like laundry in a hurricane when the air conditioning automatically clicked on.

The nightmare continued. The light pipe over the audience was hung without stiffeners, so each time a light was hung on it, the new instrument would change the balance of the pipe. It would with the weight of the new instrument and rotate all the other lights out of focus. They were not even provided a genie lift to get to this pipe and fix the problem.

Due to an incompetent design approved and "inspected" by someone in the city of Berkeley's planning office, the entire lighting power system was a dangerous fire risk. What they were given was substandard and wasted twenty-five percent of the amperage. It totally violated safety regulations. In all my years of theatre, I have never seen a space built for a white theatre group so poorly equipped. It was a blatant case of an inferior facility passed off to a deserving community.

The New Opportunity

The work I was contributing both artistically and politically through these companies was as important as *El Teatro* twenty years before. Nevertheless, continuing with these theatres was always a stretch. Therefore, I took an offer for a full-time Arts Residency at the newly formed San Francisco School of the Arts.

The director at SOTA believed in doing plays that dealt with the deeper concerns of young people. Progressive plays from the classic repertoire were as radical as we could get and still stay out of trouble. However, for this audience, they were a major ideological engine. Before I was hired, he had done *Runaways*, about runaway kids on the streets resorting to prostitution to survive. We did *Diary of Anne Frank,* about a Jewish family in hiding as Anne comes of age during the horror of the Nazi Holocaust, and *Children's Hour*, about the cruelty of children copying adult homophobic behavior. And, of course, *Romeo and Juliet* about the dangers of thoughtless hatred and love fueled by ingrained family loyalties. What more important audience could there be for these plays than young people who were soon to be voting and parenting, and who were old enough to be soldiers or activists?

Ironically, the theme in *Runaways* became personal. My daughter, then attending SOTA, announced at dinner that one of her friends had been kicked out of his house because his family discovered he was gay. Jason had been living on Polk Street, where the male prostitutes and runaways go. I got up from the table and drove down there. I found Jason with some other boys on a busy corner. I pulled over and rolled down the window.

"Jason!"

"Mister Eis!"

"Get in the car!"

"You know what this looks like, don't you?"

"I don't give a fuck. Get in the car!"

Sometimes you march with a crowd. Sometimes you go out all alone. Your action or inaction always changes the lives you touch. Jason lived with us for several months and returned to school until he was propositioned by one of his own teachers. He never returned to school. Eventually, he found a safe situation, living with a kind man in the San Francisco Bay Area.

The SOTA director also supported the production of two of my own scripts, *The Village and the Dragon*,[96] a story of children who save their village from a corrupt town council, and *Ceremonies,* a rock musical about parents and children coming to

---

[96] Ten years later, Sheri Young, an African American high school freshman I cast in the role of the water seller in this show, founded the African American Shakespeare Company in San Francisco, giving African American actors an opportunity to play important classical roles. She had heard from one of her professors who had attended the Santa Barbara workshop and was inspired to rekindle this idea.

respect each other's worldview. This show was inspired by the fateful, revealing conversation with my own father ten years before.

Because the task of the political organizer is to change minds, there can be no better situation than high school theatre to do so. This situation provided a great opportunity to introduce ideas in action in the classroom as well. In our program, young women of sixteen or seventeen regularly managed and ran entire musicals with hundreds of light, sound, curtain, and scene-shift cues carried out on their command by a small army of fellow students. I showed one young woman that with her full focus, she could drive a three-inch screw through a stack of wooden planks. She finished the job and announced to the whole room, "Maybe I *can* go to medical school!"

****

I now began to write and produce work for my own theatre, the New Company. We produced a rock version of *King Ubu* and a new show, *All the Right Moves*, a prophetic show about a Kennedy/Nixon/Ford-like president who pardons himself for murder. The New Company also did a professional version of my script, *Ceremonies,* as a benefit for a shelter for runaways. It was great work ideologically and good artistically, but I lost my shirt on every show.

During this hectic decade, I lived in the Latinx *barrio*. I marched with my neighbors against the death squads in El Salvador and then marched with my students and my own teenage daughter against the war in Iraq. Marching with my own family and young comrades provided a sense of depth and connection to the act of taking over the street to make a better world. It was the same but different from when I was one of the younger movement pioneers. I knew this was something of an adventure for them. It was something we shared but each experienced in different ways.

Then, as we turned the corner and faced the black-suited riot cops and brown-clad deputies with clubs in their hands, itching for some action, the newsreel changed. The awareness of danger and harm—of the price of activism—gained a new coinage. The responsibility of a movement to accept the result of the rhetoric always must be weighed against the action taken. In this case, with the government trying out an exercise of imperialism on a new generation to see if the younger people would let them get away with it, the rage in the streets was right. A return to considering the price of activism was the right thing for me at the time as well. The cops were also new at this and seemed surprised at the size of the demos. Luckily, this time they let us pass by, and the plotters in Washington learned that the new generation had paid attention to the lessons from the last revolution.

A Wonderful Reconnection

While at SOTA in 1987, I did freelance lighting work. I was doing the design for Sha-Sha Higby, a dance/performance artist at a theatre in San Anselmo, a town fifteen miles north in Marin County, who was notorious for jokes about meditation and "mindfulness."

Sha-Sha said a friend named "Bright Wolf" had offered to help with the lights. I just hoped this guy wasn't a total stoner who'd walk away to talk to the mushrooms when I needed him to hold the ladder. I pulled up to the theatre space and there, sitting on the brick wall, was Jim *Bertholf*, my old friend from San Jose State in 1964 and again during the Soledad Brothers project in 1970. He had changed his handle to the more easily pronounced Jim *Brightwolf*. I hadn't heard from him for more than fifteen years. I was so glad to see him that I hugged him and cried like a lost child.

Jim had recently returned from South Africa where he had smuggled an anti-Apartheid Black theatre company into the USA and gotten them asylum. Jim was just then working with the Sanctuary Movement for refugees from El Salvador and with Bay Area antiwar boat owners, planning a seagoing guerilla action using small sailboats and yachts to disrupt the United States Navy's annual Fleet Week in San Francisco Bay. Only millionaire ex-hippies could come up with such a plan. During Fleet Week, these plucky little yachtsmen sailed their tiny craft between the big Navy ships, blowing air horns and flying banners. Leafleters circulated among the crowd onshore. Their shenanigans made a mess of the Navy's maneuvers.

Jim's unorthodox, pirate-esque, David and Goliath demonstration made the national news. Jim's ability to energize political activism through any and all means available belies the excuses that the tools for activism aren't at hand. In light of my reconnection with Jim, I had an itch that I was back on the FBI's radar. It didn't matter.

A New Character in My Life

In 1988, I was a single father with my teenage daughter living with me. I had a vacant room in our apartment, so I put an ad in the *San Francisco Chronicle* for a housemate. The ad noted, "Housemate wanted, male or female, anti-Bush, non-smoking, pro-cat." I really wanted a woman in the spare room so my daughter would feel safer. A few days later, I got a call from the office of Herb Caen, San Francisco's most famous columnist since Mark Twain. Herb wanted to quote the ad in his column as something "typically San Francisco." I gave them the go-ahead. It appeared with a brief quip about me as a typical San Francisco resident with typical quirks

This is how I met Toni Paulette Labori. Toni, who responded to the ad, was a sweet-spirited woman with a quiet demeanor that hinted at something deeper. (DOCUMENT #81: Toni Labori, hanging out, Berkeley, 1989) We were married nine years later.[97] We're still married. It's really cool.

Toni tells me, "I grew up in a household both a bit bohemian and eccentric. My mother was a legal secretary who did volunteer work for the John F. Kennedy campaign, and my stepfather was a Cuban-born musician who was pro-Castro. I grew

---

[97] In 1997, we invited Herb Caen to the wedding.

up with talk of politics always around, which exploded with the Watergate hearings. Starting in my teens, I volunteered with the Democratic Party in my hometown of Santa Barbara. Then in my twenties, I worked with Sane Freeze and did support work for sufferers in the AIDS crisis, as well as Amnesty International and Doctors without Borders."

Despite the fact that Toni is fourteen years younger than I am, we have a strong political *simpatico*. Toni is extremely well read. Her leftist politics and her feminism are not tied to a particular party or faction. They are grounded in direct expressions of empathy. We have marched together against the death squads in El Salvador, Tiananmen Square, and the war in Iraq, defended bookstores against right-wing protests, and donated to Doctors Without Borders.

She tells a great story of walking home alone after a demonstration against the Iraq War in San Francisco. "Joel was working late in a theatre in San Francisco. There was a curfew after the second big demonstration against the invasion of Iraq. Seeing that I was walking alone on my way to our flat in the Mission District, three Queer women came over and offered to walk me home. On the way, we stopped in front of the lit-up windows of one of those Mission shops that had everything from inexpensive kitchenware to lingerie, which was a bit on the gaudy side. We were laughing at the various undergarments and talking politics. Suddenly, four cops on motorcycles surrounded us and demanded to know what we were doing out in violation of the curfew. One of the women said, 'Oh, officer, you know how we girls can't help but stop and shop for lingerie!' The cops remounted their bikes and roared away. We were not arrested."

Running a bookstore puts both of us in the crosshairs of political discussions daily. Though she usually holds her own with discretion, I have heard her show more than one strident right-winger the door. She is my kitchen table cadre for advice and support.

CHAPTER 45: UNDER MY OWN STARS: SOME LATE REVELATIONS

It was not until the early 1990s that my Uncle Joe and Aunt Pauline shared stories about my parents' political involvement during the Great Depression and in Washington, D. C., during the McCarthy Era. Many of their friends were progressives, laborites, and "worse." Uncle Joe told me that as a youngster, I'd played in his backyard with ten-year-old Carl Bernstein, whose parents, heavily involved in union organizing, were family friends. My own folks had mentioned their friendship with a man named Arty Manoff, a television writer blacklisted during the McCarthy Era. I'd often wondered if their connections went deeper.

My dad had told me vaguely of his life in the years before joining the Army in 1937. My Uncle Joe now filled in the details. The full story was that Dad wanted to join the Partisans fighting the Fascists in Spain. It was 1934. He was just out of high school. He'd done a short stint with the Communist Labor Theatre. Their mother forbade him to go to Spain, so he ran away and hitched around the country instead. He claimed to have been at the docks for the general strike in San Francisco in 1934. He said he'd shared a ham sandwich with Harry Bridges. With his affiliation with this specific Communist affiliated labor theatre in the mid-1930s, and his passion for the Partisan struggle in Spain, it was clear my father probably had a Communist Party affiliation.

Only a few years before this conversation with Uncle Joe, I'd told Mom I was working on a production of *Room Service*, a 1937 farce made famous as a film by the Marx Brothers in 1938. She casually remarked that she'd seen the show with the man she dated before she met my dad. He was the reviewer for the *People's Daily World*, the Communist newspaper. My folks had been in deep even before they knew each other. This must have been part of the common ground of their lives.

An Opportunity in Diaspora

I'd left my gig at SOTA in 1991. The period from 1991 to 1996 was a stormy one. Opportunities to work for socially relevant theatre dropped to near zero, but I needed to earn a living. I was living the life of an artist/wage slave, putting miles on my car and eating a lot of burritos and Chinese food from strip mall takeout spots. The dearth of companies doing relevant theatre encouraged me to write, direct, design, and produce my own work. The shows all got quirky reviews and lost money, though I made sure the cast was paid. It felt good, but I couldn't keep it up. I looked into getting the now-required MFA and qualifying for university teaching.

I needed to invigorate my own work with an approach that appealed to a younger audience. I opted for an MFA in Performance Art/New Genres at the San Francisco Art Institute, the best art school west of the Mississippi. Performance art was becoming more theatrical *and* more political, taking up the banner where traditional theatre had left it on the way to the funder's board meeting.

My study at SFAI focused on the fact that younger audiences had changed their expectations of what they wanted from an art experience. Interaction with the SFAI students' wildly nontheatrical slant kicked my ass in terms of creative approach. They were also the perfect sample audience for my current and future work. One Friday night, I got a latte and took myself out to the balcony deck over the SFAI cafeteria. It was a clear, cool evening. The northern end of the Golden Gate Bridge was just visible beyond the hills. My dad had died the year before. I felt very much on my own. I mused, *Art School at fifty years old. I am in another full circle. What I have to say to this new audience is my dad's advice—as artists, not to take the bait of commercialism.*

For the art students trying to find themselves and what they had to say, jockeying to become "The Next Best Thing" was a very seductive rabbit hole. Nothing gets in the way of an artist finding themselves more than judging their work against the current flavor of the month. It dooms you. You will always be behind someone else's vision. Much like the work of *El Teatro* for farmworkers, the play created in Westwood, and the productions for students at SOTA, I sought to make work that spoke to the needs of my immediate audience. It had to come out of my own current struggle and search for self-awareness.

Commentary on "the game of success" became a major theme in my work, highlighting the insidious encroachment of careerism into artistic choices. I focused four or five major projects exploring this theme. For my final MFA piece, I filled the entire space of SFAI's main gallery with an interactive "game of success" for artists, played out in real time. (DOCUMENT #82: "The Big Game" interactive sculpture at S. F. Art Institute, 1997)

As in a table board game, the players tossed giant dice into the air. The game table was the real world. They then moved on the game board that covered the floor in order to "win the game" and become "successful." There were punishments for landing on a bad square and unexpected advancement for landing on a "Chance" square. The "Heredity" squares were real wild cards. Quite a few players discovered that playing the game was eerily close to their own decision-making process for their future careers. Fittingly, the mural on the wall of this large space was made by Diego Rivera, the renowned political artist with Labor/Communist affiliations who leveraged the world through his art. Diego and I made a good team.

Ironically, while completing my school projects, I revised, directed, and designed a professional production of *Hamlet*, the watchword show of my life.

From my exposure to installation and performance art, I'd absorbed a new approach to what could be said and done in text-based performance and beyond. I'd worked in large theatres, important art theatres, and had teaching experience. I'd stayed true to my purpose as an activist and artist.

I now needed a paying gig…again.

CHAPTER 46: OFF TO DO MY THING, SOMEWHERE

My first teaching post was at an almost unknown university just outside of Atlanta, Georgia. To say the least, rural Georgia was vastly different from "leafy-left," organic California. The students in Georgia pour Coca-Cola over their morning sugar cereal instead of milk. Grits are served with everything. There is a local delicacy called "fried pie" made by deep-frying a sugarcoated Hostess fruit pie. 'Nuff said.

Any progressive movement in university education had dried up years before.[98] Amazingly, despite the unlikely location, I made a great connection. Dr. Stephen Earnest was a young, dynamic director who shared my love of Brecht. His aesthetic was based on dissolving the traditional boundary between the audience, the experience, and the text. We were a pair of fish who were definitely up the wrong creek. With somewhat savage abandon, we made the most of the situation while we could.

We both firmly believed that the rural and suburban, predominantly white students—many of whom were the first in their families to go to college—needed to be brought up to speed for the fast-approaching twenty-first century. We also believed that in order for them to understand theatre, they had to experience it as

---

[98] While at this teaching assignment, I reconnected with my older cousin and mentor, Dr. Doris Adler. Doris was retired emeritus from the Chair of the English Department at Howard University. When Doris was a young professor in the 1960s, she had hidden radical students and Black Panthers from Howard on the run from the FBI in her farmhouse in Virginia. The house had once belonged to an Abolitionist who had hidden slaves escaping across the Potomac to Washington, D. C., before and during the Civil War.

participants. Among the shows we did in two years, two were highly political in an unorthodox way. They generated an unexpected experience of engagement for both the performers and the audience, much like that of street theatre. The last of these was the Millennium Project, performed just weeks before the end of the millennium. We may not have been smashing the State, but we rattled the placid cages for an unsuspecting audience in desperate need of broadening their perspective.

Millennium Piece

Millennium Piece was very much a direct application of my work at SFAI. It was a large performance art/installation piece far beyond traditional theatre in every aspect. It was performed in the school's gymnasium by nearly three-hundred students from our combined "Intro to Theatre" classes. It was a meta-theatrical, ritual/historical work about the migration of peoples, a dominant human experience for the last thousand years, hence the title.

It was about why and how our students' ancestors got here. The common experience of our ancestors puts all of us in the same boat. Unless you are First People, we all have a common past of adjustment from political upheaval, famine, or war. *Millennium Piece* was supposed to do what progressive works of art do—change the perspective of the actors and the audience. With almost three-hundred students in this crazy project, word of mouth was all the advertising we needed.

Our classes were divided into smaller rehearsal units that performed specific actions, much like the work of Anna Halprin, that were moving in their simplicity. One group of former cheerleaders (we had about twenty of those from the sororities) led a section of the audience in a cheering contest with the succession of slogans used to gain support for the wars of the last century and a half.

Another group was assigned to fill a backpack with what they would carry if they had to migrate from another country, much as their own ancestors had to do. They had to take these items out and show them to segments of the audience as they progressed around the gymnasium and stopped to rest. The point of this performance art/theatre event was to illuminate for the students and the audience that it was their ancestors—and now them—who made history, not "great leaders." It showed that they were now bearing witness to times when participation was essential.

We added in a worldwide-connected live chat with communications projected on the big overhead scoreboard, tying this backwater town into the whole planet at that moment in history. Another group carried "junk bells" made of gallon cans filled with rocks. They grouped around the three-story scaffold tower at the center of the room and clanged them in an "amen" litany at the end of a poem about the children killed in all the migrations and wars brought on by adult politics. This was quite powerful.

In the finale, the three-story scaffold tower was rolled to the center of the room. The entire audience had been handed hundreds of colored ribbons as "tickets" when they entered the gym. They were then asked to bring their colored ribbons down to the performance area and tie them to the giant rolling tower, making a wish for their own future and for the world. When this was finished, the tower was festooned with hundreds of colored ribbons. The message/experience of the *Millennium Piece* was that history is personal.

Saving One Man's Life

Toni and I bought a home in Georgia in a middle-class neighborhood with firefighters, schoolteachers, small shopkeepers, and nurses all around us. Our property was so large that I had to hire a man with a small tractor to mow the lawn. I felt downright *residential*. There were perhaps two or three Black families in the enclave, and there was a palpable undercurrent of friction. One white neighbor said, "This neighborhood is gettin' too *dark* for me if you get my meanin'…" I can only image the shock if they ever figured out that yet *another* Jewish family lived right next door to us.

There was, however, one welcome Black visitor. When the weather warmed up and the roaring katydids came out in the woods, Joseph, a college student from West Africa, brought his ice cream truck around. Some of the families would not didn't let their children come out to the truck.

Aside from his very, very African, very blue-blackness, Joseph advertised his *otherness* in a way that seriously hindered his business. One evening, my chance came to help him fix his blunder.

Joseph spoke English with precise pronunciation and an African lilt. "How you doing today?"

"Fine, Joseph. How about you?"

"Okay, I guess." He leaned over and spoke in a conspiratorial tone. "You are like me. Not from around here."

"That's true."

"I see some children never come down to de truck. I wish I could do sometin' bout dat."

I seized the opening. "Joseph, do you know about the Civil War in America?"

"I read about dat. In the last century, de North and de South? About slavery of Black people."

"Yes. The South lost the war. Anything that reminds them of this defeat makes them *very* angry." My concern for Joseph was by no means unfounded. I'd seen clear evidence there were active cells of the KKK in the area.

"What does dat have to do wit my truck?"

"Joseph, the song you're using, 'Battle Hymn of the Republic,' was the anthem of the Northern Army. It's one of the most hated songs they know."

Joseph's gaffe was potentially very dangerous. "Oh, my goodness! Thanks. Here, have a Fudgesicle on me."

He did change his tune. Literally. The next time he came rolling through, his truck was blaring *Yankee Doodle Dandy*! I was out to his truck like a hornet on a mission. I stuck my head in the window and yelled, "Joseph, that's the other song they hate! For God's sake, play *Dixie*!"

****

My students at the university in Georgia complained that they were not finding their graded papers in the box by my door. The box was clearly labeled. I talked to the head janitor.

"Hey Ellis, my students don't find their papers in the box outside my door. I labeled the boxes. What's going on?"

Ellis sighed and said, "Them labels don't do no good, Mister Eyes." Ellis pronounced my name "Eyes."

"Why not?"

"Probly a third of my crew can't read or write. They think them papers in the box is trash."

I sent a letter to the governor of the state demanding a literacy program be available to these men and women as part of their employment at the university. I'll bet a plate of cheese grits that word of this letter got back to my boss. This protest was probably the torch for my burning.

For this and a list of unacceptable conditions and incidents, Steve Earnest, myself, and three other professors—over half of the department—resigned at the end of the year. I was sure that anyplace else would be better.

A Coffee Break

My next teaching gig was at a posh private women's college in Lynchburg, Virginia. The town was named for the owner of the biggest plantation in the area. It's where we get the word "lynching" from, based on his reputation for how he treated rebellious slaves.

One day, I was having coffee in the sun out on the dock behind the scene shop. Winston, the head janitor, liked the dock for a quiet smoke away from the students. Winston was easily pushing seventy. He'd lived in that town his entire life. I told him of my experiences in the 1960s. I then asked him what I thought was an innocent question. "What are those half-buried stone walls in the park on Rivermont Avenue by the James River?"

His face grew somber and clouded. His cigarette burned, neglected in his hand as he unwound his memory. "That used to be th' swimmin' pool for white folks. Never no colored could get in there...that is, 'til the Civil Rights Act. Then the City was forced to de-segregate evrythin'."

"So why's it buried?"

"They done that to keep from sharin' it with Black folks. They said that if Black boys got in the water with pretty white girls, they'd lose control and do their boy business into the water." Now Winston laughed. "They was afraid that the white girls would all get pregnant from the Black boys' stuff in the water."

I couldn't believe what I was hearing. Winston must have been a young man when he endured the ugliness of this enraging snub. Then I remembered that there were country clubs in Fresno when I was a teen that did not allow Jews to belong or use the facilities as guests. "Wasn't it a chlorinated pool?"

"Good sense didn't matter. They filled it in so nobody could use it instead."

His cigarette had gone out. His eyes were filled with tears. "I got to get back to work. See you another time."

For a Black man in America, there are no innocent questions about the past.

When I resigned from that school after one year, the Dean had twenty-two pending lawsuits on her desk for her procedural and ethical violations from faculty. That was thirty percent of the full faculty. Her own secretary quit a week later.

Florida: Gunplay in an Art Gallery

My next gig was as design teacher and resident designer at Florida International University (FIU) in Miami. My predecessor had kissed a female student—uninvited—on the mouth. There were witnesses. There was some kind of door-slamming skirmish between my fellow teachers in the faculty hall almost every week. There are no really good punch lines about any of this.

My redemption from this unhealthy place was my involvement with the arts scene in the *Cubano* community in Little Havana. I became friends with the owner of a gallery on *Calle Ocho* in the Little Havana neighborhood. His gallery showed progressive political work from all over South and Central America.

The owner, Emilio, was showing a contemporary Latino artist whose work was critical of the powerful anti-Castro group that dominated political life in *Cubano* Miami. His work criticized their reactionary *Cubano* patriotism, like using the Cuban flag to decorate used-car lots, women in Cuban flag bikinis, etc.

The third Friday of every month was "cultural night" in the Cuban district, with live music, food, and people-watching. The opening night of his art show was held on one of these cultural nights. The gallery was packed with attendees out into the street. An anti-Castro group charged into the gallery, dragged the artist out to the sidewalk, and beat the shit out of him in front of hundreds of onlookers. The next night, they drove by and shot out the floor-to-ceiling glass windows. The cops did nothing.

Somebody was missing the point about the free speech thing in America.

A few days later, I had lunch with Emilio. He said, "No one from the press, the civil rights groups, or the arts community has come to talk to me about what happened. Only you."

Emilio put down his fork. Cubans don't stop eating for just anything. He said, "Are you an artist?"

"Yeah, I do performance work, sculpture, installation."

His expression improved to an impish grin. "Do you want to do a show in my gallery?"

Toni and I did a performance/installation called "Shooting/Gallery." We set up a small carnival booth with a paint-gun. Thirty feet away, a Bill of Rights with a target printed on it was stapled to a sheet of plywood. For a dollar, anyone could "take a shot at the Bill of Rights." (DOCUMENT #83:

"Shooting/Gallery" interactive sculpture, Miami, 2001) On the next cultural night, the gallery was packed again. Even a Cuban-American member of the Miami City Council put a dollar in the bucket and took a plug at the Bill of Rights. I was the only non-Latinx artist to show in the Cuban community. We expected trouble, but it didn't come.

****

In 2004, I'd published a well-received book on the first play in English in America, *Ye Bare and Ye Cubbe*, performed in a bar in Pungoteague, Virginia in 1665.[99] This little-noted event was, in fact, the very first act of public protest against colonial rule *and* the first political theatre in America. It turns out that I'd been in good company all along. American theatre had its roots in political protest.

At my university posts, my rapport with the students was always good. My design work was praised by the press and my peers. Because the dozen or more designs I produced each year were copyrighted, I was always one of the most published professors on campus. However, all was not well.

Leavin' Dodge City

There's a biting quip about university teaching: "The infighting is so vicious in university politics because the stakes are so low." Sadly, much like my treatment at the hands of Dr. Walker at Fresno State in my graduate school years, I discovered that this pernicious behavior was more pervasive than I ever imagined.

Any mention by me at faculty meetings of "relevance" as a criterion for seasonal play selection caused a grim silence. Even though these theatre departments were in a pivotal position as a progressive engine for their communities, this opportunity—and

---

[99] "*A Full Investigation of the Historic Performance of the First Play in English in the New World: Ye Bare and Ye Cubbe, 1665.*" Joel D. Eis, MFA, Edwin Mellen Press, © 2004.

responsibility—for the most part was squandered. Concern for this criterion put me in the crosshairs of the martinets who ran these programs like personal fiefdoms.

The choice of plays for the season by individual directors was not founded on any criteria or policy. While institutional racism and racial incidents continued, homophobic violence increased, global warming grabbed our concern, and America perpetrated micro-wars in Afghanistan and Iraq, the rare project that drew headlines for its relevance shined the spotlight on the paucity of the rest of the season.

My enthusiasm for these toxic work environments eroded like a Popsicle in a microwave. Sadly, my experience was not unique. This was probably why those before me left and those after me continue to do so.

In 2005, I left full-time university teaching.

Toni found a bookstore for sale in the perfect small town just north of San Francisco. The wheel turned again.

CHAPTER 47: AFTERWARD AND NOW

"If you don't like the news,
go out and make some of your own."
(Scoop Nisker, radio broadcaster and political pundit)

Bringin' It All Back Home: Retail and Progressive Politics

In 2005, Toni and I returned to the San Francisco Bay Area. We bought a small bookstore in the progressive, laid-back community of San Rafael in Marin County. (DOCUMENT #84: Rebound Bookstore, San Rafael, CA) The joke is that "the flag of Marin County is the yoga mat." Ironically, the Marin County Courthouse in San Rafael was the site of the tragic hostage-taking attempt by Jonathan Jackson and the terrible police massacre.

To say the least, this was a radical change in my life. While I didn't see myself joining the local Vietnam War-era gray-hairs in old college sweatshirts waving hand-painted peace placards at cars going by, I have to admit that they are a reminder that speaking up and speaking out is always in fashion. When the Black Lives Matter Movement came around, these old folks were at the front of the march. Nevertheless, at nearly sixty years of age, I wasn't fit to run from the cops.

I taught school part-time at several high schools and Sonoma State University. I also served as Properties Designer in Residence for the Main Shakespeare Company and a few small, local art theatres. The lion's share of my energy, however, went into the store. The bookstore is our weapon. A bookstore is inherently a progressive enterprise, especially when the spirit is structured with that in mind. Rather than padding off into the sunset from social interaction, I now had the opportunity to be more directly engaged in a community than I'd been in years. This post on the barricades made sense for the times.

We provide a meeting place for many causes. Every day I am able to engage in political discussions with my customers. At roughly twelve to twenty people a day, six days a week, by the end of the week, I might have exchanges with as many people as attend a small political rally.

Sometimes the exchange is viciously rewarding. Shortly after we opened the store, we got a regular customer who always bought the most right-wing, conservative books we had and asked us for more. He was short, sported a "Yosemite Sam" handlebar mustache, and rode a Harley. Bowlegged and gravel-voiced, he was almost a cartoon of himself. One day, we had a little chat.

Toni said to him, "You know we're not conservatives."

Yosemite Sam said, "Aw, hell yeah. Y'all own a bookstore. All the bookstores I've ever been in is owned by lib'rals."

I said to him, "Doesn't it occur to you that the people who actually live by the principles of free speech are always liberals?"

I may have gone too far. We never saw "Yosemite Sam" again. Then again, maybe I went just far enough…

We discovered that even in our "leafy-left" county, operating a bookstore involved some unexpected risk. The Bush/Cheney administration had enacted an executive order requiring all libraries *and bookstores* to report the names of people who acquire books on a long list of "subversive" subjects, such as the Qur'an, Islamic movements, Middle Eastern politics in general, Marxism, home chemistry projects, or military training manuals. We never made such a list. We also sold books online. That information was surely harvested by the computer equivalent of a guy in a basement with headphones. If they busted us, the publicity would be terrific for business.

The bookstore has succeeded in becoming a cultural engine for the local progressive community. We post political posters in the window. We always do a Black History Month window and a Women's History Month window. Books on relevant issues are constantly displayed. Even the gardening section is heavy into organic, pesticide-free, sustainable gardening manuals. Beyond "Banned Books Week," we display banned books in the window for a full month and cover the windows with large posters of the entire list of banned books.

Through a young intern working in the store who "came out" to us, we worked to provide a safe place for the local LGBTQ teen community to hang out. They met, draped themselves all over the furniture, and read their spoken word stuff in the store on several occasions. This was one of the most important things we have ever done.

We do author readings and lit events. We were involved with the local "Step Up to College" programs for Latinx kids. On the day of Trump's inauguration, we held a well-attended public reading of the Constitution. This turned out to be far more prophetic than we could have imagined.

As has been the miracle that recurs throughout my life, the bookstore has generated full circles of reconnection. Both Daniel Abdal-Hayy Moore, former director of the Floating Lotus Opera Company (now deceased), and David Harris, my old high school friend and Resistance comrade (who lives in a town nearby), have been visitors to the bookstore.

A Progressive Theatre Gig Out of the Blue

In 2010, I received a phone call from the University of Maryland at Salisbury on the Eastern Shore Peninsula just north of Accomack County, Virginia. They commissioned me to write a play about my book on *The Bare and Cubbe*, the first play in English in the New World that I'd proven was the first play in America, the first public demonstration against colonial rule, *and* the first instance of political theatre in America.

I said yes.

I wrote a play for them about what had driven their ancestors—ordinary citizens—to commit a dangerous act of protest against an oppressive autocratic regime. It would show that the theatre could be a valuable weapon for change. The show was performed on February 26, 2012. (DOCUMENT #85: Performance, *The Play in August,* University of Maryland, Salisbury) This theatrical event raised the audience's awareness of the tradition of political involvement.

    Soon after, I learned that at least three different theatre companies in America had transformed my academic history monograph into viable plays on the theme of citizen participation in democracy. You never know when your voice will be heard. Toni and I returned to California feeling we'd made an important contribution to the cause of citizen participation. We had no idea how important this was to become.

CHAPTER 48: BACK IN THE SADDLE AGAIN...

While our involvement is not as newsworthy as it had been many years ago, each of these actions is important in the here and now. With the nomination of Donald Trump in 2016, the telescope of history was turned around, and everything in our political past came back into frightening close-up focus. We couldn't close the store to go to the many marches in other towns, but there were marches for immigrant rights, Black Lives Matter, and other issues that went right past our door on the main street of town. We stepped out on the street, raised a fist, and joined it as it went by the store.

Other opportunities came my way. For the fiftieth-anniversary reunion of the student strike at San Francisco State, I was asked to put together a reading event for the commemoration. Afterward, I got a chance to visit classes at SFSU and interact with young Black and brown students. I heard complaints that their own Black and brown professors had morphed into craven careerists disconnected from the community, chasing tenure exactly like their white counterparts. They'd become the *vendidos* (sellouts) that *El Teatro* had portrayed in our skit fifty years before.

In short order, there was a need to get out on the line again. One Friday, I got a phone call from my old Fresno Resistance organizing friend and co-member of *El Teatro,* Don Teeter. Don, now living only a few miles away in Berkeley, was deeply involved with Revolution Books, a leftist bookstore near U. C. Berkeley and a meeting center for political coalitions of all stripes and colors.

"Hey Joel! This is Don over in Berkeley."

"What's shakin', Don?"

"The right-wing assholes are going to storm Revolution Books and try to trash it again. Last time it was pretty hairy. We could use some bodies on the line."

We had an investment in protecting their bookstore. After all, we could be next. "Hey Toni, the local *Fascisti* are going to try and trash Revolution Books. Wanna got over and help defend it?"

She blinked. "Could we get arrested?"

"Yes."

"What time do they want us there?"

A group of perhaps forty or fifty folks arrived to defend the store. We split up to watch the two entrances. There was no telling how many of the right-wingers would show up. The mob of several dozen who'd arrived a few weeks before had been rowdy but unsuccessful. They might be itching to even the score. The last time, there were some real *chingasos* (fistfights). When we got there, about sixty cops in full riot gear with machine guns patrolled near the bookstore. There were more cops in vans up the block. This could be some serious shit.

This time, the right-wing contingent that showed up consisted of a single Fascist drag queen and about two dozen supporters. Across the street, s/he prattled on for the media, strutted like a turkey in horn-rimmed glasses, big hair wig, and muumuu, then pranced up the block and disappeared. Only in Berkeley, California, can you be faced with a threat from a Fascist drag queen in a paisley muumuu. However, it could have been far worse. Toni and I got ourselves a latte and went home.

I resolved to offer my skills as a strategist, public speaker, and published writer.

I connected with Rosa del Ducca, an ex-GI who'd won her struggle for C. O. status while in the service and was then discharged. Rosa was organizing a group working to go into high schools to educate students on their legal alternatives to military obligation and the role of the Army in supporting imperialism. I invited Rosa to give a book talk in my store.

Rosa, working as a stringer for CBS, interviewed me for a forty-minute podcast on organizing in the past and today. Laurel Krause, the sister of Allison Krause, one of the four students killed at Kent State in 1970, recorded me as part of a one-hour Zoomcast. I continued writing the column for the Fresno *Community Alliance*. However, keeping the bookstore afloat became a real lifeboat project. There was not much time for anything else.

The process of reconnection with old friends to verify the stories in this document quickly evolved into a political organizing event held in Fresno on June 22, 2018.[100] It was supported by the Women's International League for Peace and Freedom, the Unitarian Church, the Fresno Free College Foundation, KFCF (the local station affiliate of KPFA), *Teatro de La Tierra*, and the Valley Peace Center. People arrived from all over California.

David Harris, organizer of the National Resistance, came to give some remarks. Augustín Lira, cofounder of *El Teatro Campesino,* and three other former members of the company were also there. The event brought together a crowd of about two hundred and reenergized them during the Time of Trump.

In the face of Trump's military brinksmanship, with former Draft Resisters and the press at this event, I decided at the age of seventy-three to burn my draft card. If the Martians showed up, they'd be better than Trump. (DOCUMENT #86: Burning my draft card at 73, 2018)[101] If the FBI was in the audience, I was back in the saddle again. I hoped they'd bust me. It would be great publicity for the bookstore...

---

[100] The population of the Fresno area has swelled to well over a million people.

[101] The federal law concerning selective service registration still in effect states that a registered male must keep his Selective Service Registration Card—his "draft card"—on him at all times. There is no age limit for this requirement and no statute of limitations on arrest and prosecution for violating it.

DOCUMENT #67: Soledad Brothers (from Defense Committee pamphlet cover. 1971) At top, John Clutchette, in the middle, George Jackson, at bottom, Fleeta Drumgo (Image courtesy Library, Univ. of Oregon, Emma Sterne Archives collection)

DOCUMENT #68: Emma Gelders Sterne, 76 years old in 1970, member of the Communist Party since 1954, supporter of the San Jose Peace Center, author of 26 books, producer of *Say "Uncle" Sam!* in San Jose, California. (Photographer: Thomas Valentine)

DOCUMENT #69: Jonathan Jackson holds Judge hostage in a hostage negotiation plot for The Soledad Brothers, Main County Courthouse, in San Rafael, Ca. August 7, 1970. (Photo, Roger Bockrath . Permission, San Rafael Independent Journal)

In exclusive photos showing fury of the attack, Freedom Rider Thomas Valentine is snatched from the car (top), hurled . . . . . . through the air (center), then dumped to the ground in a heap as unidentified members of mob move in on him.

DOCUMENT #70: Tom Valentine from the Soledad Brothers Defense Committee in San Jose, beaten by a mob, McComb, Mississippi, Jet Magazine Dec. 14, 1961. (Photographer unknown)

DOCUMENT #71: Original *Say "Uncle" Sam!* show poster. (Image courtesy of Emma Gelders Sterne Archives, Oregon State University)

DOCUMENT #72: *Folklorico* kids in the back yard of the *Folklorico* rehearsal house in San Jose's East Side, near corner of King and Story Road, 1970. I lived in this house to keep it from vandals, rehearsed in it for my own agitprop theatre group, "The People's Players." (Photo: Joel Eis)

DOCUMENT #73: Westwood California, Lassen County, in the winter (Photographer unknown)

Westwood California in the summer, 1973. Row of buildings "downtown," were once rooming houses for loggers. Now retail. and apartments. Note: wooden sidewalks. (Photo: Joel Eis)

Actors prepare for war. Children's rhyme/game. Note tumes, helmets, rope--Act II, scene 4

DOCUMENT #74: *King Ubu* (Jarry/Eis), Humboldt State University 1977. Political theatre in a period of rampant careerism. Note simple set, expressionistic costumes. garbage bags for uniforms, paper diapers for helmets. In ths scene they skipped rope to the cadence of the rope slamming the floor. Whimsical map of territory to conquer is painted on the stage floor. (Photo: J. Eis)

DOCUMENT #75: Bob "B" (Robert Kieth) Hobbs and me, about 1978-79, in Berkeley, California. Both of us are feeling very good in this picture. Ripped our of our heads, would be closer to it. (Photographer unknown.)

DOCUMENT #76: Outside of Eureka Theater, ca. 1972 in the basement of the Trinity Methodist Church (Built 1926), opened as a theatre 1972, destroyed by fire - 10/11/1981. Image # AAA-868 (Photograph, Permission: property of San Francisco History Center, San Francisco Public Library.)

DOCUMENT #77: Trinity Methodist Church, Noe & Market **1930, May** 17. (NOTE: Automobile at lower left stands in front of the door to the basement assembly hall, later to become the Eureka Theatre.. Photo ID Number: AAB-1545 (Permission granted: property of San Francisco History Center, San Francisco Public Library.)

DOCUMENT #78 Trinity Methodist Church, site of the Eureka Theatre after the fire, October 12, 1981 (Photo: permission of the S.F Chronicle)

Black theater allows designer to stay committed to pluralism

IFA BAYEZA
Bulletin Correspondent

A year after the "Freedom Summer" of 1964, Joel Eis was sitting at a lunch counter in Memphis. It was shortly after the bodies of three slain civil rights workers had been unearthed in Mississippi, just a week before the civil rights law was to be passed by Congress.

Eis was a 17-year-old Jewish volunteer for SNCC, the Student Non-Violent Coordinating Committee, putting himself on the line for the equality of blacks.

"I spent the whole time with my head down, looking at my plate. Because if you sat up, you would get slapped with unlawful assembly, resisting arrest and all the unsolved murders in the county for the last six months," he remembers.

Half the people involved in the civil rights movement were Jewish, he says.

Eis also recalls "the first day the civil rights law went into effect. I was in East Texas, at a bus station, at 5 in the morning. A black janitor, holding a screwdriver, walked across the floor, climbed a stepladder and slowly took down the 'Whites Only' sign. When he walked back the other way, his entire body had changed. He gave me the biggest smile. I remember thinking to myself, 'The Civil War just ended.'

"It's not over yet but that's the way it felt then."

Eis' life as an activist, coupled with his roots as a Jew and as a child of the theatrical world, ultimately led to his working hand-in-hand with African Americans.

Among his first show business memories is the fact that "my father was a member of the Labor Theater in New York." So it was no great leap for Eis to become a student actor-activist with the San Francisco State Agit-Prop Theatre Group.

From there, he moved into the realm of technical design with the Farm Workers Theatre, where he was able to remain committed to the racial pluralism he espoused.

"I've always had multiracial friends," he says. "My Jewishness comes through in that regard. And my background is acted out in how I treat people.

"One of the most important parts of the Jewish liturgy for me is the Passover service. It teaches that when we deal with other people, we must remember when we were slaves in Egypt."

Cultural connections, says Eis, can be found in the

See JEWISH, Page 44

Jewish technical director brings activism to theater

Continued from Page 42

everyday details of our lives. While working with the Farm Workers Theatre, he remembers, "a couple of Latinos came over one night and were going through my refrigerator. They found some horseradish and tasted it. 'Now I can understand how you can eat Mexican salsa,' one of them said."

Today Eis, now 47, is working as technical director on a Lorraine Hansberry Theatre comedy production, *Steal Away*, combining his talents with artistic director Stanley Williams and executive producer Quentin Easter.

On and off, he's worked with them since the theater's start, in 1980, "when I slept on their couch and they ate [by using] my food stamps."

His job on *Steal Away* — a period comedy set in Chicago during the Depression about five upstanding church women who are driven

Joel Eis

Eis, whose parents are longtime members of Temple Beth-Israel in Fresno, where he had his bar mitzvah after the family moved from New York City, also talks of the need for a healing between the African American and Jewish communities.

He suggests that healing must

DOCUMENT #79 News Media make note of my involvement with Black Theatre. (Photo appears permission of the Jewish Bulletin)

Document #80: Transitions for a Mime Poem, LHT, 1982. Ed Mock and Debra Allen. Cutouts above represented "the pubic" as George Jackson's and Angela Davis' relationship was tried "in the court of public scrutiny." I was making up the lighting effects as I went along. (Photo, J. Eis)

DOCUMENT 81: Toni P. Labori, My girlfriend at the time, now my wife. 1990 (Photo J. Eis)

DOCUMENT 82: MFA Piece: The Big Game, 1997. interactive game board on the floor, the rules on the wall, big dice, upper right. A lot of these people were supposed to be in class. (Photo: J. Eis)

DOCUMENT #83: A guest at a *Calle Ocho* (Eighth Street) Cubano Arts District Gallery in Miami, Florida puts a dollar in the bucket and takes a shot with a paint gun at the Bill of Rights in the performance installation, "Shooting/Gallery," 2001, after Cuban right wing activists vandalized the gallery and beat up the artist. (Photo, J. Eis)

DOCUMENT 84: Rebound Bookstore, San Rafael, CA Owner takes a knee during the Black Lives Matter Movement as a demo march moves past the store front, 2018. (Photo, Toni Labori)

DOCUMENT 85: *American Play*, (*The Play in August*) about the first political play in America, 1665, staged at Univ. of Maryland, Salisbury. 2012 (Photo. J. Eis)

DOCUMENT #86 Joel D. Eis burning his draft card, Fresno, CA, June 22, 2019. Destruction of this document at any time is a federal crime. This law has no statute of limitations. (Photo: T. Labori-Eis)

CODA: AFTER A HARD RAIN...

There are names of my high school and college friends on the Vietnam
Veterans Wall in Washington, D. C. Their gravestones tell us that History is personal. These young men didn't have to die. If things go the way the ruling class plans, there will be bigger war memorials yet to come. This will be your fight.

Today my generation is by no means silent. We write books and articles and advise younger groups. Our political activism consists of sharing our experience and serving as an example. We are still active gears in the machinery of change. The political seeds we planted two generations ago have come to harvest in the resurgence of the militant Black, Latinx, and Asian community power movements. The work of Angela Davis, the Black Panthers, the Chicago Seven, the Kent State Four, and David Harris are in the news again. The fight over voting rights has been rekindled. Climate change requires a militancy that has yet to be energized. Our reward for a life of activism is seeing millions in the streets again.

I am sometimes asked about the price that I paid for being a political fighter and radical theatre artist instead of pursuing a career in New York or Hollywood. I answer, "What's a career worth in a ruined country?" How one lives one's life *is* one's politics. Don't be disheartened because you don't see yourself as somebody else's idea of an activist. You may not be able to do everything, but you should do everything you can. This is especially true if you are an artist. You have tremendous power in your hands to move the world away from the dark side and encourage people to stand up for themselves. We may need to put ourselves in harm's way for a worthy fight again, but don't fear confrontations with authority. The fact that we will never go away, never stop speaking out, is what the ruling class fears the most. No one else can fight and win this battle. History is always personal.

    The battles now are the rise of the Black Lives Matter and climate change movements, the voting rights, gender equality, pro-choice, and Women's Rights movements, and especially the uprisings in support of the LGBQT community, currently under terrible assault by the retrograde forces of reaction. All of these righteous struggles need to unify and dig in for a long struggle that will go beyond election years or individual provocations. Everybody has to come out all the time for each other.

    The forces of repression and exploitation are a united front. The foot soldiers of the Right are among the most oppressed people in History. They are throwing themselves on the line for the good of their own oppressors. The challenge is to change dangerously ignorant or apathetic minds Rage has its place in a movement, but smashing a bank window because it happens to be on your march route. What would be more revolutionary would be to convince the employees to walk against exploitive policies.

    The hard target in this war is liberating the undereducated, media-saturated population concerned with their material needs and their scapegoat hunting of imagined enemies. Most Americans believe their chains are charm bracelets. They imagine a shimmering, twisted fantasy that their grandchildren will get the chance to screw over the grandchildren of the guy who's screwing them. But the grandchildren of the bosses will inherit the keys to the factories. Our grandchildren will inherit the keys to a secondhand truck and an old house. Their grandkids will go to Harvard and Princeton. Our grandkids will go to state and community colleges and inherit our debts.

    Look at those old demonstration photographs. The people in those pictures are students, truck drivers, moms, teachers, bank clerks, waitresses, musicians, bookstore owners. This is not happening to somebody else. No matter what we tell ourselves, we are all politically engaged. Our taxes pay for war and the surveillance of our own lives.

In the political upheavals since 2016, the people have come out in the street. The photos show demonstration crowds are so large that they extend beyond the frame. This says it all. I am also informed that the number of university theatre departments offering classes—and even degrees—in Afro-centric/Latinx/Indigenous Peoples' social action theatre is on the rise. Also, as a result of the Black Lives Matter Movement, the Me Too and Women's Movements, and Asian, Brown, Native American, and LGBQT political activism—all direct legacies of our activism in the 1960s—hundreds of universities are revising and retooling the totality of their programs for more inclusion. Perhaps that young woman interested in International Business out in the sunshine at Chico State who harangued my generation for quitting on them became part of the changes.

My contact with young people in the store has become particularly important. They will be voting in the next presidential election. The COVID crisis has given rise to an unexpected phenomenon. Young people captured had to stay home and watch the news. They sat with their parents to watch neo-Fascism play out in their own lives. They have seen more real governmental and right-wing corruption than we could ever have shared in a lecture or a film. Theirs is the new unity experienced in America.

****

I have requested my FBI file under the Freedom of Information Act of 1988. I'd already seen it on two occasions. I received a letter from the FBI claiming the file didn't exist. There was only one reason why they'd come up with this whopper ... the file was still active.

****

If you don't like the news, go out and make some of your own. Your time has come.

...About the Author of *Standin' in a Hard Rain*

Radical politics is in his DNA His grandfather was an organizer for a Garment Workers Union before WWI and his grandmother was an early suffragette. His father tried to volunteer for the Abraham Lincoln Brigade during the Spanish Civil War and worked for the labor theatre in the Great depression, the ended up on the docks during the General strike in San Francisco. Before she married his father, his mother dated the drama critic for the Communist newspaper in New York

History for him has always been personal. He set off a "prayers in the schools" case at age 13.

After finding himself in the most violent campus strike in American history (San Francisco State College ,1968) he joined both El Teatro Campesino *and* the National Draft Resistance. He had a bayonet at his throat at People's Park. He participated in Eldridge Cleaver's escape from America and ran security for the Angela Davis defense Committee.

His particular weapon in the struggle was political theatre he worked with such progressive groups as El Teatro Campesino, The S.F. Mime Troupe, the Pickle Family Circus, and his own progressive theatre companis in San Jose and San Francisco. He became a university theatre professor focusing on progressive theatre.

He and his wife Toni now own and run a bookstore in San Rafael, California. He notes, "A bookstore is a progressive cultural engine. I probably get to talk politics with thirty people every week. It's just another front in the struggle."

He is an award-winning author of three books on theatre and politics, dozens of articles, and plays produced.

.. He was followed and informed on He was shot at. His phone was tapped. An army helicopter circled his house and took pictures. He did some time in jail. Even though he's seen it twice, the government claims his FBI file doesn't exist.

…About World BEYOND War in the Director's own words

World BEYOND War was founded on January 1st, 2014, when co-founders David Hartsough and David Swanson set out to create a global movement to abolish the institution of war itself, not just the "war of the day." If war is ever to be abolished, then it must be taken off the table as a viable option. Just as there is no such thing as "good" or necessary slavery, there is no such thing as a "good" or necessary war. Both institutions are abhorrent and never acceptable, no matter the circumstances. So, if we can't use war to resolve international conflicts, what can we do?

Finding a way to transition to a global security system that is supported by international law, diplomacy, collaboration, and human rights, and defending those things with nonviolent action rather than the threat of violence, is the heart of WBW. Our work includes education that dispels myths, like "War is natural" or "We have always had war," and shows people not only that war should be abolished, but also that it actually can be. Our work includes all variety of nonviolent activism that moves the world in the direction of ending all war.

THE ORGANIZER'S PAGE

Lessons from the last Revolution…

Contact the author at Wanderfoot@aol.com to schedule a live event or ZOOMTALK on organizing.

JOEL D. EIS, MFA

Discussion available on choosing and organizing effective actions, successful engaging your members (old and new!) achieving goals, making more of meetings, making the media work for you, and building a movement beyond the street!

SEIZE THE TIME!

www.ingramcontent.com/pod-product-compliance
Lightning Source LLC
LaVergne TN
LVHW011941060526
838201LV00061B/4178